Merchants and Companies in Bengal
Kasimbazar and Jugdia in the Eighteenth Century

Merchants and Companies in Bengal: Kasimbazar and Jugdia in the Eighteenth Century offers a fascinating glimpse into the world of the South Asian merchants as well as the organizations of the textile trade in Bengal in the first half of the eighteenth century. Heavily archived from French and English sources, this book tells the story of the silk merchants at Kasimbazar and the cotton traders at Jugdia prior to EEIC's takeover of Bengal. The fragility and instability of a mercantile economy, the commodification of goods and the role of capital–both indigenous and external–are highlighted in this volume.

'This book marks a new strategy for studying Bengal's eighteenth-century economic history. Instead of focussing on broader themes such as agrarian trends, trade, or even transition from indigenous rule to colonial stultification, it micro-analyses two quite different trade centres. One is in the heart of Bengal's late Mughal administrative centre, Kasimbazar near Murshidabad, nodal for the distributaries of the Ganga/Padma/ Bhagirathi rivers. The other is far south-east part of the trade between eastern Bengal and Arakan, Jugdia, close to another trade outpost Luckipore, in the estuarial reaches of the Feni river. The comparison and contrast of the socio-economic data culled out of the French archives is very useful for understanding not only the sub-regional history of Lower and Eastern Bengal and Arakan (on which very little research exists for this century) but also the crisis in Bengal's economy caused by colonial intensification, and the way in which smaller trading towns declined by the end of the eighteenth century.' – Barun De, Member, Indian Council of Historical Research.

Rila Mukherjee obtained her doctoral degree from Ecole des Hautes Etudes en Sciences Sociales, Paris, where she worked on the silk trade at Kasimbazar. She was a Fellow in the Centre for Studies in Social Science, Kolkata from 1986 to 1989 and since 1992 she has been teaching in the Department of History, Jadavpur University, Kolkata. Areas of her research interests include the pre-modern South Asian economy, late medieval Europe, pilgrimage studies and the role of spatial categories in the making of history. She has published three books on Europe : *Europe Transformed-1350 to 1789; The Lost Worlds of Europe* and *Rupantarito Europe* (in Bengali). In 2005 she co-edited a volume called *Europe in the Second Millennium: A Hegemony Achieved.* Her forthcoming publications include *Strange Riches: Bengal in the Mercantile Map of South Asia* (Cambridge/Foundation Books). She is currently working on Bengal-Arakan relations in the seventeenth century.

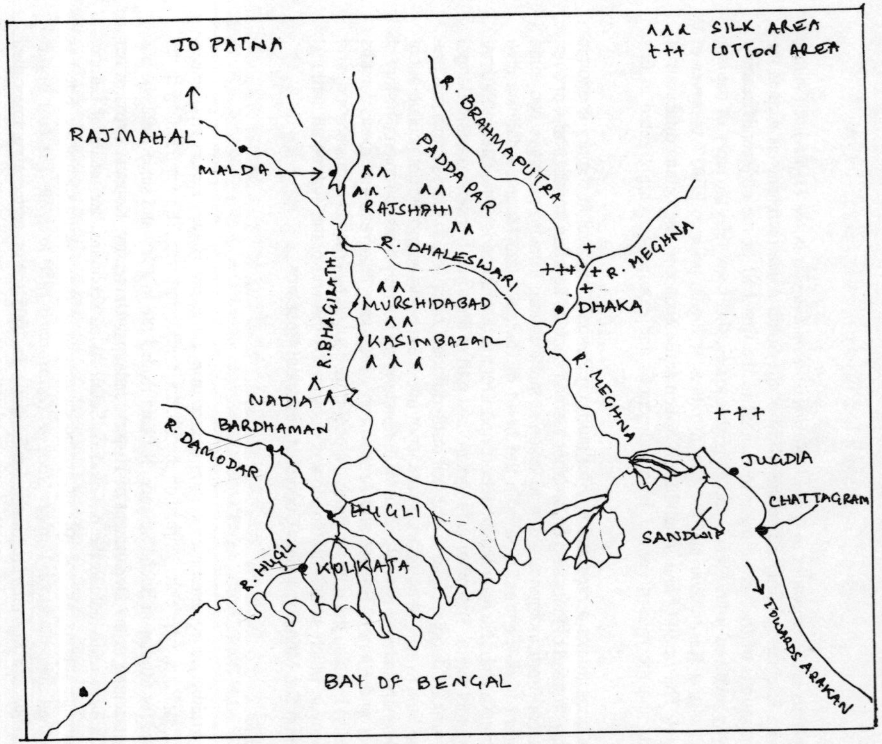

The Fluvial System of Eighteenth Century Bengal and the Places Mentioned

Hand Drawn Map: Not to Scale

Merchants and Companies in Bengal

Kasimbazar and Jugdia in the Eighteenth Century

Rila Mukherjee

PRAGATI PUBLICATIONS
NEW DELHI

First Published 2006

ISBN: 81-7307-109-8

PRINTED IN INDIA

Printed and published by Vikas Kapoor for Pragati Publications
4382/4B Ansari Road, Daryaganj, New Delhi 110 002
e-mail: pragati1@ndf.vsnl.net.in

For My Father
Professor Ramkrishna Mukherjee

Contents

Preface

Small books normally have small beginnings; and *Merchants and Companies in Bengal: Kasimbazar and Jugdia in the Eighteenth Century* is no exception to this rule. It grew out of the dissertation on the silk trade of Kasimbazar that I wrote for the Ph.D degree at the Ecoles des Hautes Etudes en Sciences Sociales, Paris from 1981–1985. This was undertaken under the supervision of Prof. Denys Lombard and presented in 1985 as 'Commerce et Marchands Autour de Kasimbazar: 1704 to 1757'.

Further documents on Kasimbazar for the period after 1757 were collected later on and the material on Kasimbazar first appeared in 1994 in *Review*, Fernand Braudel Center, SUNY, Binghampton, Volume XVII, No. 4 fall issue as 'The Story of Kasimbazar: Silk Merchants and Commerce in Eighteenth Century India.'

My discovery of Jugdia was by accident. I stumbled upon Jugdia, figuratively speaking, when working at the Pondichery archives on Bengal-Coromandel trade! The French were one of the first to set foot in this remote part of southeast Bengal and maintained a factory at Jugdia for much of the eighteenth and nineteenth centuries. Part of the section on Jugdia appeared in *The Indian Historical Review*, 17, nos. 1–2, 1990–91 as 'The French East India Company's Trade in East Bengal from 1750–1753: A Look at the Chandernagor-Jugdia Letters'. Material on Jugdia after 1753 was collected between 1990 and 2000. The French material on Jugdia is voluminous, but most of it had to be gleaned from series other than on Jugdia at the archives at Pondi and Aix. A visiting professorship in France in 2004 enabled me to collect further material on Jugdia so as to continue the story until the nineteenth century, and I wish to acknowledge my gratitude to the Maison des Sciences de l'Homme, Paris and to Professor Maurice Aymard and Dr. Gilles Tarabout there who made this possible.

The present book is therefore a revised and extensively enlarged version of the original thesis. The four main archives used here are the India Office Library and Records archives now in King's Cross, London, the Archives

Nationales, Paris, now at the Centre des Archives Outre Mer at Aix en Provence, the Goethall's Research Institute and Library at the St. Xavier College, Kolkata and the French documents at the Bibliotheque Romain Rolland at Pondichery. The London archives provided rich documentation on Kasimbazar, understandable since the English maintained a presence there from the end of the seventeenth century, while the French holdings in Pondichery and France were invaluable in reconstructiong the story of Jugdia. The Goethall's archive houses a remarkable collection of rare books and manuscripts on the seventeenth and eighteenth centuries, some of which have been used here.

I had a personal stake in writing the portion on Jugdia not only because it lies in a frontier area that exhibits some of the most intriguing facets of Bengal's trade but because the Jugdia area, Jugdia-on the-Feni as I choose to call it, was home to my mother's family before they migrated to West Bengal. Today the area of Noakhali, in which Jugdia lies, is only known to students courtesy the Partition industry. An attempt has been made in the second part of this book to restore Jugdia to her rightful place in the history of medieval Bengal. Therefore Kasimbazar and Jugdia have been revisited and the focus has shifted considerably from the initial monographs. I hope the reader will find this of greater interest.

Two persons were instrumental in designing the original dissertation and I wish to acknowledge my deep gratitude to them: the late Denys Lombard and my father Ramkrishna Mukherjee. Prof P.J. Marshall commented incisively on the M.S. and the conclusion owes much to his comments. My thanks also to Professor Barun De who graciously associated himself with this work from the very start. Despite his busy schedule, he kindly went through the manuscript and made constructive suggestions. Rudrajit helped me check and re-check the many tables and prepared the graphs in the volume. Any errors and inadequacies of this book are, of course, my responsibility alone.

Kolkata RILA MUKHERJEE
March 2006

Introduction

1. INTRODUCING KASIMBAZAR AND JUGDIA

1.1. The Trade of Kasimbazar and Jugdia in Eighteenth Century Bengal

The story of Kasimbazar-and the story of its silk-is situated in Bengal *subah* in the eighteenth century. So is the story of Jugdia and that of its cottons. Kasimbazar in the west (it is today a small town in the Murshidabad district of West Bengal in India) and Jugdia in the east (in what is present day Bangladesh's Noakhali District) form two focal points for the study of differing polities, social practices and trade in the pre-colonial history of Bengal.

Kasimbazar, by virtue of its proximity to Murshidabad, the capital of eighteenth century Nawabi Bengal, was not only the principal commercial centre of Bengal, it was also a leading financial centre. Because of its proximity to the mint at Murshidabad many financiers were located at Kasimbazar. The EEIC, at least, disbursed their funds throughout Bengal through their factory at Kasimbazar. It were the Kasimbazar factors who were in charge of negotiating with the Seths, the principal bankers of Bengal, for funds for other factories within Bengal as well as for disbursement of funds elsewhere.[1] The section on finance and credit brings this out very clearly. Jugdia on the other hand was located far away from either a political or a financial centre in eastern Bengal. The closest mint to it was at Dhaka, some days journey away. It would be seen from our data that though trade there was difficult for the EICs it was attractive because it was the last unregulated commercial frontier of Bengal.

While this study deals with Kasimbazar and Jugdia in the eighteenth century, attempts have been made (as far as the sources allow us) to follow the tale of their merchants, production and trade from earlier times. We have traced, therefore, for Kasimbazar, an almost continuous story from the 1680s to the 1780s from European and Indian sources. Sources for Jugdia are more scarce but I have attempted to reconstruct a picture of this southeastern trade for the whole century and beyond as well.

One of the main assumptions of this volume is that systematic silk cultivation was introduced into Bengal from Husain Shahi times so that it could function as a commodity in the Islamic commercial network of the early sixteenth century. Silk was therefore a relatively new commodity. The case of cotton was different. Cotton cultivation existed in Bengal from ancient times. Cottons featured in Indo-Roman trade. Trade in the various types of fine cottons was boosted when the Muslims established their base in Bengal; this fact is borne out by the names of the various grades of cotton textiles. The names of the various grades of muslins from the Dhaka region such as *abrawan, tanzib, malmai shahi, shabnam, padshahi-dar, kaghazi, hammam*, and *shahbarga-buti* show more of Persian and Arabic influence rather than Bengali or Sanskrit. This leads us to suppose that the imposition of Muslim rule in Bengal stimulated an already existing industry. That market considerations induced the Muslims to further trade in the finer cottons from eastern Bengal is borne out by the fact that terms in use by the weavers of Dhaka for warp, shuttle and loom are Sanskrit while later improvements such as reed, reed frame and spinning wheel are Persian.[2]

This study of Kasimbazar and Jugdia is the story of the commercial fortunes of silk and cotton and of the merchants dealing in them. Special attention has been paid to the following: First, this study focuses on *the dadni merchants.* Pre-colonial Indian economic history is littered with references to the '*dadni*' merchant; so much so that the '*dadan*' (or advance contract system) has acquired an universal acceptability for the whole of Bengal. We thereby assume that the whole of South Asia worked on the basis of this contract which was a variation of the Islamic *hidaya.* This was not merely a promise but an agreement to deliver, or in other words, a contract for sale.

Why was the *dadni* merchant so called? He was so called because he worked on the basis of a contract or *dadan.* When did the practice of *dadni* start in India? Irfan Habib feels that it started during the time of Ala-ud-Din Khalji when trade expanded from the twelfth to the fourteenth centuries between India and the Red Sea.[3] But an older method of buying that was not so regulated existed along with the *hidaya.* This was the system of spot-buying or ready money sales; usually the norm in those areas that had not become as integrated to specific long-distance markets. Tapan Raychaudhuri notes that two types of procurement existed: spot purchases (what we shall see were called ready money sales by the EICs) through *dalals* and traders, and the system of advance contract (*dadan*) through agents. It was the latter system that became more pervasive throughout the Mughal Empire by the second half of the seventeenth century. Moreover, he adds, the EICs, with their more coordinated networks of procurement, probably contributed to the development of the latter phenomenon, a view that agrees with our findings.[4] The system of contracts was useful in that it helped the *arangs* keep pace with expanding demand, as well as in regulating production to EIC dictates and standardizing it as far as possible; some commodities were simply not procurable without it since the producers were unable to comply without advance money as their resources were scarce. The advance contract system helped both sides but the advantage lay with the buyer. By means of the contract system competition was reduced, it bound the producer to a particular buyer and moreover it synchronized supply and demand and thereby reduced market instability. This was the system that the EEIC valiantly attempted to impose in Jugdia and Kalindi where the spot purchase system predominated. They were not too successful in this unlike at Dhaka and Kasimbazar.

It is possible that different procurement systems had their own agents and intermediaries. The data in this volume therefore indicates that *dadni* merchants operated primarily in western Bengal despite historical assumptions to the contrary. Trade in eastern Bengal—in the main production centre of Dhaka-Suvarnagram—was carried on through the medium of 'dalals' or middlemen, and sometimes by *pykars*. The different nomenclatures were not always allied to correspondingly different functions. Indeed K.K. Datta identified *dalals* as *dadni* merchants and refers to the Calcutta dalals with their own association in 1752.[5] N.K. Sinha favoured a more nuanced view of *dadni* merchants, *dalals*, *gomasthas* and *pykars*.[6]

While both '*dadni*' merchants and '*dalals*' were middlemen, '*dadni*' merchants were different in that they operated on the basis of a '*dadan*' or advance which they then distributed to the weavers under their jurisdiction. This indicates that specialized production for a specific market (be it Asian or European) had come into being in the western part of the province.[7] This specialized production came to be directed almost fully towards the European market by the 1730s and the *dadni* merchant played a crucial role in the *creation of the idea of a concrete European market* within the rural mind of western Bengal. This was essential if production was to be redirected. Europeans wanted larger sizes of textiles, they also needed different colours. Most important, they tended to invest in the medium and coarse grades of textiles. Production was reoriented towards the new market accordingly. This 'new' production was carried on through the system of advances. In time the system of advances arrived in the east as well. It worked well for the Dhaka *arangs* of Titbadi, Dhamrai, Jangalpur, Narayanpur etc.[8] But in the east the advance was called '*pattan*' and not '*dadan*'. We do not have, however, 'pattani' merchants; merchants supplying goods to the European companies in the eastern region were called, as we noted, 'dalals' or 'pykars'.[9]

Data gathered for this volume leads to the speculation that western Bengal's production of silk is possibly of relatively recent origin and introduced under Islamic rule, although wild silk cultivation had existed in Bengal long before that date. More specifically, a systematic cultivation of silk was started only under Husain Shahi aegis in Bengal in the first half of the sixteenth century. In the course of the seventeenth century silk production accelerated under Mughal rule. It then was enhanced further by European demand.[10] Since, apart from cottons, silk was the major export commodity from Bengal in the seventeenth and eighteenth centuries, can we assume that, like silk, the *dadni* merchant too was a novel phenomenon in late medieval Bengal?

Second, this study investigates the *different contracts* in vogue in mid eighteenth century Bengal. We will see that trade in Jugdia continued on a more random basis right until the end. Jugdia was not part of the 'Dacca aurungs'. Its distributive outlet was linked to Chattagram and not Dhaka. Invasive merchant capital had not been able to make inroads here although Jugdia's lineage was older than that of Kasimbazar as a production centre. European companies were not familiar with it. Jugdia was a no man's land, and its turbulent history dictated that it should remain thus. Since the sixteenth century, when we have the very first records affirming to the existence of Jugdia, it was either a part of Tripura or of Arakan. In the eighteenth century Jugdia became the last administrative frontier of the Dhaka *niabat*; yet it was not under the economic jurisdiction of Dhaka. Jugdia was the last commercial frontier of Bengal, as the French East India Company discovered to their cost.

Here there were neither *dadni* nor *pattan* merchants; ready money sales were the norm by which individual company *dalals* procured goods for the companies by buying direct from the producers. This indicates that European capital had penetrated less invasively in the east. In the 1750s the system of trading at Jugdia changed; there was an attempt on the part of a ring of five merchants known to the English as the 'Dacca Dellols' to corner European investments and to control contacts between the *arang* and the companies. At the same time the English (in 1752) attempted to bypass all *dalals* at Jugdia and set up their own base at Kalindi; a market-town for textiles close to the *arangs*. It is likely that they hoped to introduce the Agency System here later on.

Jugdia's trade in textiles continued, therefore, to be conducted on traditional lines at a time when procurement was organized differently in the west. Even after the *dalals* were eliminated, the *gomastha* system was poorly applied in eastern Bengal from the middle of the eighteenth century as Prof. Anisuzzaman's Bengali letters in the English factories tell us.[11]

The practice of *dadan* therefore was not a universal phenomenon in Bengal and the imprecise nature and insufficient quantity of historical data often leads us to make generalizations that are misleading in reconstructing a picture of trade practices in Bengal. Since sources indicate that trade was organized differently in the east from the west we find no definitive transition from one system to another in Jugdia as was the case in Kasimbazar. Jugdia's trade in textiles continued to be 'disorganized' even after the mid-century crisis.

Thirdly, this study focuses on *the mid-century crisis in textile production in Bengal.* The mid-century crisis in production in Bengal, consequent problems in procurement and their impact on finance and trade are crucial to our understanding of the nature of the precolonial economy. Moreover, the ramifications of this 'crisis' are central to our study here because their immediate result was a change in the middlemen's fortunes. The 'crisis' affected both the procurement methods of the English and French East India Companies and the final assortment of textiles for the European market. And most importantly for us here, most middlemen-*dadni* merchant or *dalal*-vanished with this mid-century crisis in production.

Some of the merchants reappeared in the EEIC's books as *gomasthas* in the new agency system. Others became salaried supervisors at Kasimbazar. The repercussions of the 'crisis' resulting in a changeover in procurement methods saw a massive encroachment of the EEIC into *arangs,*[12] this was the insidious Agency System whereby Company servants directly accessed goods at the *arangs* with the help of their *gomasthas.* While N.K. Sinha has worked on the economics of the Agency System,[13] there has been very little work on the 'crisis' leading to its inception after K.N. Chaudhuri[14] despite innumerable instances in company records as well as in our received history of Bengal.

Critics may argue that an over-emphasis on the mid-century crisis is the outcome of an excessive dependence on European records and that the 'crisis' manifested itself mainly in the sphere of English trade in Bengal.[15] The fact is that the crisis was the direct outcome of a massive jump in the demand for textiles by the European East India Companies; since the end of the seventeenth century demand for Bengal silks and cottons had been growing steadily at London, Paris, Amsterdam, Ostend and Copenhagen. This growing demand had already switched much of the production away from the internal and regional markets in Bengal. The stories narrated from Kasimbazar and Jugdia reveal that the crisis deeply affected the internal market; in the case of Jugdia just a few of the older textiles continued to be woven for the Asian market; among those woven for the European market quality suffered since the English now dictated production, the investment was invariably delayed throughout the 1740s and in both cases there were few 'independent' merchant/procurers who had not gone bankrupt as a result of the crisis.

Fourth, this study focuses on *the social milieu of the changeover to the Agency System.* Evidence from both Kasimbazar and Jugdia reveals that a major mercantile bankruptcy had occurred in Bengal by the 1750s, both among the merchants and the EEIC; this had a direct bearing on the implementation of the agency/*gomastha* system. Again despite the pioneering works of N.K. Sinha little attention has been paid either to this changeover in the method of procurement or to the social implications of such a bankruptcy. I have shown, from the EEIC records of Kasimbazar, that many of the old players continued to dominate the new system as *gomasthas* but with one difference; these *gomasthas* enjoyed a clearly unequal relationship with the English Company. I was able to do this because of three remarkable documents which traces the fortunes of the *dadni* merchants of Kasimbazar in 1752, 1755 and 1756.[16] In the case of Jugdia I have shown from FEIC sources that there were probably two sets of *dalals* operating there in mid-century,[17] these were replaced in their turn by the more powerful 'Dacca Dellols' who moved in to corner the Jugdia trade at a time when the existence of all *dalals* in eastern Bengal was uncertain because of the growing economic might of the English East India Company. Soon after, the 'Dacca Dellols' too vanished. In both cases I was not concerned with the dynamics of the agency system as such but with the players in this new system.

Fifth, we see that *the data from both Kasimbazar and Jugdia reveal that 1753 is not universally acceptable as the date of the ending of the dadni system and the introduction of the Agency or Gomastha system.* The official date for the ending of the *dadni* system and the introduction of the agency system is given as 1753 in our history books. Both N.K. Sinha and K.K. Datta accepted this date and this date is taken as a significant marker in the economic and political history of Bengal insofar as it introduced a new method of procurement.[18]

Investigations into Kasimbazar and Jugdia reveal that the year 1753 is not uniformly the year when the agency system was introduced all over Bengal. It was introduced at Kasimbazar only in February 1754. Again the Agency System, when introduced in 1754, did not apply to all textile items. The Kasimbazar Factory Records (henceforth K.F.R.) tell us that the Agency System was introduced for silk piece goods only from 1756. It appears from records that the changeover of 1754, while radical at the time in the eyes of the Court of Directors in Britain,[19] was not such a definitive break with earlier systems as we think; documents quoted throughout this book indicate that the agency system was conceived of in a period of crisis and was applied on a piecemeal and trial/error basis in Bengal throughout the 1750s and 1760s.

From 1769 the *dadni* system was re-introduced in Kasimbazar on Becher's recommendations. No date in history is final.

New facts that come to light challenge older assumptions which have remained uncontested. Just as we find that the changeover of 1754 does not display spatial uniformity in Bengal, so too we find that the year 1754 does not automatically portend the limited political control over Bengal that was won by the English East India Company at Plassey in 1757. The changeover does not presage the passage of the pre-colonial polity into the colonial. The 1750s and 1760s were a period of intermission before the resumption of absolute political and economic control by the English in Bengal from 1765. This period witnessed an era of experimentation by the English in Bengal by way of the attempts to maximize revenue from both agriculture and trade. This short-sighted economic policy climaxed in the Bengal Famine of 1769-1770 which signified the final breach with the past. From then on the economy of Bengal followed a downward trajectory. Society was radically reordered. It is noteworthy that the *dadni* system, resumed at Kasimbazar in 1769, could not stand upto this ultimate catastrophe of the famine; by 1771 the *dadni* system finally gave way to the *gomasthal pykari* mode of textile procurement. Taylor's account of Dacca tells us that the 'Dacca Dellolls' who controlled the trade from Jugdia had vanished too from the scene by this time.[20] Om Prakash traces the 'diappearance' to 1746.[21] That year may well have seen the replacement of one set of 'Dacca Dellols' by another. In any event this date seems very likely since 1746 augured the height of the 'crisis' at both Kasimbazar and Jugdia. 1754 as an overall economic marker for the economic history of Bengal may therefore be misleading.

What did the events of 1754 actually portend? 1754 saw the entry of the EEIC into the *arangs* of Bengal where the company could negotiate directly with the weavers, thereby bypassing middlemen. This allayed constant English fears of fictitious price-rises and the cornering of the market by Asian merchants. It brought down prices and it allowed the EEIC to dictate production according to the dictates of the European market. This was a right the company had pleaded for from the very beginning. At the start of the century the Surman Embassy had asked this privilege from Emperor Faruksiyar and not been granted it.[22] The EEIC especially had attempted unauthorized entry into *arangs* even before 1754.[23] 1754—even in a limited sense—was not therefore just an economic triumph for the company; it signified a social revolution within and without the *arangs*. The old commercial order had passed.

Sixth, this study highlights *the absence of a distinct commercial realm in Bengal.* The question of the existence of at least two differing modes of procurement in Bengal (*dadni* and *dalali*), frequent European complaints of a lack of a regulatory mechanism for the market and the sudden disapperance of the *dadni* merchant brings us to the perplexing issue of whether there was a distinct commercial realm in the province. Instead of a bewildering complex of rights and possessions was there a purely economic realm where the merchant functioned? And if there was, as seems to be the case in eighteenth century Kasimbazar, who exercised control over Bengal's trade? Was there any consortium of merchants, or financiers or indeed a central authority such as the state as in the city states of the Malabar, helping to organise production, transport and sales? Why was the merchant class of Kasimbazar so fragile, and why did they vanish overnight?

The *dadni* merchants of Bengal claimed to have been trained in the business since childhood. A Dutch document of 1687 noted that:[24]

> The merchants—are exceptionally quick and experienced. When they are still very young—they already begin to be trained as merchants. They are made to pretend to engage in trade while playing, first buying cauris, followed by silver and gold. In this training as money changers, they acquire the capability of engaging in large scale trade. They are always sober, modest, thrifty and cunning—They have the exceptional capability of discovering the humour of those who are in a position to help or hurt them.

This passage is significant in two respects: it identifies the merchants of Bengal, whether *dadni, dalali,* or *pykari,* as a group apart and it emphasises their twin roles, as merchants as well as moneychangers. Both these aspects are also emphasised in the K.F.R. We shall see this as we progress through this volume. The K.F.R. also refers to the merchants as having been bred in this business (that is, supplying silk) since childhood.[25]

But while the merchants may have emerged as a distinct group in seventeenth century Bengal, a group that displayed the markedly Renaissance characteristics of education whereby parents and tutors attempted to instil education through play, was there a similar coming into being of a distinct commercial realm where the merchants could function? In other words was there a uniform Mughal and post-Mughal economic realm operating in Bengal?

Of course an economic realm does not come into being through state intervention; in fact, the opposite is often the case. But commercial growth can be fostered through state policies, one of which is the avowed recognition of its 'own' merchants. This happened to some extent in the case of Gujarat because its ports controlled the Red Sea and Persian Gulf trades and Mughal interest in Mecca and its links with Persia, the East African coast and to some extent the Ottoman Empire, fostered these links. But Gujarat was different from Bengal in that there was a clearly defined hierarchy of ports and hinterlands, with corresponding trade routes and control over procurement of commodities by merchants from the sixteenth century there.[26] Mughal control over trade from Hugli (despite its being dubbed a royal port) was nominal at best. Chattagram, the only deep water port in the province was practically never under Mughal control and thus it was never a 'Mughal' port. Also, there was no indigenous merchant community operating here as was the case in Surat or the Coromandel. Most overseas and inland trade seem to have been in the hands of Bihari, Marwari and Gujarati merchants[27] and at the end of the seventeenth century, Bengal's long distance trade was controlled by Mughal subahdars only in a personal capacity. The fact that there was no continuous and resolute Bengali control over shipping and trade—despite a distinguished heritage in mercantile and sea-faring activity—may be ascribed to the fact that there was no stable maritime centre in Bengal after the Husain Shahis.[28]

Seventh, we may assume that *the presence of many contesting nationalities in Bengal may have hampered the emergence of a merchant class.* The various ethnic groups (Arab, Persian, Turko-Afghan, Afghan, Portuguese,[29] Arakanese,[30] Bengali, Mughal) that were present in Bengal's ports from the sixteenth to the eighteenth centuries could only mean that contending interest groups based on ethnicity and race (old Arab interests over Turko-Afghan interests, or older Persian interests versus Afghan interests, or again Portuguese interests versus Arakanese interests in the sixteenth century, or the newer Iranian interests in eighteenth century Bengal versus older Muslim interests are examples)—rather than a single ethnic mercantile group—had to be accommodated at any cost. Each 'national' group of merchants exercised priority over trade with its 'mother' country and consequently there was intense competition over trade routes. The ruling class in Bengal, beset by the same factions, pursued therefore a policy of open seas for all.

But there were indications that this state of affairs was changing. A regional Islamic identity and a 'regional' merchant class was emerging under the Bengal nawabs in the eighteenth century. Under their rule the Iranian group emerged as a considerable force in politics and trade in Bengal. This group also maintained close links with Surat and Basra and there is every likelihood that a major portion of Bengal's westward trade was monopolized by the Iranian group.[31] Finance was becoming an integrated realm at this time and the Hindu merchants and financiers at Kasimbazar maintained close links with courtiers in Murshidabad. The section on the market economy in Bengal explores this in greater detail.[32]

But, historically, the emergence of this mercantile class was slow; moreover by the time it gained some clout it was already too late. And the emergence of an indigenous Bengali mercantile class was even slower. M.R. Tarafdar's contention of the limited cultural area of the Bengal Muslims as hindrance to the development of trade networks, or H. Sanyal's notion of the lack of social mobility within Hinduism as a whole that hampered the growth of the Vaishnavite merchant in sixteenth century Bengal may be taken as pointers to the fact that a local mercantile elite failed to emerge in medieval Bengal.[33]

But this changed by the time our story starts. Our study of the merchants of Kasimbazar shows that many of the *dadni* merchants were of the Vaishnavite faith. The weaver sub caste, *tanti*, was almost entirely Vaishnav, so were the *telis* of whom there were plenty as merchants at Kasimbazar.[34] In any case mostly merchants of the so called 'low' castes figured in the Kasimbazar lists, as we see from Table 8.

Many of these were now ascending the social scale as shop keepers, traders, merchants and moneylenders. Like the Bagdis of Bengal, many members of which caste featured as merchants in the Kasimbazar investment lists but who were originally cultivators and had moved on to become palanquin bearers, earth workers and small traders and moneylenders by the late seventeenth century, the Telis too had moved on from being oil pressers to becoming bankers, money lenders, cloth dealers and shop keepers.[35] The Meherchurn Matar of the raw silk investment list for 1750 was probably Mehecharan Matia, Matia being a sub caste of Bagdis in Bengal[36] (See Table 7). Therefore some amount of mobility must have been present in late medieval Bengal, contrary to what Sanyal stated. But for some reason these merchants could not make the quantum leap necessary to become a great merchant.

The Portuguese presence on Bengal's shores, and their monitoring over trade and shipping in this part of the Bay could have been yet another factor that cut off the growth of a native Bengali merchant class beyond a certain point. Although more recent research tends to minimise the Portuguese impact on the trade of the Indian Ocean,[37] and certainly that of the Bay of Bengal, it was also certain that the Portuguese storming of Malacca in 1511 signalled long term changes in the trading world of the Bay.[38] The *cartaz* system that they introduced in the eastern Indian Ocean ultimately became too expensive for the small merchant. They concentrated instead on riverine networks. But it seems that the Portuguese were active in the inland trade of Bengal as well by the end of the sixteenth century,[39] and it is not known how far this may have impeded riverine trade. References in Bengali literature to

Portuguese piracy (*harmads*) are indications that riverine routes in Bengal had become unsafe by the seventeenth century. After the Portuguese, the English East India Company's increasing control over the riverine network in Bengal from the 1730s ensured that English merchant capital was able to reach internal markets unimpeded and influence production patterns in the villages even before the agency system was introduced. From the 1740s a new factor entered this chaotic arena—the Marathas. Their raids continued until 1751 and completely destroyed the economy of western Bengal.

The Arakanese factor, first as ally in medieval Bengal and then as foe from the seventeenth century, is crucial for our understanding of the seeming passivity of the Bengali merchant in the early modern period. Commonly dismissed as 'magh' raids over Bengal, Arakanese piracy impacted on the political economy of Bengal since much of eastern Bengal from the sixteenth to the eighteenth centuries was under their control. In fact, as we shall see later, Chattagram was treated by the Arakanese as a frontier post and Feni, the river of Jugdia, was deemed the boundary between Bengal and Arakan. Seventeenth century southeast Bengal was subject to two expansionist forces: the Mughals from the west and the Arakanese from the east. Jugdia was caught in this tussle.

Dermigny characterised the Magh (Arakan-Portuguese) piracy as just one element in the greater incidence of piracy that menaced the Tropics from the Caribbean to the Far Eastern Seas.[40] Taken in that sense, piracy often complemented official trade, a point made in *Strange Riches*.

Arakan collapsed in the eighteenth century and contributed in no small way to the decline of native Bengali commerce.[41] Since no history of southeastern Bengal is complete without reference to the Arakanese intervention an attempt has been made in this volume to reconstruct the story of south east Bengal's unwilling tryst with its eastern partner as much as the sources allow us.

Finally, this study underscores the fact that the *dadni* merchant of Kasimbazar was different from *dadni* merchants in other parts of Bengal. By reason of his proximity to Murshidabad and by virtue of the fact that the merchant maintained close links at court, the *dadni* merchant often had considerable political clout. Vakil, diwan, moneylender, financier and merchant could often be the same person. The *dadni* merchant of Kasimbazar did not just operate with political sanction, he often *was* the political sanction. Courtiers traded through the *dadni* merchant of Kasimbazar more than at any other place. The section 'The Merchants' World at Kasimbazar' explores this in greater detail.

1.2. Locating Kasimbazar and Jugdia within the commercial history of Bengal

Kasimbazar is in the west of Bengal. In the eighteenth century it was right next to the seat of Nawabi power in Murshidabad; today it is a small town, almost a suburb, to the south of Murshidabad. At that time it lay in the heart of the silk-producing area of Bengal. By the very virtue of its location, trade and politics at Kasimbazar was oriented westward towards the middle Gangetic plain by the time the Bengal Nawabs made their home in Murshidabad.

Murshidabad probably owed its origins to the sixteenth century. It started off as a market town producing 'aftabas', 'chellamanches' and belts.[42] Its population was estimated at 1,500,000.[43] It lay among mango orchards at the heart of the silk growing region of Bengal and was situated along the banks of the Ganga. It was 5 miles long and about 3 miles wide. Its twin city was Mahinagar on the opposite side. Filled with beautiful buildings, the city boasted many palaces—the chief one was on the river, while the country palace, or Motijheel, was in the middle of a lake. Yet another was Hirajheel on the opposite side of the river from the main palace. There was a great oval shaped market place called the *chowk* which contained many shops.[44]

The city was originally called Maksudabad but when Murshid Quli chose it as his capital he changed the name to Murshidabad. As a burgeoning provincial capital, soon to be the capital of the *nizamat* of Bengal, it assumed the trappings of an imperial city. Salim noted that 'it (was) a beautiful city. Its inhabitants in the society of the Subahdars, being thrown into contact with the people of Delhi, in point of refinement of manners and conversation, resemble the people of Hindustan unlike those of the other parts of Bengal'.[45]

As at Murshidabad, political beliefs, social styles and cultural mores of the Islamic ruling class influenced daily life in Kasimbazar in the eighteenth century. Its streets were crammed with so many palaces, a contemporary observation ran, that one never saw the light of day.[46] Tribute was sent from Bengal to Delhi (until Nadir Shah sacked Delhi and all 'successor states' stopped sending revenues there) through Patna, Allahabad and Awadh. Kasimbazar's trade with Agra lay on this route, and it was through the mechanism of its trade in silk that part of the tribute was sent. Apart from silks being sent as part of tribute, revenue from the silk trade lubricated the process whereby silk was converted into tribute. Merchants and financiers were the agency through whom the silk was transformed into cash. Therefore, Kasimbazar's trade was oriented mainly towards the west to Surat through its main port Hugli and to West Asia overland through Bihar, Awadh and Agra.

Kasimbazar's production of silks and silk piece goods was also oriented towards the internal Indian market as we saw; early on in the seventeenth century Kasimbazar 'goods' were sold at Patna.[47] Bengal silk was also sold at Agra. From the end of the seventeenth century this Indian and West Asian trade network was diverted to meet the demands of the European market. The European market expanded further in the eighteenth century. Consequently, European presence became prominent in this area. Major European companies, such as those of the Dutch, English, Ostenders (Belgians) and French, were active in the textile trade at Kasimbazar in the eighteenth century. So were the Armenians.

However, records are not clear as to when exactly the silk boom started in Kasimbazar. We get occasional mentions of Bengal (Kasimbazar) silk (manufactured as opposed to the wild variety) only from the sixteenth century and that too from European sources. Our reading of the story of Kasimbazar will show that silk was a relatively recent import in Bengal and that it did not have the same distinguished lineage as the muslins of Dhaka or the cottons of Jugdia.

Unlike Kasimbazar, Jugdia was far away from political currents emanating from Delhi. It was also aloof from European presence for it was situated far in the east. Indeed Jugdia was in southeastern Bengal, close to Chattagram and located opposite the island of Sandwip that was ruled by Kedar Rai, the Mughals, the Portuguese and the Arakanese. European trading companies had a minimal presence in this region. Unlike the cluster of companies along the Bhagirathi in the west, European presence in the eastern region was confined mainly to Dhaka. Jugdia was located far from the great cotton production centers of Dhaka and Suvarnagram as it lay nearer Chattagram. Through its river, the Feni, it connected with the river of Chattagram, the Karnaphuli, which flows south into the Bay. Through its proximity to Tripura Jugdia connected with the intricate fluvial system of the Brahmaputra which goes north into China.

We do not know much about Jugdia's production and trading system, but we may surmise that being located in the disputed area which both Tripura and Arakan fought over in the sixteenth century, it was more oriented towards the east through Arakan. Jugdia came to be linked to the commercial realm of Dhaka under the pressure of European demand only in the middle of the eighteenth century.

Records indicate that Jugdia's commercial lineage preceded that of Kasimbazar in history. The Dhaka-Suvarnagram manufacturing area is mentioned in early history. From very early times this area was an active trading area and continued to be so through the early days of Islamic conquest of Bengal as well as during early Portuguese mercantile adventurism on the east coast in the sixteenth century. By the late seventeenth century the name Dhaka had become synonymous with exquisite quality muslins. We therefore get an almost uninterrupted chronology of the cotton manufactures of this area for over a thousand years. Jugdia is first mentioned in a Portuguese notice of 1521 as a township,[48] soon after it is mentioned as a port in the *sarkar* of Suvarnagram in the *Ain-i-Akbari.*

Historians of classical antiquity have referred to the fine cottons (muslins) produced in this area and we know that Jugdia produced fine cotton goods, too. These were, however, inferior to those of Dhaka-Suvarnagram and were mainly known as *baftas.* Jugdia produced fine *baftas* similar to those produced by Tripura in the area known as the Tippera Hills.

We said that Jugdia's traditional political and cultural links were oriented more towards the east and radiated mainly in the direction of south-east Asia. They were also inclined more towards the sea—through this area's great port of Chattagram. Jugdia, being located in the extreme eastern part of Bengal, was quite unaffected by pressures originating from either Delhi or Murshidabad. Unaffected even perhaps by those from Dhaka until the midle of the eighteenth century!

Jugdia gained in stature from the seventeenth century as Dhaka shot into prominence as a temporary Mughal provincial capital. Subahdars such as Islam Khan, Qasim Khan, Mir Jumla, Shaista Khan and Azim-us-Shan established their HQ at Dhaka in an attempt to patrol the eastern borders of the Mughal state and the Mughal Nawara fleet was stationed there to defend the eastern frontier against Magh (Arakanese and Portuguese) raiders.

By the time the Bengal Nawabs appeared on the scene in the eighteenth century Dhaka had evolved into a second capital. It became the seat of the Chhota Nawab (usually a close relative or a favourite of the reigning nawab at Murshidabad) and from then on until the close of the century Dhaka's political importance was almost as great as that of Murshidabad, the capital of eighteenth century Nawabi Bengal.

This emergence of Dhaka was not an isolated event in the history of Bengal *subah.* The region was a commercial conduit to South East Asia. The Dhaka region, and further east, had traditional links with northern South East Asia (the Kamrup/Arakan/Ava/Pegu/Laos/Cambodia region) while the Coromandel was more known for its interactions with southern South East Asia or the Indonesian archipelago in ancient history. The driving force in the early history of Bengal came from this region.

The evolution of the two regions—the west and the south east—indicates that Kasimbazar and Jugdia symbolized two 'Bengals' in the eighteenth century.[49]

1.3. *Placing Kasimbazar and Jugdia within the Historical Geography of Bengal*

Sources tell us that while there really were two 'Bengals' (Lakhnawati in the west and Bangalah in the east, as Ibn Batuta saw them in the fourteenth century, or Purb and Pattan as Edward Terry and William Baffin saw in the seventeenth century)[50] in actual fact as late as in the eighteenth century, 'Bengal' still denoted an amorphous zone which contained within it various Bengals.

Just as there have been many 'Bengals' in recorded history there have been, within each of them, 'diverse' Bengals. The area we refer to as Bengal today comprised various small states (in the order north to south) in ancient times known as Pundra, Varendra, Rarh and Vardhamana in the west and Harikela and Samatata in the east. The dividing line between the two regions was Pundravarmana which comprised within it the area called *Vanga*, most of *Varendra* and a portion of *Samatata*. These distinct geographical and political units, inhabited by particular peoples with specific tribal attributes and social attitudes, were therefore designated within a particular place/time context that varied over time.[51] Harikela or the easternmost area became an addendum to samatata and its history is neglected to this day for the most part. Although *Harikela* was an expanding area in the tenth and eleventh centuries, from what we know from inscriptions found, not much is known about the geographical contours of this region. We know that in the eleventh century *Harikela* embraced Sylhet as well.[52] This area's turbulent history remains outside the ambit of historical research even now. Jugdia lies in this fluid area of *Harikela* opposite the island and port of Sandwip.

Sandwip, at the mouth of the Meghna, was an important port in medieval Bengal. It was under Kedar Rai. In 1602 he had 'liberated' Sandwip from the Mughals and placed it under the Portuguese Carvalho. Cesare Frederici visited Sandwip in 1569. Lahori tells us that there was a substantial Portuguese colony there during the seventeenth century. Later in the seventeenth century the Mughal subahdar of Dhaka 'liberated' it from the Portuguese Gonzales and gave it to Arakan as *jagir*. Jugdia lies in this contested area that was constantly 'liberated'. Politically, it was first under the rule of Tripura, for some time it was part of Husain Shahi Bengal, then under the rebel government of Ananta Manik of Bhalwa (Noakhali) and finally under Mughal rule from the late seventeenth century. But the Arakanese laid claim to it throughout the seventeenth century.

Kasimbazar lies in the area that was known as *Vanga*. In time *Vanga* assumed dominant status-at least iconographically-over other regions in Bengal. We do not know the reasons for the hegemony of *Vanga* but it seems likely that its fame as the most productive rice growing region within Bengal as well as its proximity to *Varendra* (Gaur or the political nerve centre) was responsible for its new status. From Maurya times the region of *Vanga* or the western part of the lower gangetic delta, co terminous with the ancient kingdom of Gangarides, home to the ancient port of Tamralipta and wealthy in terms of natural and material resources, claimed dominance over the regions of Pundra, Radh and Varendra in the western half. By the time of Samudragupta the entire western area was conquered and reunified as Vanga.

We can say that by the time the Guptas consolidated their empire in eastern India the great 'eastward migration' of the *Aryas* had reached the last frontier. The term 'Vanga' became a common noun describing the entire state of Bengal except its eastern part—*Samatata.* Only parts of *Harikela* (north of Samatata and contiguous with Kuch Bihar and Tripura), *Samatata* and Kamrup remained to be aryanised.

But this area was never aryanised completely, and consequently we have only local histories based on the artefacts found with local kings. The one exception was the rule of the Chandra, Pala and Varman kings from Dhaka-Bikrampur who have left behind a good number of inscriptions which help us to construct a regional history of early medieval Bengal.

The successful articulation of political power in Bengal has always based itself on two stark realities-control over surplus grain and control over the waterways.[53] Waterways play a vital role in the economy of Bengal, Bengal has one of the largest fluvial systems known to history. Ports have sprung up throughout the Bengal coast from *Vanga* to *Harikela.* Control over the resources of the hinterland have been both facilitated and hampered by the river valleys to the interior. With time therefore the flat riverine plains of Bengal saw the rise of a divine political economy and validating philosophy in this distinct topographic zone—what Lombard calls a 'rice culture of divine right'[54] based on the successful appropriation of legitimising models for lineage construction and the economic control of the area. Such a model had to operate within societies that were organised *hierarchically* (and not *spatially* as had been tribal societies) on the basis of *varna,* with *jati* being used as a mechanism of incorporating newly conquered peoples.[55] This happened first during Gupta rule and continued despite the Buddhist affiliations of this area. Successive dynasties, the Palas and Senas in the west or the Khadgas, Chandras, Devas and Varmans in the east, sculpted Bengal into two distinct political entities known as west and east, or Lakhnawati and Bangalah as they came to be known from the fourteenth century.

Under the Ilyas Shahis, throughout the fourteenth century, Bangalah was gradually brought into Lakhnawati's orbit. Now, expansionist tendencies became marked in Bengal. The Ilyas Shahis made conscious efforts to extend hegemony over Kamrup, Kamta, Tirhut and Nepal to the north and the powerful Ganga state (medieval north Orissa) to the south. Inscriptions found in Kamrup indicate that a portion of Assam at least was brought under Muslim control by the time Sikandar Ilyas Shah and Ghiyath-al-Din Ilyas Shah were on the throne of Lakhnawati.

This expansion to the north east was dictated by two factors. One was to secure the frontier against possible future invasions by foreign (Mongol) powers. The other was to tap both Assam gold and Yunnan silver.[56] Aloes wood from Kamrun (Kamrup) and Sylhet was another attraction for aloes was an item greatly in demand in the medieval world. Courts from the Chinese to the West Asian ones sought aloes wood. But Jugdia still lay outside Ilyas Shahi control in the fifteenth century.

Ilyas Shahi expansion to the east was reflected in the location of their mint towns. They issued coins from Lakhnawati and Satgaon in the west, and from Mu'azzamabad (Mymensingh), Khalifatabad (Bagerhat) and Chawalistan/Kamru (probably Sylhet) in the east.[57] After the Ilyas Shahis, the Husain Shahis too sought to expand the north eastern frontier. In this they were more successful than the Ilyas Shahis. They also enhanced trade within their own domains by connecting Triveni (in the older *Vanga* which had evolved into the cultural and economic heartland of *Varendra*) with *Vanga's* chief port Saptagram by way of a bridge in 1506. This bridge connected Saptagram and Triveni with the main channel of the Bhagirathi because the Saraswati had dried up.

Saptagram of course was not just the port of the Bengal sultans. Its antecedents go far back in history and it probably started functioning as a port from the end of the ninth century. At the end of the fifteenth century Vipradas described the mercantile dynamism of Saptagram. It was inhabited by Hindus, Mughals and Pathans; it contained a dazzling array of houses and conducted trade with Ceylon (Sarandib) and Orissa. This area therefore forms the direct ancestor of the Kasimbazar-Murshidabad area that we shall study later here.

A definite core area thereby began to take shape in western Bengal, linking the economic region with the political nerve centre by way of the intellectual capitals of Triveni and Nabadwip. As under the Ilyas Shahis, mints were established at Gaur (successively called Firuzabad, Shar-I-Naw, Jannatabad under the Ilyas Shahis, and Husainabad, Muhammabad, Nusratabad under the Husain Shahis) and Saptagram. Under the Mughals, mints were established at Dhaka, Rajmahal, Patna and Murshidabad. Taking the Sultani and Mughal periods together we get the names of some twenty five mint towns in Bengal.

How did the Husain Shahis view the east? The east had been a valuable conduit for the eastern trade from early times. It had greatly expanded during the Ilyas Shahi period in Bengal. Chattagram—the chief port in the east—conducted this trade with Arakan and China.[58] But with the conquest of Chattagram from Tripura by Ala-ud-Din Husain Shah in 1516, this area, including Jugdia, was brought into the ambit of Sultani rule in Bengal as well.

But two events in the eastern Indian Ocean foredoomed the eastward trade that had been initiated by the Ilyas Shahis. The first was the official Chinese withdrawal from the eastern Indian Ocean by the middle of the fifteenth century. The second was the Portuguese take over of Malacca in 1511. The Husain Shahis, therefore, began to concentrate more on the trade of the western Indian Ocean. Despite this shift, the east still retained its commercial vitality, a fact made evident by the fact that it housed more mints than the west. Mints in the east were in Fathabad, (Faridpur), Chattagram and Suvarnagram as well as Mu'azammabad and Khalifatabad. We thus have at least six mints in eastern Bengal as opposed to two in the west during the sultani period. In the seventeenth century a mint was established at Dhaka by the Mughals. The mints at Fathabad, Mu'azammabad and Khalifatabad were probably discontinued, as we find no coins with those mint names during the Mughal period.

Under Husain Shahi regime therefore a new urban complex emerged in western Bengal. Gaur was the capital, Saptagram its port, Triveni its religious hinterland and Nabadwip its cultural centre. Vanga thus saw a new phase of urbanization. Nabadwip attracted immigrants from Sylhet (a well known intellectual centre of *Harikela*) and Chattagram and soon evolved into the scholars' centre of *Vanga.* By 1560 Nabadwip had evolved into a well-known market town as well; merchants were settling there and selling goods from locations as far off as Kashmir in the north to Kanchipuram in the extreme south. From this time on textiles (mainly cottons and some silk piece goods) began to be manufactured in the towns along the lower Bhagirathi. These supplied the market towns along the Bhagirathi and provisioned the trade conducted from Saptagram.

We know that Saptagram ceased to function as a port with the establishment of Hugli as the chief port on the Bhagirathi in 1580. However, the impetus of urbanization in this region continued unabated and Hugli took over the functions of Saptagram by connecting long distance trade with the hinterland.

During this time Bengal came to be integrated more closely with northern India through Sher Shah Suri's efforts to reorient the trade of Bengal from the east to the west. This meant that Bengal had another outlet for its manufactures apart from its riverine/oceanic trade. The construction of the Grand Trunk Road—which exists to this day—ensured that Bengal would no longer remain a marginal sultanate. This road which was built by Sher Shah (1538–45) and finished by Akbar connected Bengal permanently with Delhi via Allahabad, Benares and Awadh.

Unlike the west, we find no similar evidence of an urban complex emerging as a result of political intervention in southeastern Bengal in medieval times, other than around Dhaka. But unchecked urbanisation continued nevertheless as more and more areas around Dhaka were drawn into a market economy. Mubarakabad and Mu'azzamabad to the south west and south east of Dhaka, Fathabad (Faridpur) and Khalifatabad (Bagerhat) appeared during the sultanate period. Urbanisation continued subsequently and two Sherpurs, one in Bogra and the other in Mymensingh, were founded during Sher Shah's time.[59]

But in the early history of Bengal this area was probably one of the first on the eastern coast to undergo extensive urbanisation. Mahastan, in Bogra district in Bangladesh, was inhabited continuously from about the third century BC until the seventeenth century AD. Mahastan, capital of the Pundra people and of the state known as Pundravardhana, was a well known Buddhist centre. This early urbanisation was accompanied by trade. Mahastan was an important trading centre in the Buddhist commercial network by virtue of its great river Karatoya which connected it with the Brahmaputra and thereby with Buddhist Burma and China.[60]

It was also a Hindu sacred spot because the Karatoya and its branch Tista contained within it Bengal's ancient *Varendrabhumi*. With time *Pundravardhanabhukti*, as it appears in the Gupta inscriptions, ceased to be a mere administrative designation and denoted instead a sacred zone with continuously expanding frontiers. By the time of the Chandras in littoral Bengal in the tenth century the territorial notion of Pundravardhana was sufficiently enlarged for them to apply the term to a portion of *Samatata* as well.[61] Chandradwip, the port of the Chandras, connected littoral Bengal to the upper reaches of Pundravardhana. Chandradwip becomes known to us as Bakla (in Bangladesh's Backergunge district) from the twelfth century. Bakla was an important port in deltaic Bengal in medieval times. Therefore this area saw considerable urbanisation throughout the ancient period.

It is, of course, significant that the borders of today's Bangladesh correspond to the old divisions of *Samatata* and *Harikela*. In ancient Bengal this was primarily a Buddhist dominated zone spanned by a pilgrimage and religious circuit linking Pagan in the east, Ceylon in the south and Nalanda and

Bodh Gaya to the west. The Dhaka-Bikrampur area was host to the Buddhist kings of eastern Bengal in the fifth century and before the coming of a definite Islamic ruling class in the shape of the Ilyas Shahi kings to Bengal displayed a markedly different culture: witness the Deva, Khadga and Chandra kings who ruled quasi-independently from the region. The cross border affiliations of this region were marked. The 'small kings' of this region maintained links with Arakan, Pagan, Ava and Yunnan by way of over land routes that ran through Kamrup into China (Tibet and Turkestan) or by way of sea (witness the Pattikera kingdom's links with Arakan in the early medieval period).

In the wake of the instability produced by the takeover of Lakhnawati, the last Sena king, Lakshman Sena, ran away to this area; later in the post-Mughal actions leading to a tempoary take-over of Gaur, dispossessed Afghan/Turk adventurers also fled there. This area was brought into the political realm of Bengal only in the middle of the seventeenth century by the Mughals. The Bengal Nawabs in the eighteenth century transferred their less favoured officers there. In time the Dhaka-Bikrampur region ceased to be a separate political unit and became instead an extension of Nawabi Bengal.

Eastern Bengal was always the last frontier as Eaton notes[62] but this frontier was not the creation of Islam. It was repeated endlessly throughout the early history of Bengal as well. This Turnerian frontier was a continuous creation through religious and political forces from the time of the spread of Buddhism in the early centuries of the first millennium. It was pushed forward relentlessly nevertheless throughout the centuries until Mughal control of this frontier put a stop to this in the seventeenth century. Diverse faiths, different religious affiliations and the prevalence of many tongues and races still mark the east from the rest in Bengal. By the eighteenth century, when our story starts, Assam (including the defunct Kamrup) and the old Koch kingdom (now Cooch Bihar) delineated the final frontier of Bengal. The south east had been incorporated. And Kasimbazar in the west and Jugdia in the east had become part of the same trading system that governed Bengal in the eighteenth century.

1.4. *Kasimbazar and Jugdia in the Market Economy of Bengal: From arang to port by way of market and mint towns*

Bengal manufactured textiles from a very early time. By the medieval period production was concentrated in various *arangs* (manufactories) situated all over Bengal. To date we do not really know what the constituents of an *arang* were, how it came into existence or who financed it. However an entry in the

K.F.R. indicates that some *arangs* had evolved into royal *karkhanas* (manufactories under royal supervision) in the eighteenth century. On April 2, 1739 the EEIC broker, Bali Katma, informed the Kasimbazar Council that the merchants were uneasy with the accession of Sarfaraz Khan and that they were unwilling to contract for more than half the proposed EEIC investment in silk piece goods. The reason given was that the silk piece goods were produced at Murshidabad 'under the nawab's eye'. This suggests the establishment of at least one royal *arang* manufacturing silk piece goods in the Murshidabad region. In fact the merchant-courtier nexus at Kasimbazar, and the fact that the leading members of the court traded as *dadni* merchants with the EICs, indicates that a substantial amount of control may have been exercised over the *arangs* by the court at Murshidabad. There are indications in the K.F.R. that certain *arangs* around Murshidabad, especially those producing silk piece goods, catered almost totally to the commercial interests of the royal elite.

Much of the production of the *arangs* was sent to ports for export by sea. Some was sent to the collection points on overland routes such as Patna and Agra for transhipment to Central Asia and Persia. This trade, whereby the products of the *arangs* reached distant markets, was made possible by the market towns where these goods were sold against agricultural produce, and was lubricated by the bullion that was melted down as coins at mint towns. The market and mint towns fuelled this commercial revolution.

At the base of this commercial revolution lay the commerciali-sation of agriculture. The commercialisation of agriculture was initiated by the trade cycles in the Bay between the thirteenth and fifteenth centuries that greatly expanded trade between Bengal, Burma and China.[63] Between 1400 and 1630, Bengal, Arakan, South East Asia and China saw an intense commercialisation in the agricultural arena as Mukherjee, Wicks, Reid, Marks and Bin Wong point out.[64] In Bengal this commercialisation was reflected in the reclamation drive of the Bengal sultans in the fourteenth century. Wang Ta Yuan wrote in 1349-50 that vast tracts of alluvial land were being cleared for cultivation.[65] In 1340, when Ibn Batuta travelled in southeast Bengal, he saw orchards, water wheels, gardens and villages dotting the landscape.[66] In the seventeenth century, when Bernier came to Bengal, he saw extensive fields of rice, sugar cane, vegetables, mustard and sesame fields for oil and mulberry trees.[67] This was echoed by a French visitor, de Gennes de la Chanceliere, who visited Bengal in 1743.[68] Between the fourteenth and eighteenth centuries commercialisation of agriculture climaxed in Bengal.

Mulberry trees for silk worms were grown in central and north Bengal, mainly in the Murshidabad and Rajshahi districts, while the fine cotton grown on the banks of the Lakhiya and Dhulasary rivers as well as on the shores of the Brahmaputra and in Bhawal, Jessore and Rajshahi dotted the landscape in eastern Bengal.[69] The state actively promoted mulberry cultivation and not just for reasons of commerce and the corresponding benefices. Murshid Quli Khan noted in 1706 that mulberry cultivation had to be promoted as mulberry lands were taxed at Rs. 3 per bigha while rice lands and land for pulses were taxed at Rs. 0.75 and 0.37 per bigha respectively.[70] The benefits accruing to the treasury from mulberry cultivation were immense. For the Bengal Nawabs capitalist agriculture became an indispensable part of state policy.

The commercial revolution was reflected in the activities of the mart and port towns from the end of the sixteenth century. Ralph Fitch mentioned Suvarnagram, Sripur (Chandpur) and Bakla (in Backergunge district) as ports which traded in cottons, rice, oil and ghee.[71] We do not know much about the origins of Kasimbazar, but we are told that at its inception in the seventeenth century it was a small mart town for silks and silk piece goods. Its emergence was linked to the commercialisation of agriculture that dotted the Bengal landscape in the seventeenth century.

Therefore the most striking feature of urbanisation in eighteenth century Bengal was the emergence of small and medium sized market-towns as a result of this commercialisation. These towns were based on wholesale markets (*golas*) and *bazaars* as opposed to semi-regular *haats*. The latter were set up by local political magnates.

The commercialization of agriculture from the late seventeenth century in Bengal resulted in economic wealth in the countryside and a correspondingly growing assertiveness on the part of local zaminadars and chiefs. Manrique, Bowrey, Tieffanthaler and de Gennes de la Chanceliere tell us that the banks of the Bhagirathi and its tributaries were filled with market-towns.[72]

The Bengal nawabs tried to bypass the traditional *haats* and semi-regular markets established and controlled by the zamindars by putting up *golas* (wholesale markets) such as Bhagwangola in Murshidabad as well as their own *bazaars*.[73] Later on they tried to control the little markets that the Europeans set up within their domains, often without success.

There was consequently a new spurt of urbanization along the Bhagirathi belt from the end of the seventeenth century as the European companies left Hugli and founded their own settlements. It is to be noted that all these urban clusters were port-settlements along the Bhagirathi, the chief channel of western Bengal at this time. The settlements—in order of ascent—were

Calcutta (English), Baranagar (a subsidiary Dutch settlement) both on the right bank, Srirampur (Danish) on the left bank, Barrackpur on the right bank, Bankibazar also on the right bank (the Ostend Company of the Belgians), and then Chandernagar (French), Chinsura or Chunchura (Dutch), Hugli, and Bandel (Portuguese) on the right bank leading to the now defunct Saptagram.

By tradition, the bazaars (*ganjs*) or *golas* were established on rent-free lands by permission (called *sanad*) from the ruler. Obviously such permission was only given to favourite courtiers, close relatives or important merchants with a considerable presence at court. Sometimes the markets were owned by the nawab or held in the name of one of his family. The state therefore took a leading role in establishing these new markets.

The *bazaar* was a unit for the Mughal economy that produced revenue. But it was also an indicator of status. If we go through the *bazaar* rents we find that the 'rent' had little to do with the volume of sales that the particular bazaar generated. Thus, in Mughal economic thought, ownership, rent and value occupied different meanings. *Bazaars* in pre-colonial South Asia were not only sites for the demonstration of social power; they were equally sites where various kinds of economic and social relations could be observed at play.

Unlike the eighteenth century English political economy that based itself on labour and property as indicators of productiveness and wealth, Mughal political economy based itself on a complex of rights, possession and forms of property that was central to the Mughal economy. This complex rested on two basic supports: the status of persons and the disposition of rights over land. Value in pre-industrial political economies was differently determined.

The fact that bazaars in post-Mughal India evolved naturally out of the social demands of all strata of the population; and that they developed further with the growth of trade and a money economy within South Asia point to a well articulated policy on the part of regional governments and the Mughal state. That the Mughal and the post-Mughal state was the guiding spirit behind the foundation of *bazaars* and the ultimate owner is clear from the fact that often, if the owner owed moneys to the state, his *bazaar* was seized by the government.[74] In the final analysis ownership of a *bazaar* was subordinated to the wider social relations of superiority and subordination that the Mughal order generated. The bazaar was an expression of Mughal property just as the complex of rights, possession etc. were essential to the Mughal economy. Yet this domain was largely unregulated throughout the seventeenth century; the culture of the market was different from that of Europe.

In the eighteenth century, this complex of rights, possessions and forms of property underwent a subtle change. This occurred with the intensive commercialization of agriculture in the seventeenth century. *Bazaars* now became a form of property in their own right and not subordinated so much to wider social relations. Value acquired a monetary meaning although here too the leadership came from the political elite.

When *ganjs* sprang up in eighteenth century Bengal and became a new feature in the urban landscape they frequently combated the role of the older urban complexes.[75] New rulers, as they carved out their political domains, sought to establish new markets and thus control the resources of the area. In Bihar Hajiganj (established in 1752) was owned by Haji Ahmad's family. Haji Ahmad was the brother of Nawab Alivardi Khan of Bengal and the de facto ruler of Bengal and Bihar after 1740. His role as the *eminence grise* of politics in eighteenth century Bengal and the undisputed power behind the throne led him to play an enormous role in commercial affairs, especially in silk and salt petre contracts from Kasimbazar and Bihar until 1748.

Again a similar situation prevailed in Dhaka where the Mughal conquest had seen the establishment of *bazaars* by ruling subahdars. In the seventeenth century, Ibrahim Khan the Mughal subahdar established the *bazaar* of Rehmat Gunge.[76] This practice continued into the eighteenth century with the nawabs and their favourites controlling these mart-towns based on rent-free lands. For Dhaka's markets in the eighteenth century we have the following data:[77] there was Burran Gunge established by Jesarat Khan the Naib Nazim, Emam Gunge belonging to the same family, Bazar Kartalab Khan established by Murshid Quli Khan the first Nawab of Bengal and Narain Gunge and Lakhi Gunge established by Benur Thakur during Muhammad Reza Khan's tenure. Establishing *bazaars* was profitable and continued throughout the eighteenth century. Bazaars Jupsah, Colipara and Motibari were established before 1765; *haats* Sowapur and Burnah were set up in the same period. Unfortunately, we have no data as to the names of their founders or the dates of their establishment except that they were founded before the Diwani of 1765.

For Murshidabad we have the following data on *bazaars* for our period: J'afar Ganj was established by J'afar Ali Khan (Murshid Quli Khan) in 1708, Maqbara Ganj was established by Kasim Ali Khan the same year, Bibi Ganj was established by Majum-ud-Daula in 1749 and Haat Sripur was established by Mughal subahdars in 1700.[78]

It is clear therefore that from the seventeenth century there was an explosion of market towns on the urban landscape. The process gathered momentum in the early eighteenth century when the Bengal Nawabs attempted a monopoly on agrarian resources; more market towns came to be concentrated around urban nodes such as Murshidabad and Dhaka. It was under these circumstances, when excessive European demand was fuelling an extraordinarily profitable trade in silk in eighteenth century Bengal that the *riyasat* lost control over its economy.

Right from the beginning the *riyasat* was compelled to introduce high grade cash crops such as mulberry. It had to promote a monoculture accompanied by an excessive reliance on world demand. More and more land earmarked for grain cultivation were converted into mulberry plantations. The Bengal Nawabs did little to check this shift apart from taxing the plantations at almost four times that of rice lands in order to finance their wars. This increased taxation became more marked after the Maratha invasions into Bengal. Apart from following a strict export policy in the case of rice and sugar,[79] the Bengal nawabs seem remarkably enough to have left economic matters to regulate themselves in Bengal. The 'new' economy of eighteenth century Bengal grew, not so much as a result of Nawabi policies, but as a result of the hegemony of European capital.

The markets were linked to ports for it was through the market that export goods (grain, pulses, oil and textiles) were procured in Mughal India. These were administered as per Mughal norms by the Bengal nawabs. There were four main ports: of them three were in Bengal and one in Bihar. They were Murshidabad under the Pachotra Bandar or Daroga as he is referred to in English records, Hugli under the Baksh Bandar and Dhaka under the Shah Bandar. The first controlled the imperial dues coming into the capital, the second dues from overseas trade and the third collected duties arising out of the trade of the eastern districts. The Budrekha Bandar of Patna controlled the duties from trade with the middle and upper gangetic plain. Surprisingly, we find little mention of Balasore as a Bengal port in the eighteenth century, although it was under Bengal's control in the late seventeenth century and was quite important as a port. Hugli carried on trade with the Red Sea, the Persian Gulf, and the Gujarat, Malabar and Coromandel coasts, while Balasore carried on trade with Ceylon, Maldives, Pegu and South East Asia. In the seventeenth century Master decided to concentrate all EEIC operations at Hugli, it being the 'key or seale of Bengala'.[80]

Who controlled activities at the ports? In terms of port administration, we have evidence that this was coming into the hands of a small clique of courtiers from the middle of the seventeenth century. The three main actors at the end of the seventeenth century in western Bengal with whom the EEIC clashed, were Malik Beg, the *Faujdar* of Hugli for twenty years (1647-1667), his successor Malik Kasim the *Faujdar* of Hugli and Balasore[81] and Malik Zindi, son of Malik Kasim. The *faujdars*, especially Malik Kasim along with his son Malik Zindi, effectively controlled all commercial traffic out of Bengal's two premier ports of Balasore and Hugli for almost fifteen years (1668-1681). They were in effect the 'kings' of Bengal, with Mir Jumla, the actual Mughal *subahdar*, far away in his seat at Dhaka-the regional capital. Malik Zindi, who deputized for Malik Kasim at Hugli and Balasore, was probably a ship owner himself.[82]

The *faujdar's* power derived from the fact that the upper echelons of the ruling class left day to day affairs of ports and shipping to the *faujdar*. Bowrey comments: 'The Prince now (neither did the Nabob before him) not in the least concern themselves with their ships.[83]' He noted extensive trade at Hugli, Balasore and also at Pipli: 'The Nabob and some Merchants here (Hugli) and in Ballasore and Pipli have about twenty saile of ships of considerable burthen that annually trade to Sea, some to Ceylone, Some to Tannassaree . . .[84] These fetched elephants while others, some six or seven ships, went to the Maldives for *cauris* which was very profitable.[85]

This trend continued into the early years of the eighteenth century. Om Prakash shows that despite our perception that *subahdars* withdrew from trade in the Bay in the eighteenth century, officials continued to charter ships and carry on trade on their own in the first two decades of the eighteenth century.[86] But this was over by the 1730s. Jacques Vincens states clearly that European ships traded in Bengal produce with Surat, the Red Sea and the Persian Gulf. Of these the English ships carried on most trade. The Bengal merchants provided freight. English private traders monopolised the Bengal-Malabar run, while the EEIC traded from Bengal with Pegu. The EEIC-China trade was just beginning to take off.[87]

As for merchants, we are told that the trade from Hugli was controlled by the Gujarati and Coromandel merchants while that from Balasore was in the hands of Bengal merchants.[88] But this was only until the 1720s; by the 1730s a radical change had been effected in Bengal shipping as we have just read in Vincens.

Ports were the final point of destination for the goods of the *arangs* or manufacturing centres (which could also evolve into market towns if they were strategically located, say near a river) by way of the market town. *Arangs* dotted the landscape of late seventeenth and eighteenth century Bengal. Om Prakash tells us that the hinterland of some *arangs* could extend over as many as 350 villages.[89] This was considerable. By the middle of the eighteenth century a new trend was visble within Bengal. The EICs, who had previously been denied entry into the *arangs*, now bypassed the market towns and procured their items directly from the arangs through the Agency System.

A port would prosper more through proximity to the capital and mint. Kasimbazar, the chief port of Murshidabad and the base of the Pachotra Bandar's operations, rose into prominence with the shift of capital to Murshidabad from Dhaka at the turn of the eighteenth century. It became the most important market-town for silk textiles in eighteenth century Bengal and was important enough to give its name to the Bhagirathi that flowed past its banks.[90] Originally a seventeenth century mart-town famed for its silk mix cloth, Kasimbazar formed an island bound by the Bhagirathi, the Jalangi and the Padma and this island was covered with mulberry trees.[91] It was these that contributed to the celebrity status of Kasimbazar for it was the centre of silk production in Bengal as well as the centre of all commerce in Bengal.[92]

As port Kasimbazar experienced a riverine traffic during the monsoon whose importance and variety has been called unique in the world.[93] As the centre for commerce in all Bengal it housed the English factory (established 1658-9), the factories of the Dutch and the French (at Kalikapur) and the Armenian settlement at Saidapur at a distance.

It seems that commercial possibilities in Kasimbazar were so extensive that foreign merchants such as Kashmiris, Gujaratis, Persians and Turks had permanent residences there. Kasimbazar's location was strategic; its proximity to the court at Murshidabad was another advantage for foreign merchants for they could then petition the court for grievances if any. Finally the establishment of a mint at Murshidabad was indispensable to trade. These merchants built beautiful buildings along the river, for Kasimbazar was also known for its salubrious climate in the eighteenth century.

In 1813, however this magnificent city, emblematic of thriving commerce and Mediterannean style silk, died out as the Bhagirathi changed its course. This resulted in the city being transformed into an unhealthy swamp.

We see therefore that Kasimbazar was not just a mart town close to the political centre. Kasimbazar was the chief riverine port of the Bengal nawabs throughout the eighteenth century, it commanded the most profitable trading items from its substantial hinterland, its manufactures were prodigious, and most important of all, political and financial activities at the capital were mirrored at Kasimbazar since it was situated right next to the *nizamat* and mint in Murshidabad.[94]

The financial realm needed bullion. Mughal political economy envisaged the body politic as a human body where bullion played the role of blood. For the Mughal the free and adequate flow of precious metals was necessary to maintain equilibrium in the realm much as proper blood circulation maintains the health of the human body. The health of the country was linked to the amount of wealth (specie) it could acquire. The Mughals therefore conceived of the state as a living organism where any disturbance—such as the circulation of too much or too little specie—could trigger off decay.[95] It is noticeable that Shah Shuja the Subahdar of Bengal, in 1656 at the height of his fight over trade privileges with the DEIC, exempted imported bullion from the proposed 20% customs hike at Hugli.[96] This naturally made for a situation where the excesses of the European companies could only be curbed upto a certain point.

In the seventeenth century, financial management was centred around Dhaka, the present capital, and Rajmahal, the former capital. The mint was located at Rajmahal and because of its location the Bengal-Patna trade was flourishing. Bowrey noted that:[97]

> Pattana (is) a very large and potent Kingdome. . . . This is a Countrey of Very Greate Trafficke and Commerce and is really the great Gate that Openeth into Bengala and Orixa, and soe consequently into most parts of India, Vizt. From the Northerne Kingdomes or Empires (by land), namely Persia, Carmania, Georgia, Tartaria . . .

But the money market in western Bengal was not uniform and was largely unregulated. This made trade a risky affair for strangers. Balasore, one of the important ports of the seventeenth century, had no coined money as the EEIC factors noted.[98] This bears out the assertion that the east—with Dhaka as Mughal capital—and the north—with Rajmahal as the former capital—were the focal points where Mughal finance concentrated at the end of the seventeenth century. A commercial zone, extending from Balasore and Pipli to the south, through Hugli in the centre to Kasimbazar in the north was coming into being only now in the eighteenth century, largely through Nawabi intervention, and partly due to the European presence.

The Bengal Nawabs integrated the activities of the *arangs*, mart and port towns through a fiscal administration powered by moneylenders who functioned as courtiers. The D.F.R. of 1750, the 12th of November, mentions the following financial firms in Dhaka with eastern offices: Seat Matabray (Mahtab Rai, successor of Jagat Seth Fatehchand), Seat Syroopchund (Swarupchand, or Surupchand, also successor of Jagat Seth Fatehchand), Coshaul-chund (Kushalchand, son of Mahtab Rai), Allumchund Nimchund (Alamchand and Nimchand), Onoopchund Kissenchund (Anupchand

Kissenchand or Krishna Chandra), Bularamray (Balaram Ray) and Anunderam (Anandaram). Alamchand was the Diwan and then Rai Rayan (chief minister) of Bengal in Shuja's time, his son Raja Kriti Chand had considerable financial interest in Azimabad (Patna) and was later appointed as Alivardi's Diwan. Alamchand's agent Chin Rai was appointed Ray Rayan of Bengal by Alivardi Khan. Alamchand was reputed to have controlled the finances of Bengal before Alivardi's dynasty grasped power. The firm/combine of Allumchund Gainchund figures prominently in investment lists of the EEIC from Kasimbazar. Many of the other names figure in the K.F.R. lists as well either as merchants or as bankers, such as that of Kushalchand the third Jagat Seth and Seth Mahtab Rai's son. Others are Mahtab Rai, Surupchand and Anandaram.

The presence of these banking firms at Kasimbazar, Patna and Dhaka, and the nexus between merchants and financiers indicates that an integrated commercial market was coming into existence in Bengal in the eighteenth century. And as with markets, port administration and maritime trade, here too the financial realm was powered by courtiers. During the seventeenth and eighteenth centuries, mint towns were set up at Dhaka, Rajmahal, Patna and Murshidabad. In the eighteenth century two mints dominated the financial scene in Bengal: Dhaka in the east and Murshidabad in the west. Dhaka was given the status of a second, but subsidiary, capital.

It was this economic realm that the EEIC destabilized in the eighteenth century. In 1736 the Court at Murshidabad complained to the EEIC at Kasimbazar:

> That we (the EEIC) established a Court of Our Own in another Prince's Country, That we still continue in Prison Goorbux a native of the Great Mogull over whom we can have no right and determine causes according to our own customs, where the Alcoran to the Great Grief of the Musulman is used in an irrelevant manner, That we defraud the King of His Customs, and now entered by Violence and Force of Arms the King's Fort at Hugley.[99]

Jugdia possessed none of the locational advantages of Kasimbazar. It was situated far away from the second capital of Dhaka and its mint. It lay opposite the port of Sandwip, but this was not a Mughal port, being largely devastated by the Arakanese and Portuguese pirates in the seventeenth century. Jugdia was just a small port town and a collection point for cotton goods from south east Bengal from the sixteenth century. In the eighteenth century Jugdia evolved into a mart town.

Jugdia's story is added in this volume as a counterpoint to Kasimbazar for the very reasons elaborated at the beginning of this introduction. But to experience Kasimbazar and Jugdia it is necessary to go back in history.[100]

2. ABBREVIATIONS

A.N. Paris.	Archives Nationales, Paris.
A.N.S.O.M. Paris	Archives Nationales Section Outre Mer, Oudinot, Paris.
E.F.E.O.	Ecole Francaise d'Extreme Orient.
CAOM, Aix	Asia holdings at Aix-en-Provence (previously at A.N.S.O.M.) now housed in Centre des Archives Outre Mer (CAOM).
I.O.L.R. London	India Office Library and Records, London.
Factory Records	F.R. (with the name of the factory at the beginning. For example K.F.R. refers to Kasimbazar Factory Records and D.F.R. Dacca Factory Records)
HMS	Home Miscellaneous Series.
BPC	Bengal Public Consultations.
B.N. Paris.	Bibliotheque Nationale, Paris.
R.R	Bibliotheque Romain Rolland, Pondichery.
E.H.E.S.S	Ecole Des Hautes Etudes en Sciences Sociales, Paris.
A.E.	Affaires Etrangeres.
EEIC.	English East India Company
FEIC.	French East India Company
EICs.	East India Companies
DEIC	V.O.C. or the Dutch East India Company
Company	English East India Company
The term 'company' denotes	European companies in general
BPP	Bengal Past and Present
MAS	Modern Asian Studies

1

Silk as Symbol of Substance

When and how did Kasimbazar evolve into a silk producing centre? There is no mention of either Kasimbazar, or of Bengal silk[1] as an export item prior to the seventeenth century. The mention we get of Bengal silk prior to this period refers to wild silk and silk and cotton yarn mixes. While mulberry cultivation had been in practice much before European trading companies arrived in Bengal it is, nonetheless, clear that silk cultivation was a recent import. Both Moreland and J.N. Sarkar date the beginnings of sericulture in Bengal only from the fifteenth century.[2] This seems likely because Ibn Batuta mentioned cottons, and not silk, as one of the primary exports of Bengal in the fourteenth century.[3]

Vasco da Gama wrote in his diary of Bengal: '. . . in this land are many cotton cloths and silk cloths and much silver.' This was in the very last years of the fifteenth century. This fits in with our notion of a new silk industry just emerging in Bengal. The Chinese account *Ying Yai sheng lan* mentions weaving with silk in Bengal (silk-cotton mixed yarns) and the existence of a tree (probably the mulberry) from which paper was manufactured, '. . . white; it is made with the bark of a tree, and is as smooth and glossy as deers' skin'.[4] This is corroborated by *Si yang ch'ao kung tien lu* which says that paper was made of the mulberry tree.[5] So the mulberry tree was known in Bengal in the fifteenth century.

Yet this silk industry was slow to emerge in fifteenth century Bengal. Ma Huan's mission to Bengal in 1425 does not mention silk specifically.[6] Chinese accounts *Ying yai sheng lan* (Ma Huan), *Sing ch'a sheng lan, Si yang ch'ao kung tien lu, Shu yu chou tseu lu* and *Ming-she*[7] of the fifteenth century are more or less similar in enumerating the produce of Bengal and in describing Chinese exports to Bengal. Among the products of Bengal *muslin,* and not silk, is mentioned; and in export items *silk* figures as one of the premier Chinese exports to Bengal along with blue and white porcelain, gold, silver, satins, taffetas, metals among others. It was only from the late sixteenth century onwards that silk cultivation really took off in Bengal, and it is very likely that silk yarn was introduced into Bengal from China.[8]

We know that in ancient times *kausaya* or wild silk was used in both Buddhist and Hindu ceremonies in Bengal. A Song Chinese inscription of 1022 AD records the gift of 'a kasaya, woven with gold threads' to a Buddha statue at an unspecified place in South Asia.[9] *Kausaya* was grown in marginal areas in the eastern part of South Asia and was not produced on a systematic scale. Costly silk for clothing was imported from T'ang China, white cottons from eastern India were sent as diplomatic gifts.[10]

Silk was therefore an item of luxury in ancient Bengal. This changed in the medieval period. Bengal now started making her own silk. Why did silk become so integral to the political economy of commerce in Bengal?

Xinru Liu[11] traces the anthropology of silk from its beginning as a status symbol to its transformation into a political and economic tool and finally to a commodity of everyday use in the medieval world. Silk was initially cultivated in China, in Central Asia (along the Caspian Sea) and in Armenia. In the sixth century silk cultivation was introduced in Byzantium; primarily in northern Syria by the mercantile network of the Nestorians.[12] Silk textiles functioned as status symbols in the political and religious domains of both T'ang China and Byzantium. The *Code of Ceremonies* prepared by the Byzantine Court in the mid tenth century reflected this concept of using silk to project the grandeur of the court.

Between these two world orders of China and Byzantium lay the domain of Islam. Silk production underwent a massive change within the Islamic world order. Silk and cotton cultivation had remained localised until the eruption of Islam on the world's economic stage. Both the cultivation of cotton and silk needed a vast economic domain which was unified politically. This was possible when Islam entered the Mediterranean-Indian Ocean world with its conquests. Islam had a vigorous mercantile network and it adopted this culture of silk with certain modifications. Silk cultivation spread, along with the Islamic conquests, in southern Syria, Cyprus, southern Tunisia, Sicily, and south-east Spain from the seventh century onwards.

Thus silk cultivation spread across the Islamic world. While the Sassanids had imported Chinese silk for the Iranian manufactories and for Byzantium, Chinese silk was no longer imported by the time the Islamic world had expanded from the Mediterranean into the Indian Ocean. From the late fifteenth and early sixteenth centuries on, Bengal too began to manufacture her own silk.

Along with this revolution in silk cultivation occurred a revolution in technology; the Islamic network imported dyes such as indigo, kermes and saffron from the east and reintroduced them into the great manufactories of the Islamic world. Each great Islamic textile centre now developed its own speciality; Bengal, too, was not far behind in this. Only the Egyptian world stayed aloof from this textile revolution, anchored as it was firmly in linen production.

Silk therefore became linked firmly to the dinar economy. In other parts of the medieval world also we find the same phenomenon functioning. In the Mediterrannean, silk was a cash standard. In central Asia, it was both an important tool of diplomacy and a currency to purchase horses and slaves, pay rent, taxes and tributes, and as payment for labour. Ibn Khurdadbih had noted in the ninth century that the dinar economy needed a great mercantile network that only Islam was able to establish; in areas where barter had been the prevailing norm the dinar economy now ruled.[13] This became all the more true as more and more countries became islamised. Within the Islamic world, unlike the Chinese or the Byzantine therefore, silk spanned an entire parabola of emirates, sultanates, and empires. When Ibn Batuta visited Delhi in the fourteenth century the silk robes produced there were already famous in the Islamic world. We do not know where this silk came from but I would hazard a guess. It came from Gujarat, for Ibn Batuta does not mention Bengal silks.

It was also Islam that made silk industry part of its state machinery and the Islamic world emerged as both the largest market and the largest producer of silk under state patronage. The two early modern Islamic empires—the Ottoman and Safavid—were largely mercantilist empires and their commercial policies were based on silk. Silk was an effective commercial item against the ever-hungry-for-silk Europe in the fifteenth and sixteenth centuries. These centres of silk culture were thus based on different material and ideological considerations and yet served as a link between the two older centres of China and Byzantium.

There was a last order that also adopted silk as bargaining tool. In the Mongol Buddhist world silk was a status symbol, a negotiating tool, a diplomatic gift, a ceremonial/ritual offering and an economic instrument. In 1258, at the religious conference called by K'ublai Khan at Karakorum, accommodation was reached between the Taoists, the Buddhists and Confucians. K'ublai Khan ordered a new catalogue of Buddhism to be compiled in the three languages of Chinese, Tibetan and Sanskrit. The Mongolian Buddhist Phags-pa compiled an alphabetic system for all the languages in the Mongol Empire: Mongolian, Chinese and Tibetan after 1260.[14] A new religious and commercial circuit sprang up between eastern India, Mongolia and China.

Given their need of a universal trading currency it is therefore likely that the Bengal sultans sought to establish the silk industry in their domains. In the sixteenth and seventeenth centuries Bengal became divided into two distinct textile producing zones. The west produced silks at Kasimbazar, Rangpur and Nadia (Kumarkhali) and coarse and medium cottons at Radhanagar and Bardhaman. The east remained a fine cotton producing area.

Given the comparative low cost of living in Bengal, specialized weavers', spinners' and winders' jobs—as distinct from those occupations being supplemented by agriculture—evolved early in Bengal. In the sixteenth century, we have a reference to weaving as a full-time occupation.[15] By the seventeenth century, Mughal style *karkhanas* manufacturing muslins were set up in Dhaka. Around the same time, Europeans came to Bengal and found good silks which, as Bernier wrote, if wrought with care, could rival the silks of the Levant (Beirut and Syria).[16] By the eighteenth century western Bengal became known for its silk production and *arangs* under royal patronage were set up around Murshidabad and Malda.

2

Silk and Europe

Silk, we just saw, was a prestigious commodity from very early times. In the ancient Indian and Chinese worlds, it was an item endowed with religious significance. Later, Islamic lands adopted silk as a symbol of power and prestige. Silk became an important negotiating tool between countries. Europe was exposed to the magical value placed on silk, its symbolic link with the opulence of eastern empires, and as a symbol of substance, from the time it confronted the lands of the Levant during the crusades.

Silk made the leap from prestige item to profitable commodity within Europe. Between 1230 and 1231 the commune of Bologna invited a number of foreign artisans to set up manufacturing of silk.[1] In course of time, with the foundation of the Ottoman Empire on Europe's doorstep in the fifteenth century, Europe moved closer to the diplomatic significance of this item and to the effectiveness of silk as a bargaining counter in commerce between nations. Throughout the sixteenth century silk kept gaining in popularity all over Europe. In the seventeenth century, EICs began to explore alternative sources of silk supply from the Levant and Persia.

Why was there this sudden craze for silk in Europe in the seventeenth century? The answer lies in the crop failures in the Mediterranean from 1619 to 1622 which heralded the failure of silk production in France and Italy in subsequent decades, the 1630 plague in Italy and the general economic crisis in seventeenth century Europe (which led to a disproportionate rise in the price of Mediterranean silks) that compelled Europeans to look for alternative sources of supply. By 1664 mediterannean silk was becoming an unprofitable trading item.[2] The obvious choice was Persian silk but political instability in Safavid Persia after 1650 put paid to that scheme. Other sources of supply were located in the Levant—here too the silks from Bayrut and Syria were difficult to obtain as also expensive.

In 1611 the Venetian ambassador in the Ottoman Empire warned of the collapse of the internal market.[3] Between 1623 and 1638 the Turko-Persian

War signalled the doom of the silk trade for the European market. European cities responded to this crisis by offering loans and inducements to silk weavers. Italy's premier export to the rest of Europe was thrown silk. This export-market was hit by the plague of 1630 that devastated the silk-producing cities of north-central Italy. It is estimated that 1.1 million people died of a total population of 4 million in less than two years. The following statistics underline the gravity of the situation: in 1631, during the depression and plague, the Grand Duke of Florence advanced to the silk workshops eighteen—month interest-free loans.[4] Such measures were not successful. In Como at the beginning of the seventeenth century there were thirty looms for silk; by 1650 there were only two. The silk industry in Genoa numbered 10,000 looms in 1565, 4000 in 1630 and 2500 in 1675. At the end of the sixteenth century Genoa's annual export of silk cloth was about 360,000 pounds. In the seventeenth century it was 50,000 pounds. Verona produced 150,000 pounds of silk annually in the early seventeenth century; this was reduced to less than 90,000 pounds after 1620. Milan's silk looms numbered 3000 in 1600, 600 in 1635 and 350 in 1711.[5]

Once the Cape Route was well established and feeder networks incorporated into it to make it more attractive, the Bengal coast seemed the best source of supply to the Europeans. In the early years of the seventeenth century both the DEIC and the EEIC explored the suitability of establishing trading posts in Bengal. The Dutch toyed with the idea of replacing Persian silk with Chinese silk. But once they sent squadrons to the Bengal coast in the 1620s they decided to concentrate on Bengal silk instead.[6]

Between 1620 and 1625 two English factors from Surat named Hughes and Parker were sent overland from Surat to explore commercial possibilities in the east and to assess the quality of items to be found in those parts. We can well imagine their amazement when they stumbled upon a treasure trove of textiles at the Patna market and their jubilation when informed that the very same items could be obtained from a place called Maxudavad at a much lower cost. Hughes and Parker have left us a list of the items that excited so much of their interest: They are '*dopattas, ornees, ballabands* and *ellachas* from Malda'[7] (read Kasimbazar area). These were what the EEIC came to call silk piece goods, that is, items woven from cotton and silk yarn mixes.

In the 1660s Bernier wrote about the export possibilities of Bengal raw silk 'which if wrought with a little care would rival those of Barut and Syria'.[8] Around the same time Tavernier commented on the prodigious quantities of silk and silk mixes produced at Kasimbazar in Bengal and complained about the inability of the Europeans to get a foothold in the silk trade.[9] He estimated the production to be at 22,000 bales of 100 pounds each which made for a total production of 3.1 million pounds. Out of this about 400,000 was made available to Europeans; the rest was destined for the Indian and Asian markets. Like Hughes and Parker half a century before them the French too were urging their company directors to invest in Bengal silk. By 1680 all three companies, the DEIC, the EEIC, the FEIC, established their factories in Kasimbazar, as did the Armenians who carried on a massive overland trade in silk in Asia.

3
Kasimbazar Silk

Kasimbazar, which lay at the centre of the cocoon growing, silk spinning and weaving region of Murshidabad, was synonymous with opulence in the eighteenth century. This opulence was due to its flourishing silk trade which attracted a large number of people from all over the world. Kasimbazar, or its silk, became the economic symbol for eighteenth century Bengal.

The city was not marked in records prior to the seventeenth century; and it is generally accepted that a Mughal commander named Kasim Khan established a post there which soon grew to become 'the great market town whose streets never saw the light of the sun, so filled as it was with magnificent buildings'.[1]

The city had certain locational advantages other cities lacked. Apart from being at the heart of the mulberry growing region in Bengal it was close to the political centre of Murshidabad. This enabled the merchants of Kasimbazar to maintain political contacts and use the royal mint. A further advantage was that the city lay in a triangle formed by the Bhagirathi, the Jalangi and the Padma and thus formed an important inland port connecting east and south Bengal. Indeed the riverine port of Kasimbazar took unto itself many of the functions of the lapsed royal port of Gaur-Saptagram which had silted up at the end of the sixteenth century. Kasimbazar's function as a royal port in Bengal was all the more crucial in view of the fact that the only other Mughal port in the region was Hugli. And other than some agricultural items, the chief export of Kasimbazar port was silk.

The most coveted commodity that Bengal produced from Husain Shahi times was silk in various shapes and sizes.[2] The most sought after item was the raw silk in bales which was produced in lots called *bunds* in November (the best quality), March (medium) and June/July (frequently the worst since the monsoons hampered the winding and reeling process). Other market specific varieties were the *Guzerat* (possibly because this was the variety sent to Surat for re-export), the Rangpur and the Kumarkhali (named after the areas of origin) silks.

Of a more varied nature were the silk piece goods which included *chanderbanies, charconas, romalls, taffetas* and so on. For the silk in bales, quality was the primary consideration; for the piece goods, specific colours, designs and finishing acquired more importance. It was also from the environs of Kasimbazar that coarse textiles such as *garas* (*gurrahs*) and *dusutties* (*doosutties* or calicoes) were available. Together these comprised a major portion of the textile manufactures of Bengal and these very items figured prominently on the Europeans' shopping lists when they set up shop in Kasimbazar.

As its volume of trade grew Kasimbazar changed, in the course of the eighteenth century, from a sleepy Bengali backwater to a bustling commercial metropolis filled with Muslim, Armenian, Hindu and Christian merchants of all denominations from all over the world.

We do not have figures for the value of the total pan-Asian and European trade in silk from Kasimbazar. However the growing significance of European trade in Bengal's economy is attested to by the fact that as early as in 1681, of a total of 230,000 pounds sterling to be invested by the EEIC in Bengal, 140,000 was earmarked solely for Kasimbazar.[3] The Dutch invested the following amounts (in pounds) in silk for the following years:

Table 1
Dutch Investment in Bengal Silk: 1635–1718 (in pounds)[4]

1635–1640	around 20,000
1650	50,000
1654	200,000
After 1654	100,000
1669–1670	80,000
1678–1679	128,077
1690–1691	121,096
1692–1693	171,326
1699–1700	198,944
1701–1702	263,589
1702–1703	2,124
1704–1705	185,589
1709–1710	176,208
1713–1714	142,967
1715–1716	192,078
1717–1718	212,779

Table 2
English Investment in Bengal Raw Silk 1669–1721 (in Pounds)[5]

1669	20,000
1673	21,874
1676	31,570
1679	70,680
1681	124,335
1683	172,859
1686	48,574
1689	1640
1694	45,960
1697	47,620
1700	96,340
1701	148,449
1704	7393
1707	77,066
1710	63,429
1713	31,512
1716	74,717
1718	121,298
1721	20,344

We see therefore that Kasimbazar silk began to feature prominently in the English Investment Lists from the second half of the 17th century although the Dutch clearly maintained a lead and contracted for almost double the amount contracted for by the EEIC. This prominence is corroborated by Om Prakash who himself detects a shift in the V.O.C's or the Dutch Company's activities from Japan to India, and within India, from the Coromandel to Bengal, in the latter part of the seventeenth century.[6]

Table 3 gives us an idea of the further growth of Bengal raw silk exports in the eighteenth century and the competition from Chinese silk from the 1750s.

We do not have total figures for the trade of others who were settled there, such as the Armenians and the French; nor do we have accurate figures for the massive pan-Indian and pan-Asian trade that was conducted by Gujaratis, Lahoris, Multanis, Hyderabadis, Afghans, Persians, Turks, Armenians and Mughals from Kasimbazar. We know that Kasimbazar produced around 22,000 bales every year each weighing approximately 100 pounds. In the absence of standard equivalences for weights the total production in Kasimbazar in the seventeenth century was estimated to be around 3.1 million pounds. European buyers accounted for a small percentage in this

Table 3
English Investment in Raw Silk from Bengal and China; 1725–1760[7]

Year	Bengal	China
1725	121,016	24,409
1730	113,595	N.A (1729–7214)
1732	85,539	77,063
1734	209,166	N.A.
1737	155,932	N.A.
1741	160,197	N.A.
1744	121,107	N.A.
1747	94,729	N.A.
1748	800	N.A.
1752	82,774	184,560
1753	70,634	129,777
1754	27,199	194,299
1755	60,013	194,791
1756	40,231	107,456
1757	N.A.	234,756
1758	13,581	130,833
1759	44,527	56,743
1760	43,113	66,123

scheme; they bought around 350,000 pounds of silk. (This pound was measured in the great ounce of 24 instead of the normal 16 ounces to the pound for English weights and by Dutch *ponds* for exports to Holland).

But it is quite obvious from Table 3 that after the crisis of the 1740s at Kasimbazar, Chinese silk imports registered a steady growth as against Bengal silks throughout the 1750s. The growth of Chinese silk exports to England has to be understood in terms of the crisis in production and supply from the 1740s at Kasimbazar. Our data about the price rise at Kasimbazar will reinforce this point in tables 4, 5 and 6.

4

The Dadni Merchant of Western Bengal

Merchants in early modern economies rarely speak for themselves and are consequently faceless. Therefore we do not know much about the Bengal merchant in history. Our received history tells us that they were active in overseas commerce in the fifteenth and sixteenth centuries. Ludovico Varthema, Tome Pires, and Duarte Barbosa had mentioned great communities of merchants from Bengal either trading with South East Asian countries or settled there in the sixteenth century.[1] Dow and Verelst were informed that Bengali merchants, mainly *gandhabaniks*, visited north India, Assam, Cachar, Arcot, Orissa, Gujarat, Kashmir, Nepal, Oudh, Malwa, Kathiawad, Mongolia, China, Tibet and the Coromandel and the Malabar coasts.[2] While the texts that Dow and Verelst referred to (the *Harilila* and the *Candrakanta*) were both eighteenth century works, it was also clear that they were referring to a forgotten memory. Even as early as in the sixteenth century, the Bengali Hindu merchant stayed mostly at home, as Pires observed. Most of the ship-owners of Bengal were Muslim, many flying the royal flag in the sixteenth century, as one Portuguese visitor noted. This trend continued into the seventeenth century.

Pietro della Valle has mentioned Bengal merchants trading with the Maldives at the start of the seventeenth century.[3] At the beginning of the eighteenth century, independent trade in the eastern Indian Ocean by Bengali merchants registered a decline. Riverine and coastal trade continued to be in their hands, however, and in the 1730s Jacques Vincens mentioned groups of Bengali merchants trading in *cauris* with the Maldives. But this trade was negligible in comparison to the volume of trade carried on by Bengal in earlier centuries.

Indeed we can note a decline in indigenous participation in the trading world of the Indian Ocean from the late seventeenth century. Throughout the seventeenth century traditional ports of the Indian merchants in South

East Asia were being closed one after the other. The troubled fortunes of Malacca between 1511 and 1641 diverted trade and shipping away from one major hub into a number of smaller ports into the Malay world: Pase, Acheh, Johor, Bantam, Kedah, and Perak. The second half of the seventeenth century therefore saw a shift in emphasis away from the Indonesian and Malay worlds—the traditional trading partners of Bengal—and a move towards the ports of mainland South East Asia such as Burma and Thailand. New sea lanes were consequently opened.[4]

A similar rearrangement took place in the western Indian Ocean at this time. Like Malacca in the east, the two major commercial hubs were Yemen on the Red Sea and Hormuz in the Persian Gulf. Aden (on the Red Sea) and Jarun (on the Persian Gulf) were the two ports that controlled the western Indian Ocean trade. But from the sixteenth century onwards the Karimi network which dominated trade in the Arabian Sea-Red Sea-Egypt area entered into conflict with the sultans of Yemen; by the seventeenth century the network was practically finished. Hormuz fell in 1622 to an Anglo Dutch force.[5] Commerce in the western Indian Ocean was radically affected.

Yet another reason for the decline in participation of Bengalis in overseas trade may have been due to the fact that control over shipping came to be concentrated increasingly in the hands of royal officials in the course of the sixteenth and seventeenth centuries. Also, Bengali merchants started the practice of freighting space on the various EIC vessels from the end of the seventeenth century. It seems that along with the crisis in the trading world there occurred a crisis in the shipping world of the Bay as well at this time.[6] Because at the end of the seventeenth century *subahdari* ownership of vessels suddenly ceased; *subahdari* ships withdrew from sea trade by the 1730s and the seas were left free for the English to take over in the course of the eighteenth century.

Among the Europeans, the English East India Company, from its base at Calcutta, emerged as the most prominent shipowner and frequenly rented out freight space to local merchants. Thus the practice of individual ownership of ships that had been a marked feature of Indian economic activity now gave way to a 'joint stock' operating for shipping as well. The withdrawal has been well documented in Omprakash (1988) and the possible reasons for the withdrawal has been discussed in *Strange Riches.*

Under such hostile economic conditions, at a time when traditional overseas markets were collapsing around him, the Bengali merchant had few options. He could either conduct business on his own account through the myriad riverine networks that dotted eastern India or re-invent himself as a supplier to the many buyers that thronged the Bengal coast. The former option was increasingly becoming a closed door as the Europeans, and again specially the English, were in *de facto* control of the inland waterways from the latter part of the 1730s. The options for the Bengal merchant were thus very limited in the eighteenth century. The only viable option was to become a supplier of goods to buyers.

The Bengali merchant's chief activity in the seventeenth century was destined to be a middleman for the products, especially silk, for which so many traders flocked every year to the Bengal coast. This new species of Bengali merchant acted in his own capacity, either individually or through partnerships and informal consortiums, as suppliers of goods on the basis of a *dadan* or advance from the interested buyer. The Bengali merchant thereby mortgaged his profession and came to be known in history as a *dadni* merchant.

Dadni merchants became especially important for outside buyers because of the distinctive topography and difficult terrain of Bengal. The weavers and spinners were rural-based and thus often isolated from the market. Bengal in the eighteenth century had not reached the degree of urbanisation already present in Surat; there were few urban *karkhanas* with urban based workers to produce textiles. While royal workshops had been set up in Surat, Ahmadavad and Bharuch, the only comparable one in the eastern zone was the royal *karkhana* at Dhaka which produced high grade cottons, among them muslins. This was because muslins were exported to the Mughal court as tribute from the beginning of the seventeenth century.

Other manufacturing centres were the traditional *arangs* where silk was produced. These *arangs* were located in the interior close to silk growing areas. Therefore for historical reasons the spinners and weavers of eighteenth century Bengal, who were in the process of divorcing themselves totally from agricultural work in order to meet the increased demand for silk, found themselves geographically scattered and isolated; and thus they were also unable to establish direct access to the market. A middleman who would organise the entire sale process was therefore necessary for them. It was here in his role as the spokesman for this group, in his role as chief negotiator and middle man for their manufactures, that the *dadni* merchant really came into his own.

As *dadni* merchant the Bengal merchant's name was entered into the investment lists that the EICs maintained. *Dadni* merchants, consequently, are not nameless. A list in the English Company's records dated December 1685 throws light on the *dadni* merchants operating from Kasimbazar. This list mentions the names of the following merchants: merchant from families which would one day form a coterie and dominate the English Company's Investment Lists until 1754. The list contained the names of local notables who, by virtue of sheer hard work and business acumen, established strong political links (and patronage ties) with Murshidabad, diversified into banking and invested in real estate during the silk boom in the course of the eighteenth century.

Names indigenous to Bengal such as Dutt, Biswas, Sarkar and Ghosh occurred in this list of 1685 along with Surma, Chowdhuri, and Kapri—names whose place of origins and caste occupations are more difficult to ascertain. There were featured, in this list of 1685, as many as 18 Surmas, 5 Biswas, 2 Chowdhury, 1 Ghosh, and 1 each of Kapri, Sarkar and Dutt. Another list of 1701 features a Ghosh and a Surma yet again, while the name Katma, which was to become synonymous with massive silk deals from the 1730s at Kasimbazar, comes to our notice for the first time. Until 1754, when the *dadni* system was abandoned in favour of the agency system, some 186 merchants with these names dominated the supply of raw silk to the EEIC at Kasimbazar. There were also those who were simply called by their first names, as in the case of the mighty Kushalchand or those affixed with the title Seth such as Mahtab Rai and Swarup Chand, great nephews of Fatehchand of the House of Jagat Seth. Other 'up country' names such as Alam Chand, Gyan Chand etc. featured prominently in the financial realm of eighteenth century Bengal as well as in the EEIC lists at Kasimbazar.

While these merchants were referred to in the K.F.R. as 'our merchants' they were in actual fact not so because they were also merchants to the FEIC, the DEIC and the Ostend Company. This was a fact they used to their advantage while bargaining for better prices with the EEIC (K.F.R. Consultation of March 22, 1744). They traded wherever a better margin of profit was to be found; this is indicated by the EEIC's unsuccessful bans as regarded the *dadni* merchants' trade with the Danes, the Swedes and the Portuguese (K.F.R. Consultations of June 19, 1733, September 18, 1736 and the Generall Letter of December 13, 1738 that is entered under the Consultation of August 29, 1739) as well as prohibitions on trading with merchants from 'upper India' (K.F.R. June 12, 1733). Throughout the 1730s, the EEIC was just one among many buyers in the chaotic world of silk at Kasimbazar. This situation changed from the mid 1740s.

The *dadni* merchants practised business on the basis of advance issued by the buyer. As noted, this system was not so much a reflection on the financial status (or lack of) on the part of the merchant as the desire of the EICs to 'tie' production, producers and merchants into a system where price rises could be kept in check and production parameters pre-determined. We noted earlier that the system of contracts was useful in that it helped the *arangs* keep pace with expanding demand, as well as in regulating production to EIC dictates and standardizing it as far as possible; some commodities were simply not procurable without it since the producers were unable to comply without advance money as their resources were scarce. The advance contract system helped both sides but the advantage lay with the buyer. By means of the contract system competition was reduced, it bound the producer to a particular buyer and moreover it synchronized supply and demand and thereby reduced market instability.

5

Commodities, Prices and Profit at Kasimbazar in the First Half of the Eighteenth Century

The commodities procured by the EEIC factors at Kasimbazar consisted of the following: raw silk divided into the harvest gradations of November, March and July bunds, the Gujarat silk favoured by merchants from Gujarat, as well as Kumarkhali and Rangpur silks, silk piece goods of different varieties (see Table 5) and calicoes such as *garas* and *dusutties* from the Bardhaman, Khirpai, Radhanagor and Dewanganj areas. S.C. Nandy identified Rangpur silk as the 'Guzerat' variety; but this is not borne out by the K.F.R. as the two varieties were recorded under separate headings in the investment lists for the years they were invested in.[1] The catchment area of the Kasimbazar factory was spread over *arangs* as far away as Malda and Rajshahi in the north, Nadia (Kumarkhali) in the south and Bardhaman to the west.

It appears from the K.F.R. that the best quality of Kasimbazar silk (the Gujarat among the raw silk and *jamawars* in the silk piece goods category) were not very popular at the EEIC sales in London. These fetched actually a price that was 30% lower than coarser grades in London. The reason was the finishing at Kasimbazar—a matter that became cause for serious complaint after the 1740s. The finishing necessary at the London sales for the best type of Kasimbazar silk made this category too expensive to sell. The main EEIC demand was therefore for the middle range of silk, as well as for the more coarse category from Kasimbazar. Tables 4, 5 and 6 below show us the prices of the different categories of silk textiles and the index of price rise between 1733 to 1750.

It is evident from Table 4 that the Kumarkhali silk registered the sharpest rise in prices, followed by the Gujarat variety. We see from tables 5 and 6 that plain taffaties and the silk *lungi rumals* registered the most rise, followed by most categories of *bandanies*. The price of *dunedars* and *chanderbanies*

Table 4
Price in rupee per maund of RS for November Bund (NB), Guzzerat (GUZ), Commercolly (COM), from 1733 to 1750 as well as the average price and index (100 for 1739)

	Price in rupee per maund				Index (1739 = 100)			
Year	NB	GUZ	COM	Average	NB	GUZ	COM	Average
1733	6.28	5.00	3.75	5.01	126	90	77	97
1735	5.00			5.00	100			100
1736	5.25	5.37	4.87	5.16	105	97	100	100
1737	3.75*	5.37	5.06	4.73*	75*	97	104	92*
1738	5.18	5.75	5.00	5.31	104	103	103	103
1739	5.00	5.56	4.87	5.14	**100**	**100**	**100**	**100**
1740	4.87	5.43	4.68	4.99	97	98	96	97
1741	5.25	5.81	5.06	5.37	105	104	104	104
1742	5.50	6.06	5.31	5.62	110	109	109	109
1743	5.50			5.50	110			110
1744	6.06	6.62	5.87	6.18	121	119	121	120
1745	5.87	6.43	5.68	5.99	117	116	117	117
1746	7.00			7.00	140			140
1748	6.75			6.75	135			135
1749	7.00	7.56	6.81	7.12	140	136	140	139
1750	7.40				148			

* The figure probably refers to 80% of the price.

remained constant but we should note that they were not always invested in. *Jamawars* were invested in only twice, in 1736 and 1741, probably because they were the most expensive among the silk piece goods.

Moreover, we see from tables 4, 5 and 6 that the price rise started in 1744; the rise is quite sharp for the raw silk of the November Bund, 'Guzerat' and 'Commercolly' varieties. This rise happened possibly because of the Maratha raids in western Bengal around this time. Parts of Nadia—a prime silk and cotton producing area-were left devastated by them. This may have triggered off a crisis in the production sphere that was already under strain due to the excessive demand by EICs.

Table 5
Price in Rupees for Silk Piece Goods (SPG) from 1736 to 1748.

(Key: TP Taffaty Plain, TS Taffaty Striped, BO Bandannoes Ordinary, BF Bandannoes Fine, D Dunnedars, C Chanderbannies, SLR Silk Lungee Romalls, J Jamawars)

Year	TP	TS	BO	BF	D	C	SLR	J	Average
1736	-	-	3.50	4.00	16.50	2.75	5.75	12.12	7.44
1737	-	-	3.50	4.00	16.50	2.75	5.75	-	6.50
1738	-	-	3.50	4.00	-	2.75	5.75	-	4.00
1739	7.00	7.25	3.37	3.87	16.50	2.75	5.75	19.00	8.19
1740	7.00	7.25	3.37	3.87	16.50	-	5.75	-	7.29
1741	7.00	7.25	3.37	3.87	16.50	-	5.75	18.50	8.89
1742	7.50	7.75	3.50	4.00	-	2.87	6.12	-	5.29
1743	7.00	7.25	3.25	3.75	-	-	6.37	-	5.52
1744	-	8.25	3.75	4.25	-	-	-	-	5.42
1745	-	-	-	4.37	-	-	-	-	4.37
1746	9.50	-	-	-	-	-	-	-	9.50
1748	9.50	9.25	4.12	4.68	-	-	8.06	-	7.12

Table 6
Index of Price Rise (Base year =1739) from 1736 to 1748

(Key: TP Taffaty Plain, TS Taffaty Striped, BO Bandannoes Ordinary, BF Bandannoes Fine, D Dunnedars, C Chanderbannies, SLR Silk Lungee Romalls, J Jamawars)

Year	TP	TS	BO	BF	D	C	SLR	J	Average
1736	-	-	104	103	100	100	100	64	95
1737	-	-	104	103	100	100	100	-	101
1738	-	-	104	103	-	100	100	-	102
1739	**100**	**100**	**100**	**100**	**100**	**100**	**100**	**100**	**100**
1740	100	100	100	100	100	-	100	-	100
1741	100	100	100	100	100	-	100	97	100
1742	107	107	104	103	-	104	106	-	105
1743	100	100	96	97	-	-	110	-	101
1744	-	114	111	110	-	-	-	-	112
1745	-	-	-	113	-	-	-	-	113
1746	136	-	-	-	-	-	-	-	136
1748	136	128	122	121	-	-	140	-	129

de Gennes de la Chanceliere noted at the height of the Maratha raids, in his voyage from Chandernagore upto Kasimbazar in 1743, that.[2]

> It (Shantipur) seemed to have been totally destroyed the year before by the Marathas . . . one comes across the village of Nodia (whose) Raja Quisim-Cha (Krisna Candra) has escaped being pillaged by the Marathas by paying two lacs of roupies . . . It is a pity that all this land, fine and fertile by itself was sacked by the Marathas . . . The country is still smouldering from the fires and damages which these barbarians have inflicted to the areas round the Ganges from which they have taken contributions . . . This has led to the near complete ruin of the inhabitants of these fertile regions . . . On approaching Cassenbazar and Moxudabad, the famous capital of the kingdom of Bengal, the country seems to have suffered a little less of pillage . . . there was at that time (in Murshidabad) a camp of six thousand cavalrymen in order to oppose the insult of the Marathas who had thought of taking the town last year.

The price rise therefore ties in with our evidence further on in this volume about the crisis in textile production in the region in the mid forties.

In their silk dealings the *dadni* merchants made a profit ranging from 2% to 4%. (Consultations of December 9, 1741; January 6, January 31, and February 3, 1742). We are also informed that they made a profit of Sicca Rupees 0.20 to 0.25 a *seer* for raw silk and between 1 and 3 annas for the silk piece goods (Consultation of April 6, 1737). While this may not sound much we should remember that 40 *seers* made a *man* and that some merchants supplied over 200 *mans* at each Investment.[3] This gives us an idea of the enormous amounts of money at stake in the silk trade at Kasimbazar. Whether the merchants made the same rate of profit after the price rise from 1744 is debatable. Our evidence later on in this volume suggests otherwise.

In reality, under the surface of Company records, there seethed something very like a *politics* of investment. The economic viability of each European company at 'home' depended on despatching the best textiles at the least possible price to the home countries; this was possible only if the stuffs in question were contracted for well in advance. The amount paid in advance depended on a well organised espionage system in the countryside and manufacturing centres (*arangs*) regarding prices and quality of *patni* or filament which would in turn determine quality in the final delivery.

The economic strength of each company on the spot depended on the amount of money it could lay out for investment and the time of investment. The two were interlinked. For example, in the early 1700s the EICs had to race against the Gujarati and other merchants who often bought up the filaments (*patni*) earlier. Late buying meant higher prices and inferior quality.

The rate of advance fluctuated between 75% and 85% from 1733 to 1750; however in lean years such as 1738, when the English Company was strapped for funds, the merchants operated on the basis of an advance of 59%. Yet again in 1740 advances for the November Bund and the Kumarkhali silks rose as high as 94% and 95%. As regards silk piece goods we notice fluctuations ranging from 67%–80% for *bandannoes*, between 86% and 94% for silk lungee romalls, advance for the plain and striped *taffaties* varied between 69%–77%, *dunnedars* ranged between 71% to 77%, *jamawars* between 82%–89%, *chanderbannies* went for a 94% advance, *gara* advances ranged from 70%–85% and *dusutties* between 60%–70% (Mukherjee 1994: 513–4). In general the rate of advance was fixed at 80%.[4]

Actually, the rate of advance fluctuated according to political and economic imperatives: the amount of cash in the hands of both parties, the Company's financial situation, the time of investment, and the relative strengths of the two parties, as well as the political situation in Bengal. For example, the English silk investment suffered in 1739–1740 because of the fluid political situation that the EEIC termed a 'revolution' in Bengal.

The company merchants—and more specifically the broker—were also buyers of European goods from the factory *kuthis*. These sales, while negligible in comparison to the volume of the sales of Bengal silks and cottons in Europe, were nevertheless significant in that they helped the EICs supplement their funds in Bengal. Firearms were in great demand, so were European broadcloth and woollens, and some velvet and damask. Some port wine and Madeira were sold. Prices of these commodities remained fairly constant from 1733 to 1750. The prominent buyers of European goods were the Katmas, Biswasses, Dutts, Surmas as well as a few other leading individual merchants.[5] The ruling elite in Murshidabad was becoming accustomed to European consumption patterns; and the accelerating sale of firearms in the 1740s, (as recorded in the K.F.R.) points to a new kind of war society coming into being in the western part of Bengal. As a result perhaps of frequent Maratha raids from this time, townsmen felt obliged to defend their lives and possessions.

The *dadni* merchant was not, we noted, a primary producer. He furnished the EIC (and Asian) investments at the company's *kuthi* (or warehouse) at the stipulated time, with the requisite specifications. Any deterioration from the quality stipulated in the sample resulted in the final price being lowered, or at least there was an attempt by the EIC concerned to do so. This issue of deteriorating quality and consequently lower prices became a bone of contention between the buyer and supplier from the 1740s, and was one of the reasons for the switch to the *gomastha* system whereby an official of the EEIC supervised the actual production at the *arangs*.

The *dadni* merchant was essentially a middleman in sales between India and Europe. But as a businessman, he possessed a clearly defined identity; he claimed that he had been 'bred in the silk business since childhood' (K.F.R. February 28, 1744); and he was, until the mid century crisis, generally in a strong enough position to withstand English interdictions on trade with Indian merchants and other European companies (K.F.R. 1733, 1736, 1738, 1744). At times he formed partnerships and informal consortiums to reinforce his position as a bloc against the European joint stocks; and his opposition tactics were referred to as a 'ring' in the K.F.R. This growing conception of the 'common good' was cut short by the production crisis of the mid eighteenth century.

6

The Dadni Merchant of Kasimbazar

Table 7 gives the names of merchants, in descending order, according to the rank in the English Investment lists from 1701 to 1750 at Kasimbazar in raw silk, silk piece goods and calicoes ('*gurrahs*' and '*doosutties*') in the years for which information is available. The original spellings of the names have been retained. An explanation of their probable origins and caste affiliations follows the table.

Table 7
Name According to Rank for Different Categories of Textiles

Raw Silk (RS), March and April Bunds	Silk Piece Goods (SPG)	Gurrahs and Doosutties (G&D)	Rungpore Silk
1701	N.A.	N.A.	N.A.
Kissore Ray			
Nundookissore Goo (Ghosh?)			
Chuckosow (Saha?)			
Bobanund Surma			
Kinno Cutma			
Damorai			
Kissenkinkar Goos (Ghosh)			
Nunderam Coit (Kayet?)			
Girderay			
Jaggernaut			
Juddam Coit			
Gopaul Tillee			
Bridgebullub Kibul			

1733 RS	1733 SPG	1733 G&D	1733 Rungpore Silk
Beley Cotma	Sudanund Cotma	Paunchue Cotma G&D)	Udachund
Booban Mahaun	Paunchue Cotma	Herre Surma (G)	Bridgebullubdass
Kissenpersaud Biswass	Nutmull	Ramnede Surma (G&D)	Bissenautdutt (Bisnadutt)
Takoo Biswass	Praunkissen	Paunchue Bose (G)	Sudanund Cotma
Radgebullub Biswass	Golol Pana	Radakissen Sircar (G&D)	Gocul Biswass
Sudanund Cotma	Kissenpersaud Biswass	Bisnadutt (G)	Rogonaut Biswass
Coosalchund	Kelleram Topaull	Urjun Surma (G)	
Kissenchund Biswass	Nundoosaud	Bridgemahaun (G)	
Ozeram Biswass	Gosseram		
Keveleram Surma	Coshaulchund		
Gocul Biswass	Ramsing		
Coolean Biswass	Ballkrishna		
Saulput	Nosena Ramdeb		
Bisnadutt	Bisnadutt		
Ball Krishna	Bickul Chowdree		
Ody Coshall	Diaram Teal (Teli)		
Sovelchund	Kissenchund Cotma		
Harrybullubdass	Russick Chowdree		
Commellochund	Debbe Persaud		
	Hernaut		
	Ruttunchund / Huttichund		
	Kissenchund Biswass		
	Seve Cotma		
	Nunderam Sircar		
	Onoop Kertee		
	Bobboo (Bobun?) Cotma		
	Radanaut Biswass		
	Nainduss		
	Doolol Berry		
	Nonet (Noni?)		
	Saulput		
	Harrybullubdass		
	Bridgebouhan Cotma		

1736 RS	1736 SPG	1736 G&D	1736 Muctadooties
Kissenpersaud (Biswass)	Nundooram Sircar	Sutchy Cotma	Diaram Teal (Teli)
Suddanund (Cotma)	Gopee Surma	Nundecomar Surma	Russick Chowdree
Bridgenautdutt	Sutchy Cotma	Petumbergose	
Deveramdutt	Jugmohun	Luckynarransain	
Bobun Mohun	Killeram Toppull	Jebbun Surma	
Takoo Biswass	Kergolin (?)	Orjun Surma	
Paunchue Biswass	Balkissen	Ramnede Surma	
Prawnkissen	Diaram Teal	Radakissen Sircar	

1736 RS	1736 SPG	1736 G&D	1736 Muctadooties
Ojuderam (Biswass)	Ramsing	Harry Surma	
Ram Tagoo (Thakur?)	Gosseram	Bridgemohun	
Bridgebullubdass	Russick Chowdree		
Nimdass	Nemydutt		
Petumbergose (Ghosh)	Anunchund/Nutmull		
Coosalchund	Mautobray/Surroopchund		
Mony Sadasib	Bridgebucun Cotma		
Kissenchund	Kincar Coppree		
Ramdeb	Kissenpersaud		
Goberdun Biswass	Radanaut Biswass		
Balkissen	Radakunt		
Bissenautdutt	Onoop Kirkee (Kertee?)		
Sisteduss (Sasthi Das)	Joyram Pundit		
Keveleram Surma			
Cullion (Kalyan) Biswass			
Nemidutt			
Durgaram Dutt			
Ramnarandutt			
Ramchund Pundit			

1737 RS	1737 SPG	1737 Additional Investment in SPG	1737 G&D
Kissenpersaud Biswass	Nemidutt	Kinkar Coppree	Sutchy Cotma
Ozuderam Biswass	Sutchy Cotma	Ramsing	Sirbis Sir
Nainchurndutt	Balkissen	Gosseram	Kissen Surma
Bissinautdutt	Bissenautdutt	Coosalchund	Dokoor Sen
Cossenautdutt	Jackernaut	Commull Coppree	Callean Surma
Maudeb Surma	Munsook Coppree	Diaram Teal	Petumber Gose
Teko Biswass	Nundoo Son	Deby Persaud	Deby Persaud
Sutchy Cotma	Sadassib Chowdree	Bulleram Acharge	Bissenautdutt
Ruggonaut Biswass	Killeram Toppull	Niandur	Nemidutt
Narran Biswass	Ramdeb Dutt	Ody Biswass	Ramnarandutt
Praunaut Pundit	Gopee Surma	Nunderam Sircar	Nemidutt/ Sutchy Cotma/ Bissenautdutt
Collean Biswass	Coosal Gautum	Jeyram Pundit	
Nimdass	Saum Cotma	Ramkissen Morgine	
Ram Taggo	Ragenchurn	Gopee Gautum	
Keveleram Surma	Kissenpersaud Biswass	Mautobray/ Surroopchund	
	Russick Chowdree	Anunchund/Nutmull	
Balkissen	Bocun Cotma		
Nemidutt	Radakunt (Coverage?)		
Petumber Goss	Onoop Coppree		
Goberdun (Biswass)	Radakunt Biswass		
Bolleram Acharge			
Coosalcoond			

1737 RS	1737 SPG	1737 Additional Investment in SPG	1737 G&D
For RS March Bund done in June:			
Kissenpersaud Biswass			
Ozederam Biswass			
Maudeb Tockur			
Sutchy Cotma			
Nainchurndutt			
Ramdebdutt			
Doolol Tockur			
Coorall Tockur			
Rogonaut Biswass			
Coosalchund			
Petumbergose			
Naran Biswass			
Nemidutt			
Prawnaut Pundit			
Bolleram Acharge			
Keveleram Surma			
Goberdun Biswass			
Nimdass			
Mozooley Sing			
Coosalchund			
Collean Biswass			
Balkissen			
Deby Pursaud			
Bridgebullub Dass			
Ram Tagore			
Bissenautdutt			

1738-RS	1738 SPG	1738-G&D
Sutchy Cotma	Prawnkissen	Sutchy Cotma
Ramdebdutt	Ramdebdutt	Bissenautdutt
Nainchurndutt	Sutchy Cotma	Ramnarandutt
Maudeb Tockur	Nundooson	Nemidutt
Kissenpersaud Biswass	Jaggernaut	Sirbis Sir
Ozuderam Biswass	Gopee Gautum	Dokoor Sow
Rogonaut Biswass	Raddakisna	Cullean Surma
Coosalchund	Indernaran Chowdree	Nillambergose
Bissenautdutt	Coosal Gautum	Deby Pursaud
Narran Biswass	Bissenautdutt	Balkissen
Kincargose	Sam Cotma	
Keveleram Surma	Kisnachunder	
Ram Tagur	Radanaut Biswass	
Nemidutt	Nemidutt	
Sam Mohun	Comaul Coppree	

1738-RS	1738 SPG	1738-G&D
Cullean Biswass	Onoop Coppree	
Goberdun Biswass	Monsook Coppree	
Bridgbullubdass	Bocun Cotma	
Prawnaut Pundit	Balkissen	
Boleram Acharge	Niandur	
Balkissen	Sadassib Chowdree	
Nillambergose	Radachunder Peramanick	
Nimdass	Kincar Coppree	
Morooley Sing	Ody Biswass	
Deby Pursaud	Debypursaud	
Coosalcoond	Ramkissen	
	Radakunt Coveraje	
	Otteram	

1739-RS, G & D	1739 April-SPG	1739 May-SPG (March Bund)	1739 April-RS
Sutchy Cotma	Oody Cotma	Oody Cotma	Oodi Cotma
(RS, G&D)	Balkissen	Samsunder	Samsunder
Odey Narain	Samsunder	Radanaut Biswass	Sutchy Cotma
(RS, G & D)	Govinram	Balkissen	Kincar Goss
Samsunder	Sutchy Cotma	Killeram Toppull	Nillambergose
(RS, G & D)	Jackernaut	Diaram Teal	Chedam Bose
			(Cheyram
Jeyram Bose (RS)	Gopee Gautum	Coosalchund	or Jeyram ?)
Cheyram Bose (RS, G)	Kincar Coppree	Sutchy Cotma	Nainchurndutt
Narran Biswass (RS, G)	Bissenautdutt	Munsook Coppree	Coosalchund
Govinram (G)	Randchund	Russick Chowdree	Bissenautdutt
	Permanick		
Sirbis Sir (G)	Radanaut Biswass	Gopee Gautum	Maudeb Tockur
Colean Surma (G)	Sadassib Chowdree	Naran Biswass	Keveleram Surma
Rogonaut Biswass (RS)	Monsook Coppree	Naindur	Goberdun Biswass
Ojuderam Biswass	Bocun (Bobun?)	Cooshall Gautum	Naran Biswass
(RS, G)	Cotma		
	Narran Biswass	Ramkissen Morgine	Ojuderam Biswass
Nillambergose (RS, G)	Russick Chowdree	Saum Cotma	Balkissen
Kincargose (RS)	Comull Coppree	Kissenchund	Bulleram
		Chowdree	Acharge
Nainchurndutt (RS)	Chucker Biswass	Otteram Coit	Coolean Biswass
Coosalchund (RS)	Onoop Coppree	Radakunt Coverage	Kissenpersaud
		Biswass	
Maudeb Surma (RS)	Kissenchund	Radakissen	Bridgebullubdass
	Chowdree		
Dookor Saw (Shaha)	Raddo Chowdree	Sadassib Chowdree	Coosalcoond
(G & D)	Radakunt Coveraje	Chucker Biswass	Deby Pursaud
Balkissen (RS, G)	Saum Cotma	Bissenautdutt	Nimdass
Deby Pursaud (RS, G)	Cooshall Gautum	Ramchund	Ram Tagore
		Peramanick	

1739-RS, G & D	1739 April-SPG	1739 May-SPG (March Bund)	1739 April-RS
Nemidutt (RS)	Otteram Coit	Kissenchund (Chowdree)	Praunaut Pundit
Coolean Biswass (RS)		Buccun Cotma	
Bridgbullubdass (RS)		Comull Coppree	
Coosalcoond (RS)		Jackernaut	
Goberdun Biswass (RS)		Kincar Coppree	
Onoop Coppree (G)		Onoop Coppree	
Bulleram Acharge (RS)			
Moorely Sing (RS)			
Nimdass (RS)			
Praunaut Pundit (RS)			
1740 RS SPG	**1740-February**	**1740-G & D Silk**	**1740-Rungpore**
Sutchy Cotma	Sutchy Cotma	Sutchy Cotma	Huttoo Cotma
Samsunder	Odey Naran	Colean Surma	Coosalchund
Jeyram Bose	Samsunder	Odey Naran	Bissenautdutt
Bissenautdutt	Commol Coppree	Samsunder	
Naran Biswass	Balkissen	Naran Biswas	
Odey Narain	Radanund	Bissenautdutt	
Kincar Gose	Radanaut	Balkissen	
Maudeb Tagore	Kissen Chowdree	Nillambergose	
Nainchurndutt	Killeram/Diaram	Onoop Coppree	
Bridgu (?)	Sam/Onoop Mahon		
Coosalchund	Russick/Kissenchund		
Sam Mahon	Naran Biswass		
Sirbis Sir	Chuckena/ Otteram		
Ojuderam Biswass	Sam Mahon		
Kissenpersaud Biswass	Becull Tagore		
Bowannychurndutt	Coosalchund		
Nemidutt	Radakunt		
Ram Tagore	Kissenchund		
Coosalcoond	Bissenautdutt		
Goburdun Biswass	Samsunder/Odey Naran		
Balkissen	Odey Naran		
Colean Biswass	Sutchy Cotma/Jackernaut		
Nillambergose	Kissenpersaud Biswass		
Bridgbullubdass	Radakunt		
Nimdass	Naran Biswass/		
Praun Coppree	Gopee Gautum		
Keveleram Surma	Kipperam (Killeram?)		
Becul Tagore	Onoop Coppree		
Moroley Sing	1740-July Addl. SPG Invest done with same merchants mainly for the appearance of 'New Sort Romalls' at Kasimbazar		

1741 – RS	1741-March and April SPG	1741- March and April SPG, G & D
Naran Biswass	Coosalchund	Sutchy Cotma (SPG, G&D)
Coosalchund	Ramsing	Samsunder (SPG, G&D)
Samsunder	Nunderam/ Sauhibram	Odey Naran (SPG, G)
Maudeb Tagore	Gosseram	Nemidutt (SPG, G)
Odey Naran	Nundookissore	Narran Biswass (SPG, G)
Sutchy Cotma	Onoopchurn	Nunderam Sircar (SPG, G)
Nainchurndutt	Morley Sing	Nillambergose (SPG, G)
Nimdass	Kissenchurndutt	Rogonaut Biswass (SPG, G)
Nemidutt	Saum Cotma	Radakissen (SPG, G)
Rogonaut Biswass	Bridgbullubdass	Onoop Coppree (SPG, G)
Goberdun Biswass	Raudaramon	Paunchue (G)
Lollchund/ Bowannychurndutt	Jug Mohun	
Bridgusing	Keveleram Surma	
Morley Sing	Sam Mahon	
Prawn Coppree	Ramkissen Morgine	
Baramull	Ramnaut/Itchinaut	
Ojuderam Biswass	Money Biswass	
Bridgbullubdass		
Coosalcoond		
Bissenautdutt		
Sam Mahon		
Onoop Coppree		
Prawnaut Pundit		
Nunderam		
Radakissen		
Sabram Surma		
Coolean Biswass		
Nundookissore		
Becul Tagore		

1742 RS	1742 SPG
Narran Biswass	Gosseram
Bissenautdutt	Nunderam/Sabram
Samsunder	Ramsing
Rogonaut Biswass	Samsunder
Maudeb Surma	Kissenchurndutt
Harrykissen Mullick	Jugmohan
Prawn Coppree	Bissenautdutt
Ojuderam Biswass	Ramnaut/Itchinaut
Bridgbullubdass	Russick Chowdree
Doolol Surma	Money Biswass
Ram Tagoor	Nain (churn?) dutt
Onoop Coppree	Raddakissen

1742 RS	1742 SPG
Sabram Surma	Keveleram Surma
Nillamber Gose	Nillambergose
Nainchurndutt	Pudoll Ochun
Cossenautdutt	Nundokissore
Nundoo Kissore	Jackernaut Coppree
Keveleram Surma	Killeram Toppull
Praunaut Pundit	Ramkissen (Morgine?)
Odey Naran	Onoop Coppree
Coolean Biswass	Jugul Sircar
Bowannychurndutt	Sadassib Chowdree
Duccour (Sow?)	Raddo Chowdree
Sam Mahon	Radachund Peromonick
	Radacunt Coveraje
	Kissen Inder (Tagore? Or Surma?) Nusseray

1743 RS	1743 SPG
Beroofe Cotma	Gosseram
Bowannychurndutt	Radamohun Sircar
Nainchurndutt	Beroof Cotma
Seroopchund	Praunkissen Cotma
Maudeb Surma	Russick Chowdree
Coosal Tagore	Radakissen Sircar
Primnaran/Onoopnaran	Killeram Toppull
Lollchund/Annunchund	Money Biswass
Praun Coppree	Ramsing
Naran Biswass	Luckicundgose
Bobun Cotma	Nain (churn) dur (dutt?)
Rogonaut Biswass	Seerpursaud Chowdree
Roopnarandutt	Diaram Teal (Teli?)
Nundoo Kissore	Sudanund Gufft (Gupta?)
Onoop Coppree	Rajechunder Tagoor
Bridgoosing	Ramnaut/Tekinaut
Harrybullubdass	Primnaran/Onoopnaran
Seerbissinaut	Ramkissen Morgine(Majhi?)
Gurdas Dutt	Kissenunder Tagoor
Bajoochunder	Bridgoo Mahone Tagore
Bridgoomahone	Jugulldass
(Tagore?)	Bridgoo Bocun Surma
Doccour	Kisna Biswass
Sambonaut Tagore	Morley Podar
Harrykissen Tagore	Ram Chowdree
Ojuderam Biswass	Kissenchurndutt
	Jetto Tilly
	Wooderam(Udayram)Sircar
	Bridgoo Bobun Cotma
	Seerbissinaut
	Onoop Coppree

1744 February and March RS	1744 March SPG	1744 May 28th, SPG
Suroop Cotma	Coosalchund	Gosseram
Narran Biswass	Gosseram	Succoloil
Bobun Cotma	Chuckerloll	Coosalchund
Rogonaut Biswass	Radakissen Sircar	Radakissen Sircar
Maudeb Surma	Rada Mohun Sircar	Suroop Cotma
Kinkargose	Adey (Odey) Naran	Preet Cotma
Preat Cotma	Kisninda Surma	Radamahone Sircar
Onoop Coppree	Kissenpersaud Biswass	Mohun Chowdree
Prawn Coppree	Onoopnaran/ Primnaran	Russick Chowdree
Coosalchund	Collichurn Cotma	Prawn Kissen Cotma
Nundookissore	Nainchurndutt	Kissenpersaud Biswass
Harrybullubdass	Kissenchurndutt	Luckycundgose
Keveleram Surma	Russick Chowdree	Kisnanda Surma
Coolean Biswass	Luckicundgose	Odey Naran
Kissenchurndutt	Bistumchurndee	Doololl Sircar
Nundoocoomar	Becul Taggoor	Deby Pursaud
Sirbissinaut	Radachunder Surma	Rogonaut Biswass
Nainchurndutt	Ramkissen Mosunder	Ramnaut
Bowannychurndutt	Getoo Teley	Ramsurn Mosunder
Becul Tagoo (re)	Kelleram Toppull	Diaram Teal (Teli)
Duccour	Moorley Podar	Morley Podar
Money Biswass	Mohun Chowdree	Killeram Toppull
Nainchurndutt/Bobun	Harrykissen Morgine	Ram Chowdree
Cotma	Harris Chowdree	Radakissen Bobboo
Harrybullubdass/	Doolol Surma	Jettoo Teley
Doolol Surma	Jugull Sircar	Jugull Sircar
Coosalchund/Keveleram	Deby Prasad	Naindur
Surma	Doolol Biswass	Rogonunder Surma
Onoop Coppree/Prawn	Harrybullubdass	Jackernaut
Coppree	Sadanunder	Teele Teele (?)/Jackernaut
Boolchund Cotma	Samsunder	Randgedurpoore (?)
Coolean Biswass/Harris	Sibepersaud Chowdree	Kissenchurndutt
Chowdree	Ramjee Teal	Keveleram Surma
Bistumchurndee	Doolol Sircar	Sibepersaud Chowdree
Kisninda Surma	Huttonaut	Gopee Gotrem (Gautam)
Dookur	Ram Chowdree	Harris Chowdree
Morley Podar	Jackernaut Teal	Harrykissen Morgine
Luckicundgose	Nusseram	Doman Counch (?)
Becul Taggoor	Ramsur Musinder	Becul Tagoor
Ramkissen Mosunder	Gopee Taggor	Mohun Cotma
Getoo Teley		Kissenchunder Chowdree
		Otteram Coveraje
		Jugnu Surma

1745 RS	1745, March 20, SPG. May, additional investment in SPG	1745 April G&D.	1745: June-September, additional investment in *garahs*
Nainchurndutt	Coosalchund	Rogonaut Biswass	Rogonaut Biswass
Bobun Cotma	Kisninda Surma	Nainchurndutt	Samsunder
Rogonaut Biswass	Nainchurndutt	Samsunder	Odey Naran
Doolol Surma	Kissenchurndutt	Odey Naran	Prawn Coppree
Coosalchund	Russick Chowdree	Prawn Coppree	Keveleram Surma
Cableram (Keveleram)	Luckicundgose	Cableram Surma	Nyanchurndutt
Surma	Bistumchurndee	Coosalchund	Coosalchund
Harrybullubdass	Onoop Coppree	Radakissen (Sircar?)	Harrybullubdass
Onoop Coppree	Becul Taggoor	Kissenchurndutt	Radakissen Sircar
Prawn Coppree	Ramkissen Bobboo	Onoop Coppree	Onoop Coppree
Bulchund Cotma	Getoo Teley	Harrybullubdass	Kissenchurndutt
Colean Biswass	Moorley Podar	Luckicundgose	Kisninda Surma
Harris Chowdree	Harrykissen Morgine	Kisnainda Surma	Luckicundgose
Bistumchurndee/	(Majhi?)	Harris Chowdree	Harris Chowdree
Kisninda Surma	Harris Chowdree	Harrykissen	Harrykissen
		Morgine	Morgine
Doolol Biswass	Doolol Surma	*May-additional*	(Majhi?)
Kissenchurndutt	Jugul Sircar	*investment in Gurrahs*	
Duccour (Sow or Sen?)	Doolol Biswass	(*garas*)	Bistumchurndee
Morley Podar	Harrybullubdass	Kisninda Surma	Kisninda Taggoor
Luckicundgose	Sadanunder	Onoop Coppree	Harris Chowdree
Becul Taggoor	Ramsurn	Doolol Surma	Doolol Biswass
	Mosunder		
Ramsurn Mosunder	Gosseram	Coosalchund	Doolol Surma
Getoo Teley	Chuckerloll	Bistumchurndee	Ramsunder
			(Ramsunder)
	Radakissen Sircar	Doolol Biswass	Mosunder
	Radamohun Sircar	Harris Chowdree	Ramkissen
			Bobboo
	Odey Naran	Kissenchurndutt	
	Kissen Biswass	Keveleram Surma	Kissenchurndutt
	Onoop Naran/	Radakissen (Sircar)	Ramkissen
	Prim Naran		Bobboo
	Collichurn Cotma	Ramkissen Bobboo	Onoop Coppree
	Rajachunder	Ramiser (Ramsurn?)	Rogonaut
	Surma	Mosunder	Biswass
	Killeram Toppull		Ramsurn
			Mosunder
	Mohun Chowdree	Suddanunder	Luckicundgose
	Divepersaud		Nainchurndutt
	Samsunder		Doolol Surma
	Sevepersaud		Rogonaut
	Chowdree		Biswass/
	Ramjee Teal		Doolol Biswass

1745 RS	1745, March 20, SPG. May, additional investment in SPG	1745 April G&D.	1745: June-September, additional investment in *garahs*
	Doolol Sircar Huttoonaut Ram Chowdree Jaggernaut Teal Nusseram Gopee Taggoor		Coosalchund Kisninda Surma Samsunder Harris Chowdree Cableram Taggoor Radakissen Sircar Odey Naran Kissenchurndutt Onoop Coppree Nainchurndutt Radakissen Sircar Odey Naran Coosalchund Saddanunder Keveleram Surma Harrykissen Morgine

1746 June –September, RS
Rogonaut Biswass Nainchurndutt Bowannychurndutt Doolol Surma Bistumchurndee Coosalchund Bobun Cotma Harrybullubdass Mohun Biswass Praun Coppree Kisninda Surma Luckicundgose Duccour (Dass) Ramiser Mosunder Sadanunder Gosseram Morley Podar Getoo Teley Anunderam Sircar

1746 June –September, RS
Nemosene (Sen)
BridgekissoreBullub
Biswass
Devepersaud (Surma)
Onoop Coppree
Bulleram Acharge
Keveleram Surma
Coolean Biswass
Brajakissore Surma

1748 October/ November-RS	1747/8 February SPG	1748 November SPG
Allumchund/Gainchund	Cossenaut (Surma)	Gopee Taggoor
Nimmo Taggoor	Getoo Teley	Cossenaut Surma
Sevepersaud Aucharge	Nemosene (Sen?)	Morley Podar
Harris Chowdree	Nemo Taggore	Paunchooram
Jetoo Surma	Nusserai	Nimmo Sein
Monickchund	Ramanund Surma	Nusseray
Sevepersaud Surma	Morley Podar	Hollaschund
Coosal Surma	Ramsurn Gose	Nundoololl
Myachund	Doolol Surma	Jaggurdasdur
Becul Taggoor	Seebnaut Toppull	Jugul Sircar
Ramsurn Gose	Doolol Sircar	Getoo Teley
Nainchund	Gopee Surma	Doolol Sircar
Hollaschund	Susteedass	Sevenaut Toppull
Morley Podar	Ramkissen Bobboo	Ramkissen Bobboo
Jaggurdasdur	Seveparan Surma	Bullub Biswass
Sutchy Burrall		Sutchy Burrall
Oporan Ray		Susteedass
Chollychurn (Kalicharan)		Sevenaut Surma
Gose		Doolol Dur (Dhar)
Rogoo Bose		
Kissenchurndur (Dutt or Dhar?)		
Cossenaut Surma		
Jugul Surma		
Ramsurn Surma		
Getoo Teley		
Nainchurndutt		
Nimmo Sen		
Bullub Biswass		
Gouranga Biswass		
Jugoul Baddoolie		
Bobun Cotma		
Radakissen Surma		
Maherchund Matah		
Bulleram Acharge		

1749 RS	1748/9 January SPG	1749 SPG
Allumchund/Gainchund	Gopee Tagore	Cossenaut Surma
Nainchund	Paunchoosaum	Kissenchurndutt Cotma
Saome Mahone	Nimmo Tagore	Nemo Sene
Harris Chowdree	Doolol Sircar	Gopee Tagore
Sutchy Burrall	Cossenaut Surma	Jetoo Teley
Jugull Surma	Hollaschund	Nemo Tagore
Ramsurngose	Susteedass	Nusseray
	Sevenaut Surma	Nundoolol Surma
		Allumchund/Gainchund
		Doolol Sircar
		Seebnaut Toppull
		Ramsurngose
		Ramkissen Bobboo
		Jagoordasdur
		Sutchy Burrall
		Harris Chowdree
		Jetoo Surma
		Subnaran Surma
		Morley Podar/Susteedass
		Suroop Burrall/Doolol Dur
		Jugull Badooley/Jugull Surma

1750 RS	1750 SPG	1750 G
Saumahone Surma	Cossenaut (Surma)	Allumchund/Gainchund
Dudit (?) Burrall	Jugul Surma	Saumahone Surma
Harris Chowdree	Gopee Tagore	Sutchy Burrall
Sutchee Burrall	Nemosene	
Naychund (Nainchund?)	Kissenchund Cotma	
Bullub Biswass	Doolol Sircar	
Jugul Bondue (?)	Nusseray	
Nemosene	Nundoodoolol Surma	
Jagoordasdur	Allumchund/Gainchund	
Seerpursaud Surma	Nemo Tagore	
Ramsurngose	Seebnaut Toppull	
Jetoo Surma	Ramsurngose	
Biarul (Baramull?)	Ramkissen Bobboo	
Cossenaut Surma	Jaggordasdur	
Ramsurn Surma	Sutchy Burrall	
Allumchund/Gainchund	Harris Chowdree	
Morley Podar	Jetoo Surma	
Monickchurn	Radamordeb Sircar	
Ramkissen Bobboo	Morley Podar	
Mehurchurn Matar	Susteedass	
	Suroop Burrall	
	Jugool Badooley	
	Seebnaran Surma	
	Doolol Dur	

The first thing that strikes us in this list is that all the *dadni* merchants at Kasimbazar were Hindus, so far as we can make out from the names. We also see from these lists that merchants of both upcountry origin such as Surma and Kapri (who may hail from Bihar) and merchants indigenous to Bengal with surnames such as Dutt, Ghosh, Biswas, Dhar, Sarkar, Sen, Das, Bose, Boral and Ray were active at Kasimbazar. The surnames of Toppull and Kibul have not been identified with any known caste name. Morgine may be Majhi and Badooloey may be Bhaduri but this identification is, as yet, speculative.

The caste affiliations are not always certain. Acharya and Pundit are Brahman names, prolific in Bengal even today. Gautam is both a Brahman and an Aguri surname. It is a *gotra* of the *Madhya-sreni Brahmans* of Midnapur district in Bengal. *Madhya-sreni brahmans* are generally *saktas*, that is, worshippers of the *shakti* cult.[1] But Gautam is also a sub caste of the Aguri caste.[2]

Tagore, a surname that features frequently in the lists, can be either Brahman or kayastha. But the name could also be a hypergamous division of the *Maghaya* sub caste of the *Barhis*[3] which contains the *Telis* of Bihar.[4] Kaviraj is *Baidya*-the medical caste in Bengal.

Religious affiliations depended very often on the caste status. Many of the first names of the merchants featured in this list betray a Vaishnavite (*Boshtom* in Bangla) affiliation. S.C. Nandy who has published extensively on the trade milieu at Kasimbazar based on his family papers, comments:[5]

> In Cossimbazar most of the Hindus were Baishnabs and followers of the Lord Chaitanya; there were a few Shaibites and Shaktas or worshippers of Shiva and Shakti also.

And what about professions? A few surnames were traditionally linked with revenue collection and assessment, such as Chowdhury and Majumdar.But the 'Chowdree' of the Kasimbazar lists may well refer to Chaudhari Telis (occupational caste name for oil pressers) along with Nandy, Pal, Kundu, and of course De (which features in the lists as Dee as in Bistumchurndee). And Chaudhuri, along with Biswas, Dhar, Majumdar and Sen, can also be of the Barui sub caste of Bengal.[6] Again Chaudhuri, along with Poddar and Shahu (Sow?), could belong to the *Sonar* or caste of goldsmiths[7] or, along with Dutt, De and Sen, can belong to the *Tambuli* caste.[8]

Certain merchants retained their original occupational caste name, such as the surname Teli, as we see from the lists (spelt variously as Tili, Tilly, Tillie, Tellaie). It is not clear whether Kapri (Coppree) was an occupational caste name. Kapris may have originated in Bihar, and Risley comments that

Kapris are a sub section of the *Maghaya* sub caste of *Barhis* or a section of the *Banapar* sub caste of *Koiris*, also in Bihar.[9] They could also be a title of *Arayiya Telis*[10] or of the *Kharwar* caste.[11]

Hutton comments that those with surnames of Shaha (Sow?) or Teli displayed commercial abilities.[12] Some had become sanskritised such as Saha, spelt as Sow. Sahas can be *gandhabaniks*—the traditional spice merchants of Bengal— and so are the Dutt, De and Dhar.[13] But Dutt, Das, Dhar and Sens can also belong to the *sankhari*, or *sankhabanik*, caste.[14] This was a group that was also prominent in late medieval Dhaka. It had its own quarter in the city. But Dutts and Des can also belong to the *sutradhar* or *chutar* caste, which is a low caste.[15]

'Coit' is a caste name for *kayastha*, also called Kaet, Kait, Kayath and Kaya. They are generally *shaktas*.[16] Paramanik, a name that features here, is a title given to the village headman[17]. Paramanicks are usually of the milk men sub caste-called *Goala* in Bengal,[18] and as Pramanick they belong to the *Tanti* (weaver) caste.[19] Ghosh can belong to either the Kayastha caste or to the *Goala* caste. Biswas, Chaudhuri, Majumdar, Rai and Sarkar can also be *kulin kayasthas*.[20] The Berry of the SPG list of 1733 is probably *Bauri*, originally a cultivating caste of western Bengal like the *Bagdis*, which had diversified into palanquin bearing and then moneylending and petty trading.[21] Kertee is Kirtti—a title of *Dakshin Rarhi* and *Bangaja Kayasthas* in Bengal.[22]

Shah is obviously of upcountry, possibly Gujarati origin. So can be Das, often spelt as Doss in Company records. There were seven Gujarati merchants at Kasimbazar; they are referred to as Neelmoni Doss, Girdhar Doss, Govind Doss, Nuggin Doss, Golapchand, Tulsi Doss, and Jogjibon Doss.[23] The caste affiliation of the Katmas, who feature very prominently in the lists is not clear, but it is probably a weaver (*tanti*) caste. Their origin, too, is not clear. First names of other *dadni* merchants such as Alamchand, Gainchand, Anandchand, Ratanchand, Huttichand, Lahorimal and Natmall betray upcountry associations (see Table 7); but in the absence of proof it would be pointless to speculate on their origin and caste affiliations.

The traditional trading castes of Bengal are the *gandhabaniks*, *sankhabaniks* and *suvarnabaniks*. These may have been present in Kasimbazar in large numbers. Sahas along with the Dutt, De and Dhar can be *gandhabaniks*-the traditional spice merchants of Bengal.[24] Dutt, Das, Dhar and Sens can also belong to the *sankhari*, or *sankhabanik*, caste.[25] Baral, Das, Dutt, De, Dhar, Mallick, Poddar, Rai and Sen can also be *suvarnabaniks*.[26] It is likely that the weaver (*tanti*) caste featured largely in this list; Das, Dutt and De belong to this caste.[27] So did Telis: as Chaudhuri, De, Poddar, Shahu, Shaha.[28]

It is quite clear from Table 7 that many caste and occupational groups had become *dadni* merchants at Kasimbazar. The preponderance of the 'lower' castes in this list affirms our position that a new kind of mobility was evident in late seventeenth century Bengal. For example the Chowdrees and Sows may well have been of the sweet maker caste or *Halwai*[29] as well as being *Telis*, *Baruis* and *Gandhabaniks* as we just noted. Again Chaudhuri, Biswas, Boral (Burrall), Sarkar and Das can also belong to the *Jaliya* or fishermen's caste in Bengal.[30] They could equally belong to the *kaivarta* (fishing) caste.[31] The existence of the EICs enabled many of the new aspirants to be elevated social status and improve their position in late medieval Bengal, although the trend had probably started many centuries ago.[32]

Let us see which castes were probably present as merchants at Kasimbazar.

Table 8
Caste Affilations among Dadni Merchants at Kasimbazar

Surname	Caste	Likely Status
Acharya	Brahman	High
Pundit	Brahman	High
Gautam	Brahman, Aguri	High/Low
Tagore	Brahman, Kayastha, Barhi (Teli)	High/Low
Kaviraj	Baidya	High
Chaudhuri/Chowdhury	Teli, Barui, Sonar, Tambuli, Kayastha, Halwai, Jaliya, Kaivarta	High/Low
Majumdar	Barui, Kayastha	High/Low
De	Gandhabanik, Sutradhar, Teli, Tambuli, Suvarnabanik, Tanti	Low
Biswas	Barui, Kayastha, Jaliya, Kaivarta	Likely to be low
Dhar	Gandhabanik, Sankhabanik, Barui, Suvarnabanik	Low
Sen	Sankhabanik, Barui, Tambuli, Suvarnabanik	Low
Podar	Sonar, Suvarnabanik, Teli	Low
Sow (Shaha, Shahu)	Gandhabanik, Sonar, Teli, Halwai	Low
Kapri	Barhi, Koiri, Teli, Kharwar	Low

Surname	Caste	Likely Status
Dutt	Gandhabanik, Sankhabanik, Suvarnabanik, Tanti, Tambuli, Sutradhar	Low
Das	Sankhabanik, Suvarnabanik, Tanti, Jaliya, Kaivarta. Could also be a Gujarati surname.	Low
Paramanick	Goala	Low
Pramanick	Tanti	Low
Ghosh	Kayastha, Goala	High/Low
Sarkar	Kayastha, Jaliya, Kaivarta	High/Low
Rai	Kayastha, Suvarnabanik	High/Low
Berry	Bauri	Low
Kirti	Kayastha	Low grade of Kayastha
Baral	Suvarnabanik, Jaliya, Kaivarta	Low
Mallick	Suvarnabanik	Low
Bose	Kayastha	High
Katma	Tanti	Low

It is quite clear from Table 7 that many of the 'lower' caste and occupational groups had become *dadni* merchants at Kasimbazar. The preponderance of their names in Table 8 validates our claim that the late seventeenth century saw unprecedented social mobility in western Bengal.

7

The Merchants of Kasimbazar in Business

The main items of trade at Kasimbazar consisted in, we saw, various grades of raw silk (RS), silk piece goods (SPG), and calicoes such as *garas* and *dusutties* (called '*gurrahs*' and '*doosutties*' by the EEIC at Kasimbazar, and used here as G&D). The RS had three grades, the best was the November Bund which is abbreviated here to RS. But there was also a March Bund (used here as MB) and a July Bund which was the worst category because it was wound off in the rains and thus rarely invested in. There was also silk from Rangpur, entered in the records as Rungpore silk and mentioned in this volume as Rg. This variety is still produced in present day Bangladesh. Let us see the actual number of merchants supplying the various categories of textiles to the EEIC at Kasimbazar.

Table 9
Number of Dadni Merchants Supplying Silk at Kasimbazar to the EEIC from 1733 to 1750[1]

Tex	33	36	37	38	39	40	41	42	43	44	45	46	48	49	50
RS	11	23	3	19	5	18	16	17	18	14	4	28	24	2	8
SPG	25	15	27	22	23	11	12	20	27	40	20	-	16	22	13
GD	6	8	5	4	3	1	1	-	-	-	2	-	-	-	-
Rg	3	-	-	-	-	1	-	-	-	-	-	-	-	-	-
MB	-	-	5	-	5	-	-	-	-	-	-	-	-	-	-
RS+ SPG	5	3	-	1	-	3	5	7	5	18	3	-	8	5	8
RS+ GD	-	1	-	1	1	1	-	-	-	-	3	-	-	-	1

Tex	33	36	37	38	39	40	41	42	43	44	45	46	48	49	50
RS+ Rg	1	-	-	-	-	-	-	-	-	-	-	-	-	-	-
RS+ MB	-	-	11	-	9	-	-	-	-	-	-	-	-	-	-
SPG +GD	1	1	-	-	2	1	1	-	-	-	6	-	-	-	-
SPG +M B	-	-	2	-	-	-	-	-	-	-	-	-	-	-	-
RS+ SPG +GD	-	-	-	5	-	5	9	-	-	-	12	-	-	-	2
RS+ SPG+ Rg	1	-	-	-	-	1	-	-	-	-	-	-	-	-	-
RS+ SPG +M B	-	-	3	-	1	-	-	-	-	-	-	-	-	-	-
RS+ GD+ MB	-	-	1	-	4	-	-	-	-	-	-	-	-	-	-
SPG +GD +M B	-	-	1	-	-	-	-	-	-	-	-	-	-	-	-
RS+ SPG +GD+ +Rg	1	-	-	-	-	1	-	-	-	-	-	-	-	-	-
RS+ SPG +GD +M B	-	-	3	-	4	-	-	-	-	-	-	-	-	-	-

Table 9 shows the specialisation and diversification among the merchants of Kasimbazar. Most specialised in one kind of commodity-either RS or SPG. These were obviously the most paying. Combinations, that is contracting for more than one item, were rare. Few merchants contracted for a combination of the profitable items, say a combination of RS and SPG. We shall see from Table 10 that only a few specialised in two commodities and a handful dealt in three. When it came to four commodities, the number of merchants contracting for them is minimal. Only the very big merchants undertook to supply these items (see Table 7). This kind of grouping leads one to infer that there was no specialisation among merchants on the basis of commodities, rather prices and profit were the criteria.

Table 10 shows the number of merchants supplying one or more varieties of textiles at Kasimbazar. The varieties are RS, SPG, GD, Rg and MB, as before.

Table 10
Number of Dadni Merchants Supplying One or More Varieties to the EEIC at Kasimbazar

Year	One Variety	Two Varieties	Three Varieties	Four Varieties	Total
1733	45	7	1	1	54
1736	46	5	-	-	51
1737	40	13	5	3	61
1738	45	2	5	-	52
1739	36	12	5	4	57
1740	31	5	6	1	43
1741	29	6	9	-	44
1742	37	7	-	-	44
1743	45	5	-	-	50
1744	54	18	-	-	72
1745	26	12	12	-	50
1746	28	-	-	-	28
1748	40	8	-	-	48
1749	24	5	-	-	29
1750	21	9	2	-	32

We shall see from Table 11 that a smaller numbers of merchants supplying the total investment in a particular year had nothing to do with the amount of money invested by the EEIC in that particular year. For example 1733 and 1745 saw the highest investments, but the number of merchants contracting were 54 and 50. In contrast, in years of low investment such as 1746 and 1748, the numbers were still 28 and 48. And even in a really bad year such as 1749 (only Rs. 5,057,000 invested) 29 merchants still contracted with the EEIC. But 29 was the second lowest number ever recorded among *dadni* merchants contracting with the EEIC at Kasimbazar. More significantly, in 1749 only 5 merchants contracted for a combination of any two items (and none for any three or four). These were the most profitable items: RS and SPG (see tables 7 and 10). 1749 was truly a lean year.

Table 11
The Total, Average, Maximum and Minimum Sums of Money Invested by the EEIC at Kasimbazar from 1733 to 1750, Individual Merchants and the Proportion Maxi/Mini in Thousands of Rupees

Year	Total Investment	No. of Merchants	Investment Average	Investment Maximum	Investment Minimum	Maximum/ Minimum
1733	1335.96	54	24.74	166.50	1.90	88
1736	746.21	51	14.69	63.00	0.50	126
1737	888.13	61	14.56	67.25	0.50	135
1738	776.67	52	14.94	69.50	0.25	278
1739	964.29	57	16.92	101.95	0.25	408
1740	820.30	43	19.08	53.54	0.55	97
1741	723.65	44	16.45	48.26	1.50	32
1742	470.26	44	10.69	40.06	0.81	49
1743	519.09*	50	10.38	42.34	0.93	46
1744	1368.58	72	19.01	88.84	0.61	146
1745	1594.78	50	31.90	97.15	1.15	84
1746	552.74	28	19.74	54.96	2.11	26
1748	540.10	48	11.25	54.00	0.10	540
1749	50.57	29	1.74	7.62	0.05	152
1750	236.93	32	7.40	32.09	0.10	321

* The lower figure was because the Nawab had forbidden all EEIC commerce between July and September 1743.[2]

The grouping of merchants according to inequality in silk transactions as shown in tables 9 and 10 is clearly manifest in Table 11 which records the range of disparity in the volume of trade; namely the average, maximum and minimum investments of the EEIC each year by individual merchants. Table 11 brings out the inequalities among the *dadni* merchants of Kasimbazar; this inequality was reflected in consequent group formations as big, medium and small merchants. This division among the *dadni* merchants of Kasimbazar is a pointer to their vulnerability as a category vis-a-vis foreign merchant capital, because consciousness, solidarity, and common agenda could only go up to a certain point and not beyond within the mercantile context that prevailed in Bengal. But it also signifies the rise of notable (or big) mercantile families at Kasimbazar.

8

The Rise of Merchant Families

A particular method of control exercised by the English, and utilised by the *dadni* merchants, was to give out contracts for the more profitable items to favoured merchants. This is what the General Letter of February 9, 1736 remarked to the Council of the English Company at Kasimbazar:[1]

> In the division of the Investment among the merchants entered upon the Consultations of 25th July, we observe one man Sookmoy Seat had a much larger proportion of fine goods than any other, all the Cossajura Mullmulls and the Cossajura Dooreas being provided by him. These are the fine sorts which you have often represented are profitable articles to the Merchants so that in order to induce them to contract for the full quantity of Gurrahs, Romalls, Photaes and other coarse goods upon reasonable terms, all fine species should be divided among them. You may call to your mind upon recollection that it was a very large part of the charge against the late broker (probably a member of the family of Katma, and likely to be Huttoo Katma from the dates-my comment) that his relations and Favourites had all the fine goods to themselves, and our Investment was said to suffer greatly through the Discouragements the other merchants laboured under thereby.

Three things emerge from this admonitory note. First, all *dadni* merchants were not willing to contract for all items—especially the less profitable items—and they had to be induced to do so. The fact that *garahs* (coarse calicoes) were less profitable to the merchants was reinforced in the consultations of April 23, 1745.

Second, there was an attempt by Sukhamoy Seth (possibly a member of the Jagat Seths) to what was known as 'corner' the Investment to derive maximum financial advantages. He attempted this through his proximity to the broker. Third, the fact this was not new, that despite the incident of the previous broker having tried similar practices that the English at Kasimbazar allowed the practice to continue, indicated there was possibly a little scam going on between the factors and brokers at Kasimbazar.[2]

This assumption of certain merchants having a favoured status in the English investments becomes stronger in view of the flourishing private trade carried on by the English factors at Kasimbazar where the Katmas and some favoured merchants acted in private capacities as brokers to individual factors[3] despite interdictions on private trade from London. Members of the Biswas and Katma families were named as private brokers to Company servants.[4]

This practice was so widely entrenched that, unable to stop it, the East India Company in London actually organised a mini joint stock among the factors at Kasimbazar so that all might benefit and the rising prices be checked.[5] The K.F.R. Consultations of September 13 1733 noted that:

> The Company in India, in order to avoid future insolvency, has decided to carry on private trade settlement in a joint stock . . . which as it must keep the markets low by having but one Buyer and at the same time must the better conceal from the Durbar the Private Trade itself, cannot be prejudicial to our correspondents in Calcutta or elsewhere.

The new joint stock was to come into operation at Kasimbazar from January 1, 1734. The shares were divided as follows: Hugh Barker, Chief-6 shares, Samuel Fazalle(?)y identified as Fazakerly by P.J. Marshall (email of November 19, 2005), Second-2 shares, John Halsey, Third-1 share, Samuel Millechamp, Fourth-1 share, James Mill, Fifth-1 share, Samuel Bennet, Sixth-1 share. Adam Dawson and Charles Addams were not admitted into this coterie for the time being but they were each given SR 1 500 until such time as places fell vacant. Favoured *dadni* merchants too profited from the new system. Huttoo Katma became Barker's banyan, and Naran Biswas became Millechamp's banyan.

The position of official Broker or Diwan to a European Company was an important position. The EICs followed the practice of confining this crucial post to a mercantile family of good standing within the community. Thus Indra Narayan Chowdhury became broker to the FEIC in the 1730s.[6] The K.F.R. tell us that the Katmas became official brokers to the EEIC at the same time. The company merchants—and more specifically the broker—was the buyer of European goods from the factory *kuthis*. This gave them an added clout within their community as well as enhancing their reputation further with the EIC in question. The actual sales, while negligible in comparison to the volume of the sales of Bengal silks and cottons in Europe, were nevertheless significant in that they helped the EICs supplement their funds in Bengal. Firearms were in great demand, as well as European broadcloth and woollens, and some velvet and damask. Some port wine and Madeira were sold. The prominent buyers of European goods were again the Katmas, Biswasses, Dutts, and Surmas as well as a few other leading individual merchants such as Kushalchand, Alam Chand and Mahtab Rai as well as Jagat Seth Fateh Chand himself.[7]

Table 12 gives the names of merchants who scored double or more of the average total investment furnished by individual merchants from 1733 to 1750. This gives us an indication of which particular merchant (and which particular group on the basis of surname) was the most prominent in any one particular year from 1733 to 1750.

Table 12
Merchants Scoring Double and More of the Average Total EEIC Investment at Kasimbazar

Name	33	36	37	38	39	40	41	42	43	44	45	46	48	49	50
Beley Cotma	7														
Booban Mahaun	3	2													
Paunchue Cotma	3														
Kissenpersaud Biswass	3	4	2												
Herre Surma	3														
Ramnede Surma	3														
Paunchue Bose	2														
Takoo Biswass	2														
Sutchy Cotma		3	5	7	6	5	3								
Sudanund Cotma		3													
Bridgenautdutt		3													
Nundecomar Surma		3													
Deveramdutt		2													
Sirbis Sir			3	2	2										
Kissen Surma			3												
Dokoor Sen			3												
Coolean Surma			2												
Ozuderam Biswas			2												
Nainchurndutt			2						4		4		3		
Bissinautdutt			2	3				4							
Cossenautdutt			2												
Maudeb Surma			2					3	3						
Ramnarandutt				3											
Nemidutt				3											
Dokoor Saw				2											
Ramdebdutt				2											

Name	33	36	37	38	39	40	41	42	43	44	45	46	48	49	50
Odeynaran					4	2	2				2				
Samsunder					4		4	3			2				
Jeyram Bose					3										
Cheyram Bose					2										
Narran Biswass					2		3	4		2					
Govinram					2										
Coosalchund							3				3	2			
Rogonaut Biswass								3			5	3			
Harrykissen Mullick								2							
Gosseram								2							
Beroofe Cotma									4						
Bowannychurndutt									4			3			
Surroopchund									3						
Coosal Tagore									2						
Primnaran/ Onoopnaran									2						
Lollchund/ Annunchund									2						
Suroop Cotma										2					
Bobun Cotma										2					
Doolol Surma										2		3			
Bistumchurndee												2			
Allumchund/ Gainchund													5	4	
Nimmo Taggoor													3		
Sevepersaud															
Aucharge													2		
Harris Chowdree													2		3
Jetoo Surma													2		
Monickchund													2		
Nainchund														4	
Saome Mahone Surma														4	4
Sutchy Burrall														2	2
Jugull Surma														2	
Dudit Burrall															2

Table 12 is undoubtedly led by Sutchy Katma who scored six years, with Udainaran, Samsunder, Naincharan Dutt and Naran Biswas coming second, each having scored for four years. Krishnaprasad Biswas, Sirbis Sir, Biswanath Dutt, Mahadeb Surma, Coosalchand and Raghunath Biswas each scored for three years. Beley Katma scored only once, in 1733, but he scored seven times the average annual investment per merchant that year.

Of the surnames in the lists, the Surma are the most represented (10 family members), followed by the Dutts (9), the Katmas (7 family members), the Biswasses (5), the Boses (3), and finally the Barals (2). The table shows further that: One, none of the merchants was associated with the EEIC's investment all through 1733 to 1750. Some fizzled out earlier while others, such as the Dutts, Surmas, the Chaudhuris and Barals, started later and gradually consolidated their position in the Investment; Two, the merchants show a marked variation as regards the degree of concentration of investments. They score from 2 to 7 times the average investment in a particular year; Three, of the 57 merchants Sachi Katma is the only one who scores above the average annual investment for the 6 years from 1736 to 1741 and his scores are 7, 6, twice 5, and twice 3 times the average.

These merchants with such great scores over the average amount invested may be regarded as the notable merchants of Kasimbazar. Table 13 has been prepared, with reference to Table 12, dealing with merchants whose family names are not repeated or mentioned in the investment lists, and Table 14, again with reference to Table 12, deals with those who can be grouped by their family names.

The following points can be made from tables 13 and 14:

1. While for 19 merchants the family or kin grouping cannot be ascertained, it is registered for 38 merchants or double the number.
2. About the same proportion of merchants who can or cannot be grouped by family names were associated with the EEIC investments for 1, 2 or 3 years; namely 13 or 68% in Table 13 and 25 or 65% in Table 14. But the proportion of merchants associated with the EEIC's investment for more than five years (and up to ten out of the fifteen years during 1733–50 for which data is available) is marked for those who can be grouped by family names, namely 8 or 22% as against only one for those who cannot be so grouped.
3. Only 4 out of 19 or 21% of the merchants who cannot be grouped by family names score the maximum of 4 or 5 times the average investment per merchant in a year, while the corresponding score from 4 to the maximum of 7 times the average is for 10 out of 38 or 26% of the merchants who can be grouped by family name.

Evidently the incidence of repetition (or mention) of family names occurs in the case of those merchants who had the most durable and profitable association with the EEIC. These were also the *dadni* merchants who dealt with the largest volume of trade. As to details from Table 13 in relation to Table 12 it is found that Samsunder (surname unknown) heads the list, scoring the greatest numbers above the average for the three years of 1739, 1740 and 1741. The number of merchants scoring higher than the averages for three

Table 13
Kasimbazar *Dadni* Merchants with Family Names that are not Repeated (or Mentioned) Scoring the Same or Less, or Double or More, the Average of Total Annual Investment (ATAI) at Kasimbazar from the EEIC Investment Lists in a Particular Year

Name of Merchant	Number of Years of investment Corresponding to the same or less (S or L) or double or more (D or M) the total average annual investment		Number of Times over ATAI, D or M	
	S or L	D or M	Total Years	No. of Time
Samsunder	1 (1740)	4 (1739, '41, '42 and 1745)	5	4/4/3/2
Odey Naran	1 (1742)	4 (1739–41, 1745)	5	4/2/2/2
Coosalchund	6 (1736, 1738–40, 1744 and '46).	3 (1741, '45, '46)	9	3/2/3
Sirbis Sir	1 (1740)	3 (1737–39)	4	3/2/2
Allumchand Gainchund	-	2 (1748–9)	2	5/4
Harris Chowdree	3 (1744,'45,'49)	2 (1748, 1750)	5	2/3
Booban Mahaun	-	2 (1733, 1736)	2	3/2
Nainchund	2 (1748, 1750)	1 (1749)	3	4
Dokoor Sen	-	1 (1737)	1	3
Surroopchund	-	1 (1743)	1	3
Bistumchurndee	3 (1744–46)	1 (1748)	4	2
Lollchund Annunchund*	1 (1741)	1 (1743)	2	2
Monickchund	1 (1750)	1 (1748)	2	2
Govinram	-	1 (1739)	1	2
Gosseram	-	1 (1742)	1	2
Dokoor Saw	-	1 (1738)	1	2
Harrykissen Mullick	-	1 (1742)	1	2
Primnaran Onoopnaran	-	1 (1743)	1	2
Sevepersaud Aucharge	-	1(1748)	1	2

* Lollchund alone in 1741, Lollchund and Annunchund in 1745.

consecutive years is small; only two out of nineteen such merchants (Table 13) fall into this category. Five merchants supplied silks worth two to five times the averages for any two years, and the majority scored two to four times the averages for any one year. The degree of concentration varied from two to five times the average annual investment.

Table 14

Merchants with Family Names that are Repeated in the EEIC Investment Lists from 1733 to 1750 with the Same or Less or Double or More of the Average of Total Annual Investment (ATAI)

Name of Merchant and Surname	Number of Years of Investment Corresponding to the Same or Less (S or L) or Double or More (D or M) ATAI		No. of Times over the Annual Investment, Double or More	
	S or L	D or M	Total Years	No. of Time
Sutchy Cotma	-	6	6	3/5/7/6/5/3
Beley Cotma	-	1	1	7
Beroofe Cotma	-	1	1	4
Sudanund Cotma	1	1	2	3
Paunchue Cotma	-	1	1	3
Bobun Cotma	4	1	5	2
Suroop Cotma	-	1	1	2
Nainchurndutt	6	4	10	4/2/4/3
Bissinautdutt	4	3	7	2/3/4
Bowannychurn Dutt	4	2	6	4/3
Nemidutt	5	1	6	3
Ramnarandutt	2	1	3	3
Bridgenautdutt	-	1	1	3
Cossenautdutt	1	1	2	2
Deveramdutt	-	1	1	2
Ramdebdutt	-	1	1	2
Narran Biswass	4	4	8	2/3/4/2
Rogonaut Biswass	6	3	9	3/3/5
Kissenpersaud Biswass	2	3	5	3/4/2
Ozuderam Biswass	6	1	7	2
Takoo Biswass	2	1	3	2
Maudeb Surma	2	3	5	2/3/3
Saome Mahone Surma	-	2	2	4/4
Doolol Surma	2	2	4	3/2
Herre Surma	1	1	2	3
Ramnede Surma	1	1	2	3
Nundecoomar Surma	-	1	1	3
Kissen Surma	-	1	1	3
Coolean Surma	3	1	4	2
Jetoo Surma	1	1	2	2
Jugull Surma	-	1	1	2
Jeyram Bose	1	1	2	3
Cheyram Bose	-	1	1	2
Paunchue Bose	-	1	1	2
Nimmo Tagore	-	1	1	3
Coosal Tagore	-	1	1	2
Sutchy Burrall	1	2	3	2/2
Dudit Burrall	-	1	1	2

Table 14 is undoubtedly led by Sachi Katma; this heralds the arrival of the Katmas into the premier league, although Bally (Beley) and Huttoo Katma may have prepared the way by their favoured status as Barker's banyans. Sachi Katma scored some of the highest number of times over the average for the greatest number of years. Sachi's score varied from 3 to 7 times the average for the years that he scored thus.

In Table 14, while the number of merchants scoring above the average for only one year is as high as in Table 13, here the range of concentration varies from 2 to 7 times the average. In the middle stratum lie two merchants scoring above the average for 4 years, 4 merchants scoring for 3 years, and another 4 merchants for 2 years.

Table 14 shows furthermore that 7 family groups were formed by the notable merchants: namely the groups of the Katmas, the Dutts, the Biswases, the Surmas, the Boses, the Tagores and the Barals. Considered as a group, merchants belonging to these families received the highest amount of money for the investments. Also the recurrence of their family names over the years, as well as the degree of control they undoubtedly exercised over the EEIC investments, leads us to suppose that a coterie of merchants was gradually coming into being at Kasimbazar by the 1730s.

9

The Coterie at Kasimbazar

As early as in 1685, as many as 18 Surmas, 5 Biswas, 2 Chowdhury, 1 Ghosh, and one Kapri, Sarkar and Dutt each were mentioned as supplying silk to the EEIC at Kasimbazar. Another list of 1701 featured a Ghosh and a Surma yet again, as well as the name Katma. Around 186 merchants with these names dominated the supply of raw silk to the English East India Company at Kasimbazar until 1754, when the *dadni* system was abandoned in favour of the agency system.

We will now see from tables 13 and 14 that there is a persistent occurrence of the nine names of Katma, Dutt, Biswas, Surma, Chowdhury, Sarkar, Kapri, Tagore, Ghosh, Toppull, Teli, and Das. The Barals were also fairly regular. But the Toppulls, Teli and Das always contracted for amounts less than the average annual investment contracted per merchant. They therefore have been excluded from the category of the main mercantile families of Kasimbazar.

Tables 15 and 16 show us that many of the names featured in the lists of 1685 and 1701 crystallised into a coterie of merchants who were prominent in the EEIC investment at Kasimbazar.

We see from Table 14 that seven surnames occur in the lists with more than one given name; these are Katma, Dutt, Biswas, Surma, Bose, Tagore and Baral. The Boses and Barals may be excluded from our list of the 'main' or 'notable families' because they occur only infrequently from 1733 to 1750. The surname Bose features in 1733, 1739 and 1740; and Baral occurs only in the three years 1748 to 1750. Therefore, despite the fact that the Boses and Barals figure in Table 12 as notable merchants, these two names cannot form part of the 'main' or 'notable' families. Also the Boses and Barals do not record more than four merchants each over the period from 1733 to 1750.

Table 15
Important Merchant Families and their Share in the EEIC
Silk Investment at Kasimbazar: 1733–1750
(% of total investment)

Surname	33	36	37	38	39	40	41	42	43	44	45	46	48	49	50
Big Partners															
Cotma	25	13	13	15	14	15	10	-	14	15	5	4	2	2	0.2
Dutt	7	13	18	27	5	13	7	14	20	8	13	19	2	-	-
Biswass	20	10	21	16	13	11	17	21	11	11	12	16	4	-	5
Surma	14	17	12	5	9	4	1	13	6	13	14	13	22	17	31
Small Partners															
Coppree	-	0.1	1	0.3	1	1	3	7	6	8	10	4	-	-	-
Ghosh	-	-	3	5	7	1	3	2	-	4	1	3	6	7	3
Tagore	-	2	4	5	1	5	4	3	7	2	2	-	10	5	1
Big Partners	66	53	64	63	41	43	35	48	51	47	44	52	30	19	36
Small Partners	-	2	8	10	9	7	10	12	13	14	13	7	16	12	4
Total	66	55	72	73	50	50	45	60	64	61	57	59	46	31	40
Total investment in thousands of rupees	1336	746	888	777	964	820	724	470	519	1369	1595	553	540	51	237

Table 16

Numerical Strength of the Most Important Merchant Families Supplying Silk Goods to the English at Kasimbazar: 1733–1750
(% of total number of merchants)

Surname	33	36	37	38	39	40	41	42	43	44	45	46	48	49	50
Cotma	11	6	5	6	7	5	5	-	8	10	6	4	2	3	3
Dutt	2	12	8	10	5	9	11	11	10	4	4	7	2	-	-
Biswass	17	12	15	15	14	12	11	11	10	8	8	14	4	-	3
Surma	7	14	8	4	5	5	5	11	4	10	8	14	4	-	3
Coppree	-	2	7	8	9	7	5	7	4	3	4	7	-	-	-
Ghosh	-	-	2	4	4	2	2	2	-	3	2	4	4	3	3
Tagore	-	2	7	4	4	7	5	2	10	3	8	-	6	7	6
Big Families	37	44	36	35	31	31	32	33	32	32	26	39	31	24	31
Small Families	-	4	16	16	17	16	12	11	14	9	14	11	10	10	9
Total	37	48	49	51	48	47	44	44	46	41	40	50	41	34	40
Total No. of Merchants	54	51	61	52	57	43	44	44	50	72	50	28	48	29	32

On the other hand, the family names of Chowdhury and Sarkar feature consistently in the EEIC lists from 1733 to 1750. But the members of these two families are associated exclusively with the investment in silk piece goods, unlike other family names occurring in the same consistent manner. Since the amount invested in silk piece goods alone accounted for a small portion of the total EEIC investment in silk at Kasimbazar, the Chowdhurys and Sarkars may not be considered in the elite category of merchant families.

Like the Chowdhurys and Sarkars, the Tagores, Ghoses and Kapris, occur consistently in the lists from 1733 to 1750, but unlike them members of the Tagore, Ghosh and Kapri families were both RS and SPG merchants. However members of these three families never reached the status enjoyed by the Katmas, the Dutts, the Biswasses and the Surmas both as regards the proportion of the total annual investment as well as their numerical strength. The Tagores, Ghoshes and Kapris may therefore be considered as 'small' partners in the trade with the EEIC at Kasimbazar in contrast to the 'big four' of the Katmas, the Dutts, the Biswasses and the Surmas.

Tables 15 and 16 drive home two points.One, that a coterie of seven merchant families controlled the EEIC silk investments at Kasimbazar until 1750 and two, that within this group of seven a stratification was visible with the consequent division of the coterie into 'big' and 'small' merchants. Table 15 reinforces this point and shows us that the 'big four' of the Katmas, the Dutts, the Biswasses and the Surmas supplied silk at a rate ranging from 1/3 to 2/3 of the total EEIC investment of silk at Kasimbazar until 1750. Among them the Katmas led the way with the Biswas and Dutt families following closely behind. From the later 1740s the Dutts and the Biswasses left the Katmas behind. The Surmas outpaced the other three from 1748 to 1750 although they had followed the others modestly in earlier years. The low ranking of the Kapri, Ghosh and Tagore families regarding their share in the investment, and as compared with that of the 'big four' is clearly seen from Table 15.

A greater share in the investment allotted obviously went with the number of members a family group could get into the investment lists. Table 16 tells us the relative size of the families and shows that the Katmas, the Dutts, the Biswasses and the Surmas provided the greatest number of family members engaged in the business of supplying silk to outsiders.The most influential among the *dadni* merchants as formed by the seven families (that is, by adding the Kapris, Tagores and Ghoshes to the 'big four') accounted for *almost half of the total number of merchants* figuring in the EEIC Kasimbazar lists until 1750.

Therefore the 'big four' comprised a coterie within a coterie, dominating the EEIC lists year after year until the 1750s. As to where the other merchants featured in the EEIC Kasimbazar lists from 1733 to 1750 may be ranked, we have little or no idea at all.

Graphs 1 and 2 show the relative strengths of the big and small families in EEIC investments at Kasimbazar from 1733 to 1750 in percentages. Note for Graph1 that only alternate names have been marked. The names should

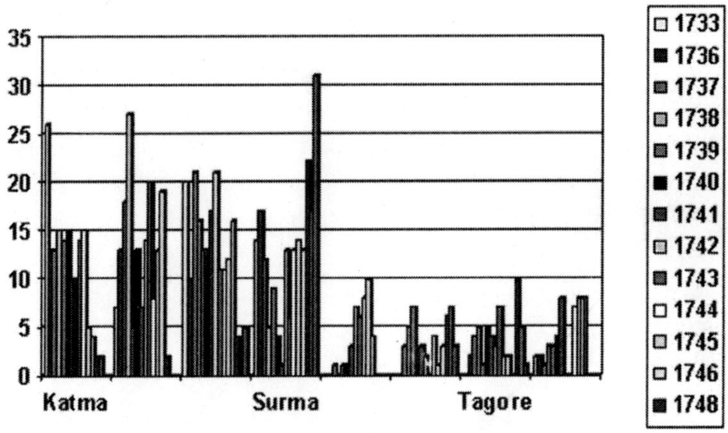

Graph 1

Relative Strength of Each Mercantile Family in Percentage Terms Year Wise at Kasimbazar: 1733–1750

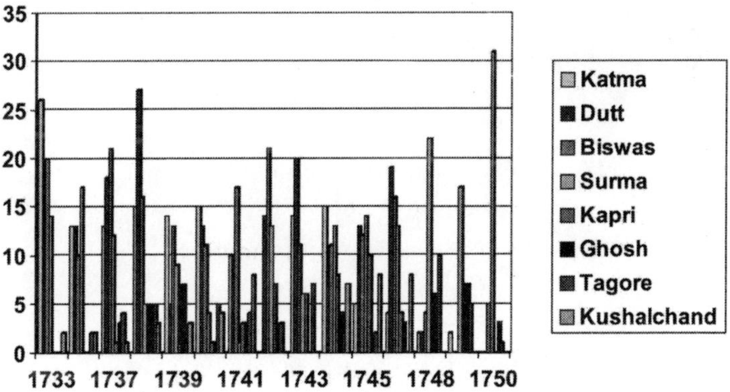

Graph 2

Position of the Families (and Kushalchand) in Relation to One Another in a Particular Year of Investment at Kasimbazar 1733–1750

read as Katma, Dutt, Biswas, Surma, Kapri, Ghosh, Tagore and Kushalchand. The years for both graphs should read as 1733, 1736, '37, '38, '39, '40, '41, '42, '43, '44, '45, '46, '48, '49 and '50. Note the leading position of the Katmas in early years and of the Surmas in the later years. Note the strong position of Kushalchand, an individual merchant, who has been included in both graphs to demonstrate that only a very powerful merchant could hope to keep up with the mercantile families at Kasimbazar.

10

The World of Finance at Kasimbazar

As trade in silk gained popularity at Kasimbazar in the eighteenth century, the high prices commanded by certain articles at the end of the seventeenth century fell considerably.[1] The EEIC investment list for 1701 at Kasimbazar mentions the price for *Silk Lungee Rumals* at Rs. 8.50 a piece. However Streynsham Master noted in the 1670s that they cost Rs. 3.50 a piece.[2] By the 1730s the price had steadied at Rs. 5.75 and remained thus fixed until 1741. After the effects of the Maratha invasions began to be felt the price rose from Rs. 6.12 a piece in 1742 to Rs. 8.06 in 1748 (see Table 5).

As the volume of EIC trade grew the practice of spot sales ceased.[3] So did the practice by EIC servants of buying goods against ready money, as did the practice of part payments in European goods.[4] The whole process of judging the nature of silk filaments, the ordering and the making of the contract, the actual buying and selling as well as quality assessment on delivery, became more streamlined. Definite procedures for each step were slowly coming into being in the commercial world of Kasimbazar.

This streamlining of commercial operations necessitated a ready flow of capital. Without a regular and assured capital flow the whole process—one where each work segment was dependant on others—would grind to a halt. Since capital was not always available from Europe an alternative source had to be found. Bengal seemed to provide an alternative but at the end of the seventeenth century interest rates in Bengal were as high as 15% to 20%.[5] Master notes that in the 1670s the rate varied between 15% and 18%.[6] It was in the region of 12% when Luiller visited Bengal around 1701–1702.[7]

Such fluctuations ceased when a major banking house—that of the Seths—established themselves at Murshidabad in the eighteenth century with the transfer of capital there. This was a financial dynasty established by the Marwari Hiranand Shah who migrated to Bengal in the seventeenth century. His son Manick Chand, sensing business oppurtunities along the Bhagirathi, left his seat at Dhaka and accompanied the new *subahdar* of Bengal, Murshid Quli Khan, to what was then Maxudabad. Murshid Quli Khan was keen to establish a strong quasi-independent dynasty in Bengal and Manick Chand played no small part in that process. In course of time the banking family of Hiranand, which was hounoured by the title Jagat Seth or Banker to the World being conferred on its third and most prominent member Fatehchand, became a vital part of the economic and political profile of the Bengal *niyabat.*

Interest rates fell from an average of 15% to a steady 9% throughout the eighteenth century.[8] More importantly, not only did the Seths furnish the capital necessary for all EICs to carry on operations in Bengal; they also undertook to change the foreign moneys brought in by the EICs into the sicca rupees that was the currency in Bengal. Therefore the Seths played the vital role of catalyst in linking Bengal to the European economy through their financial knowledge and fiscal measures. They fixed the rates of exchange between the Sicca, Madras and Arcot rupees at 100, 103 and 108.[9] The EEIC bullion was fixed by Fatehchand in 1741 at 202½ per 250 sicca weight.[10] In 1745, Fatehchand's successors, Seths Mahtab Rai and Suroop or Swarupchand, fixed ducatoons at SR 2-7annas-3 pies, and the French Crowns, Pillar Dollars and Mexican Dollars at 203 for SR 204 or 240.[11]

Fatehchand was conscious about the value of the currency that the EICs imported into Bengal but he was equally knowledgeable about their differential value. He refused, in 1741, to give the same rates of exchange for the new Pillar Dollars to the EEIC at Kasimbazar and insisted that they were equivalent to the Mexico dollars and not the old Pillar Dollars.[12] That he was right was evident as the Calcutta Council admitted that:[13]

> They (the new Pillars) might be inferior to what the pillar dollars used to be some time ago, and that about the year 1730 it was found in Europe that this specie was greatly debas'd where coin'd.

Fatehchand was a good friend of the EEIC and frequently interceded on its behalf at Murshidabad. The entry of January 3, 1745 noted:

> That on the 20th in the morning died Fatehchand, who has left his vast wealth to his two grandsons Mautobray and Suroopchund by whom it is supposed the business of the House will be carried on as usual, that we believe letters of compliment to them from the President would be proper . . .

But Seths Mahtab Rai and Swarupchand were less favourable to the EEIC. Despite having been given shelter within the English factory during the

Maratha invasion of 1745 ('it seemed necessary to us to oblige these people who are likely to have a very great interest in the government', noted the K.F.R. on Febrary 7, 1745) it was also noted on December 1, 1746 that:

> Jugut Seat's family have started fresh objections and expect their compliance with some conditions before they let us have the money promised . . . we must represent to them that we did not use to be treated in this manner by that family, Futtichund using to give orders on his house (at Dacca) when they were to receive money from him . . . however if they insist upon it we must comply therewith.

The Seths were also powerful enough to pressurize the French Government in France to force FEIC compliance with debts in Bengal. Negotiations between the Seths and the Ministry in Paris, noted in FEIC entries between 1773 and 1775, tell us they were successful. On August 18, 1773 the Seths demanded the moneys due to them by the FEIC in Bengal from the Ministry.[14] Entries of September 7, 1774 and of February 16, 1775 noted that the Seths had been paid back.[15]

Therefore a myth that has now been exploded is that the Europeans pumped in substantial sums to finance their operations in Bengal. As Peter Marshall has shown, the private British traders in eighteenth century Bengal were dependant on local sources of supply.[16] The K.F.R. tells us that so was the EEIC. But references to 'local' sources of supply tend to focus almost exclusively on the banking house of the Seths.

The House of Jagat Seth[17] is credited to have acted as the chief financiers to the European companies when their supplies of money fell short. Their loans to the EEIC were frequently of vast sums and, more importantly, for long periods. Between 1733 and 1750 this house lent the EEIC at Kasimbazar SR 4 232 278.[18] The interest rate was the standard established for Bengal in the eighteenth century.[19] This was, as we just noted, fixed at 9%.

But the Seths were not the only creditors of the EEIC. Other local supplies were loans between private individuals of EICs; in 1768 Sykes and Chevalier made an agreement whereby Sykes helped the FEIC at Kasimbazar.[20] FEIC efforts to put this on an official footing failed as both the EEIC and FEIC refused to accept the terms earlier that year.[21]

Both the FEIC at Chandernagore and the EEIC at Kasimbazar found yet another alternative source in their *dadni* merchants. Between 1772 and 1775 the Katmas were the principal moneylenders to the FEIC. Baburam, Bobun, Panchu and Poran Katma were listed as important FEIC moneylenders.[22] The Katmas had clout because we find an entry of February 16, 1775 mentioning that some of them had been paid off along with the Jagat Seths.[23]

At Kasimbazar it is remarkable that the bulk of loans to the EEIC-both in terms of amount and frequency-was furnished not by the Jagat Seths but by the merchants themselves. The names of some seventy moneylenders, with whom the EEIC dealt, are entered in the K.F.R. from 1733 to 1750.

There are both Bengalis and non-Bengalis (from upper India, as it seems from the first names) listed as money lenders in the K.F.R. Names such as 'Deochund', 'Odeychund' and 'Lahorymull' betray upcountry provenance. They account for 27% (out of the 70 names) of the moneylenders who did business with the EEIC at Kasimbazar. As in the case of *dadni* merchants, there are no Muslim names. These moneylenders lent money to the EEIC at the prevalent rate of 9%.

There were some who worked in partnership such as 'Nutmull and Roopchund', 'Lahorymull and Monsookray', 'Hernaut and Nonet' (two *dadni* merchants), 'Annunchund and Nutmull' (also two *dadni* merchants who feature in the K.F.R. investment lists), 'Coosalchund and Goolobray' (also *dadni* merchants), 'Deochund and Odeychund' and 'Kurrucksun and Kissenchund'.[24] 'Ruttunchund and Huttichund' was another partnership mentioned in the 1733 SPG investment (see Table 7).

There seem to be two Bengali combines : that of 'Ramdass and Ramchund Roy' and that of 'Nunderam Sene and Geporam'.[25] There is also an interesting association between one 'Meter Jean and Boisnaut Cowbray'.[26]

There are also those moneylenders who bear the same names as the *dadni* merchants that we just studied. These names are Katma, Dutt, Surma, Kapri, Tagore, Sarkar, Das, Poddar, Acharya and Pandit. As was the case with their merchant brethren, these names repeat themselves as moneylenders many times between 1733 and 1750. The occurrence of these names as merchants and as moneylenders is significant. We shall see that not only did a coterie of merchants grow up around the EEIC at Kasimbazar, this same coterie maintained close familial ties with the moneylenders at Kasimbazar. We shall study this under two heads: that of the merchant-moneylender family and that of the *merchant himself as moneylender.*

10.1. THE MERCHANT-MONEYLENDER NEXUS

For the Sarkars we note only one name-that of Nunderam Sarkar-who lent the EEIC SR. 25,000.[27] Among the Das, who were constantly present although not as big *dadni* merchants at Kasimbazar, we find five moneylenders: Jeytadass (in association with 'Lahorymull'), Radhakissen Dass, Durrumchurn Dass, Ramnaut Dass and Ramchurn Dass. These were probably of Gujarati origin.

How big was the Das family as moneylenders? Radhakissen Dass seems a small time moneylender: he lent money twice to the EEIC: SR 6070, 50 in 1744 and SR. 4 389 in 1745.[28] Dharamcharan lent even more modest sums: SR 1001 and SR 4232 in 1744.[29] Ramnath Das was different; he was clearly a big moneylender for he lent the EEIC a total of SR. 79000 (in 5 lots) between June 1745 and October 1746.[30] Ramcharan Das lent money only once to the EEIC; this was SR 10 000.[31]

By contrast, another moneylender Kisen Poddar, was an important figure. He was the EEIC *vakil* or the man who liaised with the *durbar* at Murshidabad.[32] In 1744 the EEIC gifted him SR.100 on the occasion of the marriage of his son;[33] and he is the only name thus honoured.

There is one Acharya moneylender, listed between 1736 and 1748 as 'Tackergee Achargee'. During this period he lent the EEIC money seven times: this came to a total of SR. 137 650.[34] He seems to be an important moneylender of Kasimbazar, at least as far as the EEIC is concerned. Jairam Pundit was also a prominent moneylender of Kasimbazar. He lent the EEIC money four times between 1736 and 1740, totalling SR. 80 000.[35]

Among money lenders with the same names as the notable merchants we find Katmas, Dutts, Surmas, Tagores and Kapris. None of the Biswas clan, who are notable as *dadni* merchants, figure as moneylenders.Three Dutts feature as moneylenders: Naran who lent the EEIC SR 8 000 in 1745,[36] Anandacharan ('Annunchurn') who lent money thrice, once in 1746 and twice in 1748 . The first time was for SR 11 350, the second time was for a sum unknown and the third time for SR 13 000.[37]

There is only one Surma moneylender listed as such in the K.F.R. Sadanand Surma lent money twice to the EEIC-once in July 1746 for SR 5 500 and once in October 1746 for SR 2 000. There is also only one Kapri moneylender, listed as Anandaram (Anunderam). He lent money twice: SR 10 000 in 1743 and SR 15 000 in 1746.[38]

Tagores as moneylender are more common; and they also seem more important. Sadanand Tagore lent SR. 5 000 on May 22, 1745; 'Ozooderam' Tgore lent the EEIC SR 4 250 on July 9, 1748. On April 1 1746 the EEIC borrowed SR 16,000 from Jiban (Jebun) Tagore. On May 4 Dayaram Tagore lent the EEIC SR 50,000. This leads us to speculate that although the Tagores were modest as merchants, they may not have been so as moneylenders.[39]

The Katmas were the most prominent moneylenders to the EEIC. As in *dadni*, the number of Katmas engaged in the business of moneylending was among the highest. Indinaran Katma once lent the EEIC SR 60,000 in 1733,[40] Golap Katma lent SR 40,000 in 1733.[41] Raghunath Katma lent 25,000 in 1733.[42] Sibnath (spelt Seepnaut) lent SR 15,000 in 1744 and SR 10 000 in 1745. Between April 1745 and August 1746 Sibnath lent a total of SR 29 181 to the EEIC.[43] Satu Katma lent SR 10 000[44] and Kritichand Katma lent SR 3 300 to the EEIC in 1743.[45]

Table 17 shows the amount of money lent by the big merchant-money-lender combines at Kasimbazar between 1733 and 1750.

Table 17
Amounts of Money in Sicca Rupees in Descending Order lent to the EEIC by the Merchant-Moneylender Combine at Kasimbazar: 1733–1750[46]

Katma	SR 192 481
Achargee	SR 137 650
Das	SR 104 692
Pandit	SR 80 000
Tagore	SR 75 250
Dutt	SR 32 350
Kapri	SR 25 000
Sarkar	SR 25 000
Poddar	SR 23 665
Surma (Sharma)	SR 7 500

Table 17 tells us not only that the merchant families that we identified before were prominent as money lenders at Kasimbazar, it also shows us that some, not identified as such like the Poddars, Sarkars, Pandits, Achargee and Das, were important moneylenders. Note however that the Tagores and Kapris had also made the EEIC investment lists as 'small partners' at Kasimbazar.

10.2. THE MERCHANT AS MONEYLENDER

Here the list is headed by Sachi Katma who let the EEIC SR 183 536 between 1732 and 1736.[47] No other person, except the Seths, had lent the EEIC so much at such short notice. Chakoo Katma is the next most important merchant-moneylender among the Katmas. On August 27, 1733 he lent the EEIC SR 50,000; he added another 30,000 on June 28, 1736. The Katmas had other lesser members as merchant-money lenders. Preet Katma lent SR 25 000.[48] Yet another was Hatoo Katma-one time favourite and broker of the EEIC at Kasimbazar-who lent the English SR 20,000.[49]

No other family had so many members in the moneylending business as the Katmas. Including those Katmas who functioned solely as moneylenders we find that there were 10 Katmas who were moneylenders to the EEIC at Kasimbazar between 1733 and 1749. From 1733 to 1746 the Katmas single-handedly lent the English Company Sicca Rupees 501,017.[50] We know from entries between 1772 and 1774 that they financed the FEIC as well.[51]

Other than the Katmas, who feature as both merchant and moneylender at Kasimbazar, there are the members of the Das family such as Hariballabh Das and Brajballabh Das who often appeared in the investment lists as partners. They seem to have worked as partners in money lending as well. On October 3, 1744 they lent SR 10 000 and again in January 1748, a lean year financially, they lent SR 756 to the EEIC at Kasimbazar.

Both of them seem to have been more worthy as financiers to the EEIC than as *dadni* merchants. In 1741[52] and 1746[53] Hariballabh Das lent the EEIC SR 10 000 and 7 000 respectively, both on his own account. Braj was an even larger creditor: he lent the English company SR 15 000 in 1744[54] and 16 000 in 1745.[55]

Some merchants with no surname recorded also feature as important moneylenders to the EEIC at Kasimbazar. The most important merchant-moneylender in this category is Kushalchand who lent the EEIC SR 50,000 in 1737[56] and SR 30,000 in 1738.[57] In both transactions he was partnered by one Golap Rai. He also lent the EEIC SR 50,000 in 1739 by himself.[58]

Other than Kushalchand, another merchant named Natmal teamed up with Rupchand and lent the English SR 30,000 in 1733.[59] The same year, Natmal, in association with Anandchand ('Annunchund'), lent the EEIC SR 12,5000.[60] Hernaut (Heeranath?) and Nonet (Noni?), two merchants who worked often together, lent the EEIC SR 6,000 in 1733.[61]

We also get the names of Govinram, Ramsing, Saulput and Praunkissen (family names not indicated) who lent the EEIC money. Govinram lent them SR 35,000 on April 24, 1743. Ramsing lent them SR 5 000 in 1733.[62] In the entry of October 13, 1733 it was noted that the EEIC paid back Saulput SR 2,500.

There is also the case of the merchant Praunkissen. He lent the EEIC SR 20 000 in 1741.[63] In the lists of 1733, 1736 and 1738 we find the name of Parunkissen entered without a surname. But in the lists of 1743 and 1744 there is a 'Praunkissen Cotma'. If Praunkissen was a Katma then the amounts lent to the EEIC by this family would be even larger.

Three points emerge from the section on merchants as moneylenders. One, as we noted, the EEIC were really very dependent on local capital sources. Marshall had already remarked on this in the case of English private traders. If we add up the amounts lent by the merchants and moneylenders we find that they were quite substantial. Between 1733 and 1750 the Jagat Seths lent the EEIC at Kassimbazar SR 4 232 278. The *dadni* merchants and moneylenders lent the EEIC a total of SR 1 311 880. This was not an insignificant sum. But there were some important differences. One, the sums were more modest than that lent by the Seths. While the Seths could afford to lend SR 250 000 at one go, none of the moneylenders could lend more than SR 60 000.This was only done once, by Indinaran Katma in 1733. Two, the moneys lent were for much shorter terms than those offered by the Seths. And finally, as in the case of trading, here too the role of the Katmas seems prominent. It is evident that there was an enormous amount of money floating around Kasimbazar in the eighteenth century. This liquid capital increasingly came to be concentrated in the hands of prominent merchants who used it as circulating capital or invested it in usury, real estate and in building up their contacts with the court at Murshidabad.

The office of broker to the EEIC, whereby 'a person of good standing' was not only the conduit for contracts and sales between the company and its merchants but also the chief negotiator between the company and merchants, also helped keep finance moving through guarantees, sureties and price fixing. The EEIC were careful as to whom they appointed. The Directors of the English East India Company wrote on July 16, 1736 that:[64]

> It is very necessary that you should be satisfied as to the ability and circumstances of the merchants to whom such large sums are advanced, and the broker may doubtless be of some service in that respect as to his being security that no bad debts fall upon us.

Yet another cautioned that:[65]

> Debashes and black servants must be confined to menial offices and not entrusted with our prosperity in any respect whatever, no confidence must be reposed in them in transacting our affairs.

Between 1736 and 1741 Huttoo and Bally Katma were the company brokers. Other than loans, the broker frequently stood surety for merchants; on March 26, 1737 Huttoo provided guarantee for the merchants to the tune of SR 30 419. This was no small sum but as we saw Huttoo was a moneylender as well as the private broker of Barker at Kasimbazar. But the broker frequently abused this privileged position by granting contracts within his coterie. The General Letter of February 9, 1736 remarked to the Council of the English Company at Kasimbazar:[66]

> In the division of the Investment among the merchants entered upon the Consultations of 25th July, we observe one man Sookmoy Seat had a

> much larger proportion of fine goods than any other, all the Cossajura Mullmulls and the Cossajura Dooreas being provided by him. These are the fine sorts which you have often represented are profitable articles to the Merchants so that in order to induce them to contract for the full quantity of Gurrahs, Romalls, Photaes and other coarse goods upon reasonable terms, all fine species should be divided among them. You may call to your mind upon recollection that it was a very large part of the charge against the late broker (probably Huttoo Katma-my comment) that his relations and Favourites had all the fine goods to themselves, and our Investment was said to suffer greatly through the Discouragements the other merchants laboured under thereby.

There was great wealth in the Katma family. When Bally succeeded Huttoo as broker the EEIC at Kasimbazar wrote on February 21, 1737:

> Having duly considered of a person for Broker we think none so proper as Bally Cotma as well through his great experience in the Company's affairs as the great wealth that is in his family which will make him a useful servant to our Honourable Masters.

Bally had been the private broker of Barker in 1733.[67] He directed the EEICs operations as broker from 1737 until 1741 when the post of broker was abolished. Bally was instrumental in creating a group of 'favoured merchants' with a steady and regular access to investments. Given this flouishing state of the money market in Kasimbazar it is all the more surprising that merchants declared bankruptcy towards the middle of the century, as we shall see later.

One reason for the bankruptcy was that mercantile capital became increasingly shy of investing further in Kasimbazar and moved on to invest in the better business ventures offered from Calcutta.[68] Yet another was the perceived crisis in the supply areas which became manifest by the 1740s. Yet another may have been that Calcutta offered better security of persons and property than Murshidabad. The issue of security gained prominence as the Marathas invaded Bengal with regularity from this time onward.

The K.F.R. notes that the Katmas left Kasimbazar and moved on to Calcutta at this time. Troubles in the hinterland, a breakdown in the supply areas, and increasingly unsettled political conditions in the *niyabat* led to this flight of capital from the land. Like the political system at Murshidabad itself, the indigenous capital market too, was caught in a moment of transition.

11

The Merchant's World at Kasimbazar

Having drawn a picture of the mercantile and financial world of Kasimbazar let us now move on to the drama that was enacted on these sets in the first half of the eighteenth century. Tables 7 to 17 offered us pictures of mercantile activity, profiles of dominant merchant groups and their financial strengths. Until 1752 the *dadni* merchants of Kasimbazar controlled a vast mercantile pyramid with a hierarchy of underlings, *gomasthas*, *banyans*, *underbanyans* and *pykars*, along with a whole host of employees who actually organised the production and sales from *arang* to company warehouse, serving under them. Others' positions were strengthened by the diversion of the bigger mercantile families into the twin branches of banking and supplying silk.

What were the political affiliations of these merchants? We saw that a ruling coterie of merchants, controlled by a dominant core, had come into existence in Kasimbazar by the eighteenth century. This dominance was enhanced by affiliations and links with the financial and political nexus that controlled the Murshidabad *niyabat.* Kushalchand ('Coosalchund') was the third Jagat Seth, the son of Seth Mahtab Rai. Kushalchand was also a prominent merchant featured in EEIC Investment Lists along with other members of the Seths such as Miachand. The partnership of 'Mahtabray-Surroopchund' featured in the SPG investments at Kasimbazar in 1736 and 1737 and Swarupchand was featured independently as a RS merchant in 1743. See Table 7. In 1743 Surupchand scored three times above the average annual investment (See Table 12).

Alamchand, mentioned simply as a merchant between 1748 to 1750 in the RS and SPG investments, was the *Ray Rayan*-Chief among Ministers-*the* Alamchand of the triumvirate of Haji Ahmad-Fatehchand-Alamchand that ruled the Murshidabad *niyabat* in the 1730s. Closer inspection tells us that far from being merely a merchant, Alam Chand was first the *Diwan* (or Finance Minister) and then *Rai Rayan* (or the Chief Minister) in the

1730s in Bengal. Alamchand was the most powerful financial figure in Shuja's Murshidabad in the 1730s, and his son Raja Kirti or Kriti Chand ('Krittichund' in the KFR) had considerable financial interests in Patna. As *Diwan* and then *Rai Rayan* Alamchand had a finger in every financial pie so that Alivardi, when he came to power, did not risk antagonising him. In fact, Alamchand and Fatehchand actively supported Alivardi against Sarfaraz in 1739–1740.[1] After his death, his protégé Chin Rai was made *Rai Rayan* and the various firms of Alamchand-Gainchand (Gyanchand) and Alamchand-Nimchand ran successful banking firms at Kasimbazar, Dhaka and Patna.[2] And after Chin Ray Raja Umed Rai, the deputy of Kriti Chand, became *Rai Rayan* in 1751. Kriti Chand became Diwan or Finance Minister of Alivardi—a title previously held by his father Alamchand in Shuja's time. Therefore between the 1730s and the 1750s—during the period of the EEIC's critical transition from an economic to a political power—Alam Chand's group was in power[3] and it is all the more significant that the firm of Alamchand-Gyanchand should come to figure in the raw silk and silk piece goods lists between 1748 and 1750.

Alamchand however died in 1740, in the Battle of Giria.[4] But as his firm continued with the name of Alamchand-Gyanchand and was important in financial affairs it is very likely that the 'AllumchundGainchund' referred to in the RS and SPG lists referred to the firm and not to any particular individual supplying goods to the EEIC.

Other merchants had links with the Court. Kissendeb Poddar, the EEIC vakil, and Harish Chowdhury were favourites of the powerful *Pachotra daroga* Hukum Beg. Kissendeb was initially Hukum Beg's diwan[5] and he frequenty mediated in conflicts between the EEIC and Hukum Beg. Hukum Beg, in his capacity of *Pachotra daroga*, frequently stopped EEIC ships. Kissendeb was held in high esteem by the EEIC as he had influential friends as well as patrons in not just Hukum Beg. He features also as a moneylender as we just noted. In the Cash Account of February 1744 of the Kasimbazar Council we find an entry detailing a gift made to Kissendeb on the occasion of his son's marriage. Kissendeb became the EEIC *vakil* in the 1750s and died in the Company's service. During his tenure with the EEIC at Kasimbazar he undertook many sensitive negotiations with the Murshidabad court.

Harish Chowdhury was noted as Hukum Beg's *diwan* in 1756.[6] He also scored twice above the annual average investment EEIC at Kasimbazar in 1748 and 1750 (see Table 12). In 1744, 1745 and 1749 he scored the same or less the annual average at Kasimbazar (see Table 13).

Ramkrishna Babu ('Ramkissen Bobboo') was the adopted son of the high official Raja Chin Rai and the protege of the Rajas Kritichand and

Umed Rai. Others such as Bakul Tagore (written in the K.F.R. as Becul Taggoo) and Umichand had patrons at court such as Haji Ahmad, the king maker of Murshidabad. A relative of Bakul Tagore kept the accounts for Haji Ahmad.[7] In 1736 when Umichand was dropped from the EEIC investment lists Haji Ahmad declared himself as Umichand's guarantor in open court at Murshidabad. Umichand profited from this association and moved on to become a substantial merchant dealing in salt petre from Patna in the 1750s. Myachund was a relative of the Jagat Seths.[8]

Political and economic clout was often indistinguishable and favours descended down the scale at Kasimbazar. Lesser merchants such as Devi Prasad (Surma) had guarantors such as Ramkrishna Babu who in his turn was the protege of some of the highest revenue officials in the land—Raja Chin Rai, Raja Kritichand, and Raja Umed Rai, as we just saw. Indirectly, therefore, Devi Prasad was guaranteed by some of the highest officials and financiers of Murshidabad. Devi Prasad's affiliations are significant in that he was the chief actor in the crisis of 1753 at Kasimbazar.

I have found no political affiliation in the case of the Katmas, but given their clout it is almost certain that they had links with the court at Murshidabad. But by 1750 they had lost political support at court. Three incidents support this view. One, in 1750 Hukum Beg asked the English factory at Kasimbazar to send up Bally Katma to Murshidabad to defend himself against charges brought against him. Two, again in 1756 Hukum Beg sent horsemen and peons to Calcutta to seize the effects of the Katmas. This snowballed into a political issue. The horsemen were turned out of Calcutta and complained at Murshidabad to Hukum Beg. The English at Kasimbazar were forced to intervene in the matter and suggested to Calcutta that protection to the Katmas might turn out to be too expensive as the factors at Kasimbazar apprehended that business might be stopped by the Nawab.[9] Again, when the Katmas died intestate there was another tussle between Murshidabad and Calcutta as the court decided to seize their effects.

Partnerships in *dadni* were common. Partnerships such as Alamchand-Gyanchand, Premnaran-Anupnaran, Samsunder-Udaynaran, Mahtab Rai-Swarupchund, Ramnath-'Itchinaut' and Anandachand-Natmal continued for some years as also those between Dutts, between Kapris and between Biswases (see Table 7). Exceptions were the partnership between Ruttunchund and Huttichund which was recorded only once for the year 1733 in the SPG investment and the one between Lalchand-Anandachand which occurred only once in 1743 for the RS investment. The partnership of Mahtab Rai-Swarupchand was active in the 1730s (two SPG investments in 1736 and 1737. See Table 7) and ceased after that, possibly as a result of the two brothers becoming the Seths on Fatehchand's death in 1744. But there is a 'Seroopchund' listed in the RS investment of 1743; and Table 12 tells us that he scored three times above the average per merchant that year in investment. After Mahtab Rai stopped trading as a *dadni* merchant his son Kushalchand became even more prominent in the investment lists. We do not know if he traded also on account of his father.

Other partnerships, such as that between Nunderam and Sauhibram was recorded for two successive years, in 1741 and 1742, and also only for the SPG investment. It is likely that some of these partnerships specialised in a particular item but the partnership of Primnaran-Onoopnaran specialised in both RS and SPG; and Allumchund-Gainchund specialised in RS, SPG and G&D investments between 1748 and 1750. We find no partnerships in furnishing the Rungpore or March Bund silks.

Partnerships were not permanent. They could last a few years, or either of the members could form a partnership with another merchant. This happened in the case of 'LollchundAnnunchund'. 'Annunchund' then formed a partnership as 'Annunchund Nutmull'. 'Lollchund' partnered Bowannychurndutt in the 1741 RS investment. Partnerships were also flexible. For example a particular merchant in partnership with another could also furnish the same goods on his own account in the *same* year. For example, in 1740 the partnership between Samsunder and Odeynaran furnished SPG, but the two merchants also supplied RS, SPG and G&D separately on their own account the same year. But I have found no two different partnerships involving the same member in the same year.

How lucrative were partnerships? Table 12 tells us that only three partnerships without family names mentioned scored double or more of the average annual EEIC investment in Kasimbazar. These were the partnerships of 'LollchundAnnunchund', 'PrimnaranOnoopnaran' and 'Allumchund-Gainchund'. But one indication that partnerships may have been extremely lucrative is provided by the fact that it was mostly members of the notable families at Kasimbazar who formed partnerships within themselves. In other words, these partnerships were not within the kin group rather they were formed along class lines.

In fact, partnerships between individuals were not always on kin lines. Those merchants with family names mentioned in partnership with another merchant did not always form partnerships on the basis of the family name. Examples are the G&D investment in 1737 where a partnership between Nemidutt, Sachi Katma and Biswanath Dutt operated, the SPG investment of 1740 where there was a partnership between Sachi Katma and a 'Jackernaut' (the Jackernaut Coppree of the 1742 SPG investment or the Jackernaut Teli of the 1744 SPG investment?), the 1740 partnership in SPG between Naran Biswas and Gopee Gautam, the partnership between Lalchand and Bhabani Charan Dutt in the 1741 RS investment, the partnerships between Kushalchand and Kablaram Surma, between Naincharan Dutt and Bobun Katma, between Hari Ballabh Das and Dulal Surma, between Kalyan Biswas and Harish Chowdhury in the RS investment in 1744; the list is endless and it is worth noting that these merchants acted in their individual capacity as *dadni* merchants in those years as well.

But we should note that 1744 was the year when the merchants formed a successful ring, and it was in this year that the most partnerships occurred. It is also worth noting, from Table 9, that 1744 was a year that saw some of the largest numbers of merchants participating in the RS and SPG investments. In 1745 there was a partnership between Bistumchurndee and Kisninda Surma in the RS investment and in the *gara* investment between Raghunath Biswas and Dulal Biswas. For all partnerships mentioned see Table 7.

What do these partnerships involving the members of the notable families tell us? We see that all four notable families, those that we termed as 'coterie', frequently formed partnerships with one another. Sachi Katma, Nain Charan Dutt, Naran Biswas, Bistumchurndee, Nemi Dutt, Raghunath Biswas, Kissen Inder Surma, Bhabani Charan Dutt, Bobun Katma, Dulal Surma, Kablaram Surma and Biswanath Dutt were merchants who had all, at some time or the other, scored at least double over the average EEIC investment per merchant (see Table 12). As had those merchants without family names mentioned who formed partnerships: LollchundAnnunchund, Kushalchand and Swarupchand (again Table 12). We can estimate, therefore, that forming partnerships was both advantageous and lucrative. But we should also remember that partnerships were most common in the 1730s and declined after 1745. (See Table 7 for more details).

Favourites regularly traded on behalf of their patrons at Court; and the merchants often formed consortiums to oppose any breach of their monopolistic position in the silk trade as *dadni* merchants. In other words, the nexus between merchants and courtiers did not just stop at cordial relations; there was an active trade with the EICs by courtiers and financial combines through intermediaries and *dadni* merchants.

In 1741 the EEIC at Kasimbazar attempted to force the merchants to contract for the raw silk at the low price of SR 5.25 a seer. Bally Katma the broker refused, so did other prominent merchants such as Naran, Gobardhan and Raghunath Biswas, Mahadeb and Kablaram Surma, Ram Tagore and Kushalchand. Only two small merchants, Nim Das and Nimo Poddar agreed to this price.[10]

The EEIC was still hesitant to bypass the coterie and on February 20, 1740/41 agreed that:

> Agreed that we stay till tomorrow and no longer to ask those merchants again whether or not they will contract at the price we have offered, as we think several of them the best and most substantial merchants and of course the properest to be imployed in providing the Honourable Company's Investment.

On February 21, 1740/41 all merchants agreed to contract for at the price offered. But at the same time the big merchants took a move to crush future attempts by smaller merchants to break the price threshold at a date on or around March 24th. This is evident from the Consultations of April 13, 1740/41 that noted:

> We now sent for the merchants who signed the paper sent hence the 24th (*not found*-my note) and required them to give their reasons for that extraordinary proceeding, to which they reply'd that they had no ill intention and that their motive for it *was their own interest, which as merchants they had a right to pursue by any methods that seemed to the Conducing to that End* (my emphasis), they said further that what chiefly induced them to sign that agreement was, that as some of them had during the troubles in December bought up some of the Putney, which to the prejudice of the rest they might possibly offer to contract for below the real market price at the time of giving out the dadney, in such case others who had slipt the opportunity might be disabled from taking any dadney or be great sufferers by it . . . These they declared were the only motives for signing said paper which they did to secure themselves from the tricks of each other.[11]

This document highlights the fact that there were different interest groups fighting for control over the silk trade in 1740. Huttoo Katma, the Consultations of January 27, 1740 noted, proved his indispensability to the EEIC by persuading the other merchants to diminish the price of silk. This fight for control over the Investment assummed greater significance in view of the troubled situation following the invasion of Nadir Shah in northern India in November 1739;[12] the overthrow of the old 'dynasty' with Sarfaraz' dispossession from December 1739 to April 1740, the start of the new dynasty of Alivardi where merchants were not sure how the new political climate might affect them, and the expected outcome of Mir Habib's overtures to the Marathas which would unleash the decade long invasion of Bengal.

Throughout that year of 1740 silk reelers and winders abandoned their homes in view of the impending Maratha invasions. The *dadni* merchants complained that no reelers and winders could be found for almost two months; consequently the 'Guzerat' variety was wound off during the monsoons. This resulted in bad quality silk.[13] 1740 ushered in changes that were to be far reaching for commerce in Bengal.

The document also shows that the big merchants formed a combine to forestall any attempts on the part of the smaller merchants to break the ring. In 1744 a similar incident occurred; this time two merchants, Hariballabh Das and Bobun Katma broke the ring by accepting a lower price in the contract. The EEIC at Kasimbazar accepted. 'as this may be a means to bring other Merchants to our terms'.[14] This apparently worked because the consultations of March 6, 1744 noted that Dulal and Kablaram of the Surma family and Raghunath of the Biswas family accepted the lowered price. Two of the three were notable merchants; the K.F.R. noted in the consultations of February 28, 1741 that Naran, Raghunath and Gobardhan Biswas, Mahadeb and Kablaram Surma, Ram Tagore and Kushalchand were the 'best and most substantial merchants'. Once Kablaram Surma and Raghunath Biswas led the way in 1744, the others soon followed.

Bobun Katma was not a small merchant. In 1744, the year he accepted the lowered price, he formed a partnership with Nainchurndutt (of the Dutt family) in the RS investment; and he also furnished RS that year on his own account. Similarly Hariballabh (spelt Harrybullubdass) formed a partnership with Doolol Surma of the Surmas that year. Bobun Katma was definitely not a small merchant; in 1744 Bobun Katma scored double over the average investment figures per merchant. Doolol Surma, with whom Haribullub formed a partnership that year similarly scored over double in 1744 and 1746 (See Table 12).

The position of broker to the EEIC was an important one, and here too worthy persons of good standing in the local community were appointed. The Katmas were prominent as brokers: from 1736 to 1740 or 1741, and this post was occupied by Huttoo and then Bally Katma. But just as we saw in the section dealing with money supplies, the merchants did not build up a sustainable credit network, and this lacuna became glaringly evident when the merchants' bankruptcy was revealed from the late 1740s. Also, dissensions within the Katma clan became glaring from 1740. Despite Bally being the company broker, the EEIC at Kasimbazar continued to favour Huttoo as he had influence over the other *dadni* merchants and was often instrumental in getting them to contract at lower prices, because his goods were better than those of other merchants, and because he offered large guarantees for his contracts.[15] Most important, Huttoo was useful in that he could be used to 'control' Bally Katma.[16] But Huttoo lost this round against Bally because as company broker Bally refused to stand surety for Huttoo for the *dadni*.[17] This began Huttoo's slide into obscurity. But Bally's ascension to the post of the head of the Katma clan[18] was short-lived. As early as January 27, 1740 the Kasimbazar Council had declared that the Katmas were 'unworthy of admittance into dadni'. On 21 December 1741 Bally Katma was referred to as 'the ancient broker of the Company'.

Once the post of broker was abolished in 1741, the Katmas lost their influence. But the EEIC at Kasimbazar could not exclude them totally from the investment. In 1741 Bally's name was there in the Rangpur Silk investment.[19] From 1743 we find the names of other Katmas: Beroofe, Bobun, Mohun, Praunkissen, Suroop, Preat, Boolchund, Collichurn, Kissenchund, Coosal and Kissenchurn in the investment list. They continued to lend money to the EEIC as well, as we saw. But none of the next generation of Katmas reached the heights of Sachi, Bally and Huttoo; they were much smaller merchants. And perhaps this explains why Bobun Katma was willing to break the ring in 1744, in a strategy reminiscent of Huttoo's in 1740.

12
The Crisis

It was K.N. Chaudhuri who was among the first to mention the 'breakdown in the supply areas' all over the Indian hinterland from the 1740s.[1] My own work on Kasimbazar (1994) and Jugdia (1991) focussed almost exclusively on the manner of this breakdown. But earlier historians did not accept this idea of breakdown. Indeed N.K. Sinha wrote in 1965 that 'this (company) talk of the economic decline of Bengal before Plassey is a myth'.[2] Following Sinha, both Richard Eaton (1993) and Sushil Chaudhury (1995) disregard the decline in production that set in prior to Palashi.[3] Indeed, the latter finds no decline in the position of the *dadni* merchants at all.[4]

The breakdown in the supply areas followed a trajectory similar to what Peter Kriedte, Hans Medick and Jurgen Schlumbohm outlined in the crisis of proto industrialisation in *Industrialisation Before Industrialisation* (1981, Cambridge). This crisis was three phased. The first was a crisis in perception of goods as commodities as the needs of merchant capital far outpaced the demands of the peasant household which was the chief unit of manufacture of textiles. This was because the world of merchant capital was ruled by the norms of exchange value which sought to enhance capital, while the world of the peasant economy was used primarily to the norms of use value. The world of the peasant had no interest in enhancing merchant capital. It did not perceive goods as commodities.

Secondly, there was a crisis in supply. Since the peasant produced textiles primarily to supplement his/her income from agricultural work, production did not always keep pace with demand generated by far off markets. Very often, in times of a trade crisis the peasants actually produced more (if they needed greater incomes than what agriculture generated) and thus contributed to a glut in the market. And the peasants did not necessarily manufacture more in times of a boom if the income generated from agriculture was sufficient for their needs at that particular moment. Therefore the world of the merchant and the world of the peasant moved in opposite directions.

The merchant could, of course, centralise manufacture, and thereby direct production in accordance with international demand. But the peasants were not ready yet to form an industrial labour force. The first precondition of such a system would be to divorce the peasants from land, whereby they would then form a reserve labour force. This was not possible in Bengal in the eighteenth century.

The *dadni* merchant therefore took the only other option open to him. In order to expand supply, he brought in an ever growing area into the ambit of production. This ultimately led to the third phase of the crisis: as more and more areas were brought under the system, the merchant found it increasingly difficult to supervise quality and ensure deliveries on time. Therefore he employed more people under him who could go into the interior and supervise production. This increased the merchant's cost per unit of production and ultimately proved prohibitive. Also, this system did not ensure either quality or punctuality. At some point or the other, Kriedte, Medick and Schlumbohm pointed out, this system was bound to collapse. It did start collapsing in the 1740s in Bengal. The first signs of trouble came in 1739–1740 when silk prices went up at Kasimbazar. This, coupled with the Maratha invasions until 1751, was the first warning bell of the crash. The crisis became even more visible from 1744 onwards.

Let us now follow the trajectory of the crisis. In 1740 the *dadni* merchants refused to contract for the silk piece goods as they apprehended wars in Murshidabad between the armies of Sarfaraz Khan and Alivardi Khan.[5] The 'Guzerat' silk of that year was of a very bad quality; the merchants affirmed that this was due to the devastation caused by the wars of succession and the fact that it was reeled off late during the monsoons.[6] The Rangpur silk that year was expensive. The EEIC had to pay SR 4.31 a seer as the investment was late due to the uncertain political situation. The Pathan merchants, anticipating trouble, had bought up all the November Bund of the Rangpur silk.[7] The Rangpur silk finally delivered at the company's warehouse was much inferior to the sample shown at the time of investment.[8]

Similar troubles continued in 1741. The November Bund and Kumarkhali silks were inferior to the samples shown; this was due, the merchants claimed, because the investment was passed late in the season.[9] Moreover the Rangpur silk price rose to SR 5.75 a seer because merchants from Gujarat and Hyderabad had bought up huge amounts.[10] The consultations recorded on January 31, 1742 that raw silk was more expensive that year due to the heavy rains of 1741. The price rose further as a big merchants' convoy had arrived from Delhi to buy silk and silk piece goods for the Mughal emperor.[11]

The merchants now reacted. The consultations of February 25, 1744 noted that the merchants demanded a higher price for the raw silk and silk piece goods contracts; in effect they demanded the same price as they had obtained from the DEIC in 1743 and 1744.[12] They were not very willing to contract for the *garas* either because the Nawab objected to EEIC trade in *garas.* This was corroborated in the entry of March 13, 1744. In 1745 the Maratha invasion of Bengal caused the price of all articles to rise and on May 15 the council noted that the merchants had hidden all the *garas* they had in the *arangs.* On October 26 it was noted that 'this year . . . the excessive dearness of putney which never rose so high in the memory of the Oldest Person here made it difficult to procure it at any rate'. The quality of raw silk suffered accordingly.

In 1746 the silk filaments (*patni*) continued to be expensive and bad. On April 3 the merchants told the council that the Marathas had ravaged the *patni* areas; moreover the Armenian and Gujarati merchants had already bought up what little was available, and that too at an elevated price. On June 1 they informed the council that *patni* would be consequently expensive that year. Moreover it would be of a bad quality because the season was advanced, the monsoon had arrived and the cloths would be washed in the water of the ponds that was now very dirty. The situation was similar in case of silk piece goods. On June 13 the EEIC was obliged to pay the high price the merchants asked for the plain taffaties.

On June 22, 1746 the Kasimbazar Council informed the Calcutta Council that the goods would be expensive and mediocre that year. There was also no guarantee for the *gara* and *dusutty* contracts. On August 12, on seeing the goods delivered, the Council averred that its fears had been well founded. The quality was terrible. The silk piece goods were equally expensive that year because they were made from the November and March Bunds which were expensive that year.

There are no entries for investments in 1747. Was it that the EEIC decided not to invest that year? On January 27, 1748 it was noted that the Gujarat variety of silk did not tally to specifications. The reason given was that the contracts had been late and that consequently the silk had been wound off in unfavourable climatic conditions.[13] But a more urgent reason for the bad quality was the impending Maratha invasion; there was anarchy and pillage in the countryside and it was said that the people of Bengal no longer trusted their government could protect them.[14]

In 1748 the distress of the *dadni* merchants became apparent. Both the November Bund and the Kumarkhali silks were delivered late that year and the merchants pleaded that they had no money, that the nawab's officers harassed them daily and that there was a scarcity of silk reelers. Moreover the financial distress had resulted in the merchants having to borrow money at exorbitant rates to pay salaries. Most were now heavily in debt to the money-lenders.[15] The Kasimbazar Council wrote to Calcutta on May 24, 1748 that the merchants would not make investments unless SR 300 000 due to them was paid by the EEIC.[16] Seth Mahtab Rai also demanded money owed to him by the EEIC.[17]

This sorry state of affairs was not excused by the Board of Directors in London which was only interested in buying cheap and selling dear. It wrote to the Kasimbazar factors (entered in the consultations of February 23, 1749): 'The Prices of Raw Silk have advanced upon us from year to year at Cossimbazar though the Buyers here complain that it grows worse and worse. We hope our Servants buy as cheap as other people get it there'.

But the EEIC and its merchants were not to blame for the sorry state of the silk trade. The instability of a mercantile economy, an instability that could be aggravated by the slightest seasonal disturbance or political disturbance, had started to manifest itself at Kasimbazar by mid century. The slightest hitch could cause the whole cycle to slow down. Financial cracks within the system now became visible. By 1750 both merchant and company were caught within a system from where there was no escape.

13
The Crash at Kasimbazar

From 1749 EEIC affairs at Kasimbazar entered a new phase. The company in London was now seriously reconsidering its decision to invest in the textile trade here. It was noted on August 11, 1749 that the Letter Generall from London felt that the price of *garas* was so high as to make investment in them unprofitable.

Gara contracts played a central role in the EEIC investment at Kasimbazar since 1733. Table 18 shows the proportions of raw silk, *gara* and *dusutty*, silk piece goods, Rangpur silk and Rangpur silk (March Bund) in the EEIC investments at Kasimbazar.

Much of the complaints of both the *dadni* merchants and the EEIC centred around the *gara* contracts. As early as May 8, 1733 the K.F.R. noted in the consultations that since the number of buyers of *garas* had increased, the prices had risen and the quality deteriorated. The Directors of the EEIC had noted in their letter of February 9, 1736 that:

> The dearness or cheapness of Cotton, the large or small demand, and the Oppression and Mildness of the Country Government influence very much the price of coarse goods . . . such as Gurrahs, Romalls, Photae . . .

But in the period from 1736 to 1741 prices of *garas* and *dusutties* had either remained stable or had actually come down. Table 18 demonstrates this clearly.

Gara prices therefore rose steeply after 1741 and reached crisis proportions in 1749. One reason for the rise in *gara* and *dusutty* prices after 1741 was the presence of Indian merchants as well as the FEIC and DEIC.[1] *Garas* were the focal point in the crisis of 1753–54.

Yet, investment in other items continued throughout 1749. On October 22 the merchants showed inferior samples of raw silk. But the price was high;

Table 18
EEIC Investment (in thousands of rupees) of Textiles at Kasimbazar
Between 1733 and 1750.

		RS (% of Total Inv)	**G&D** (%)	SPG (%)	Rg Silk (%)	RS (MB) (%)	Total
1733	1335.95	47	**32**	13	8	-	100
1736	746.21	61	**33**	6	-	-	100
1737	888.13	40	**39**	6	15	-	100
1738	776.67	52	**44**	4	-	-	100
1739	964.29	-	**82****	7	-	11	100
1740	820.30	64	**21**	13	2	-	100
1741	723.65	54	**46****	-	-	-	100
1742	470.26	76	-	24	-	-	100
1743	519.09	82	-	18	-	-	100
1744	1368.58	68	-	32	-	-	100
1745	1594.78	30	**54**	16	-	-	100
1746	552.74	100	-	-	-	-	100
1748*	540.10	98	-	2	-	-	100
1749*	50.57	72	-	28	-	-	100
1750	236.93	81	**16**	3	-	-	100

* The investment of February 1748 of the year 1747/48 is included in the year 1748. Similarly the investment of January 1749 of the year 1748/49 is included in the year 1749.

** The investment of 1739 was done together for RS and G&D. The investment of 1741 was done together for G&D and SPG. Hence the inflated figures. However Table 18 shows quite clearly that gara-dusutty investments accounted for a third to one half of the total EEIC investment at Kasimbazar.

the merchants claimed this was because the cost of the primary materials was high. For the SPG contract the merchants demanded the same price as in 1748 because the price had risen by 4 annas a seer since 1748. In October the consultations noted that the price of *patni* had risen again. On November 6, 1749 the council noted that 'Being of the opinion the Merchants cannot well afford the silk piece goods for less than last year's prices as silk is dearer' and

Table 19

Price of Each Variety of Gara and Dusutty, the Average Price and the Index 1736 to 1741 with 1739 as the Base Year

Year	Gara of 72 and 2 and ¼ cubits	Ditto of 36 and 2 and ¼	Ditto of 30 and 2 and ¼	Dusutty of 15 and 1 and 1/8	Ditto Fine of 30 and 1 and 1/8	Ditto Superfine of 30 and 1 and 1/8	Average Price
1. Prices in Rupees per Corge							
1736	112.00	56.00	46.75	48.00	123.00	142.00	87.96
1737	112.00	56.00	46.75	48.00	123.00	142.00	87.96
1738	110.00	55.00	46.00	48.00	120.00	142.00	86.83
1739	106.00	53.00	44.00	48.00	120.00	142.00	85.50
1740	104.00	52.00	43.25	-	-	-	66.42
1741	102.00	51.00	42.50	46.50	-	-	60.50
2. Index (1739 = 100)							
1736	106	106	106	100	102	100	103
1737	106	106	106	100	102	100	103
1738	104	104	105	100	100	100	102
1739	100	100	100	100	100	100	100
1740	98	98	98	-	-	-	98
1741	96	96	97	97	-	-	97

that it would be better to contract at the price offered by the merchants. For perhaps the first time in the history of the EEIC at Kasimbazar, the company and the merchants were in total accord.

The letter from London dated January 23, 1751 (entered in the K.F.R. Consultations of August 9, 1751) accused the EEIC at Kasimbazar of malpractices in the investment that resulted in the falling quality and high price of silk. The Consultations of August 20, 1752 took note of a letter from the Court of Directors in London that feared 'that unless some very Extraordinary Efforts are made by you in future the many abuses so justly complained of as well as to improve the several manufactures and reduce the exorbitant price thereof, that branch of trade that has been the most beneficial to the Company will cease to be a profitable one.'

In 1753 these fears proved well founded because the Court of Directors noted that *garas* and raw silk were so expensive that the quantity to be invested in should be reduced so as to sell in London at a profit to the EEIC.[2]

Until the end of 1753 the EEIC at Kasimbazar was beset by a combination of extraordinarily high prices and a progressively worsening quality of goods from which the *garas* and *dusutties* were not exempt, harsher pricing at the weighing in,[3] conflicts with the merchants because they refused to take back the rejected silk (K.F.R. January 13, 1752), penalties imposed on the merchants (K.F.R. September 12, 19, 1753) with the merchants pleading adverse conditions, indebtedness and penury within which they were forced to furnish the investments.[4]

It was against this background of a production breakdown that the crisis of 1753 took place. It demonstrated the fragility of the present system and the extent to which the economic and the political could become intertwined. Its repercussions marked a turning point for the economic history of Bengal.

'Davypursaud', one of the *dadni* merchants of the EEIC at Kasimbazar, was suspected to be in bad circumstances in the consultations of August 16, 1753. It was noted on September 7, 1753 that the *dadni* merchant Debi Prasad was confined by the English for non payment of debts. The consultations of September 12 noted that Debi Prasad's security, 'Ramkissen Bobboo' had also been arrested. The English suspicion of the former's 'bad circumstances' led to this extreme act in spite of the fact that Ramkrishna Babu was the adopted son of Raja Chin Rai and had other powerful allies at the durbar. It was noted on September 19 that Ramkrishna Babu was applying to the durbar for his (Ramkrishna's) release. This event, in view of Ramkrishna Babu's powerful patrons, caused a sensation within Bengal and became a show of strength between Murshdabad and Calcutta. On September 24, 1753 it was reported that several high officials such as *mutsuddis* and *diwans* and the Rajas Kriti Chand and Umed Rai had made an appeal to Nawab Alivardi Khan.

In view of the seriousness of the matter the nawab threatened immediately to attack the Kasimbazar factory if Ramkrishna Babu was not released forthwith. Because of the delicate nature of the incident the English decided to let their trusted *vakil*, Kisendeb Podar, who himself had friends in high places, handle the negotiations with Murshidabad.

Who was Debi Prasad and why were such high level solicitations made on his behalf at court? Debi Prasad was a 'prominent merchant' who featured in the RS, MB, SPG and G & D investment lists between 1733 and 1746.[5] There is no indication of his family name except for an entry in 1746 which leads us to suspect that he was a member of the Surma family (see Table 7).[6] If that is so, this explains his having such a powerful security such as Ramkrishna Babu because the Surmas became powerful in the EEIC investments from 1744 on. By 1748 the Surmas accounted for *22*% of the total amount invested by the EEIC at Kasimbazar as against the Katmas' 2%, the Dutts' 2% and the Biswases' 4%. In 1750 the Surmas accounted for 31% of the total investment at Kasimbazar as against the Katmas' 0.2%, and the Biswases' 5% (the Dutts were not featured that year). See Table 15 which details the share of the big families in the EEIC investments, for more.

The Surmas therefore out paced the Katmas in the EEIC lists at Kasimbazar from the mid 1740s, except in the field of moneylending.[7] Despite having a similar numerical strength (only 4%) as compared to the Katmas (2%), the Dutts (2%) and the Biswas (4%) in 1748 and 3% as against the Katmas' 3% and the Biswases' 3% in 1750, the Surma's activities point to a concentration of capital within their clan such as no other merchants, the Katmas included, had shown at Kasimbazar (see Tables 15 and 16, see also Graphs 1 and 2). Moreover, Debi Prasad was one of the very few who invested in more than one item (see Table 7): while investing in only one item in 1733 (SPG), in 1744 and 1745 (SPG again) and in 1746 (RS), he invested in two in 1737 (RS and G&D) and in three items in 1738 (RS, SPG, G&D) and 1739 (RS, G and MB). As we have seen in Table 10 very few merchants (and by inference only the most substantial ones) invested in three items. Debi Prasad was truly an important merchant at Kasimbazar. But we have no idea as to what happened to him ultimately.

14

The Parting of Ways

Soon after this incident, and close on the heels of rejection upon rejection of goods, two minor incidents sparked off a mutiny among the merchants of Kasimbazar. Both merchant and company had to rethink their strategy in Kasimbazar now.

On September 19, 1753 a considerable part of the NB silk was rejected by the EEIC. The merchants refused to take back the rejected silk; and on February 4, 1754 the consultations noted that the merchants had not yet decided whether they would contract with the EEIC that year as they had greatly suffered in 1753. On the same day, that is February 4, 1754, the *garas* of 72 cubits (covids) were once again rejected as sub-standard by the English Company at Kasimbazar. The entries of March 4 and 18, 1754 reiterated the merchants' decision not to contract with the EEIC at Kasimbazar. And the rejection of *garas* in February 1754 was the last straw for the merchants. It resulted in a delegation of the merchants to the Court on March 28 to air their grievances and ask for redress. We have no knowledge of the Court's reactions to this deputation.

The merchant's Punch Paper, signed on December 11, 1753, and entered in the consultations of October 21, 1954, reiterated the merchants' decision not to contract for investment. It noted that 'But if in Anger they (the EEIC) get any of us imprisoned, we do agree to confine ourselves with the Person so imprisoned: And if they happen to turn any of us out of their Business, we all do promise to quit their Business likewise'.

The EEIC in Kasimbazar felt that the merchants regarded the threat of being 'dropped from the dadney very lightly' and that 'our merchants have given us no very great signs of their valuing our Favour and Protection'.[1] What was certain was that not one merchant was willing to accept the terms offered by the EEIC. The EEIC attempted to procure the investment through the Gujarati merchants and the DEIC; this proved unsuccessful as the quality of the silks was the same as that shown previously by the *dadni* merchants, but the prices higher. Moreover the terms of the Gujaratis and the Dutch were quite unacceptable.[2] On February 5 and 10, 1754 therefore, a decision was taken by the Kasimbazar Council to buy directly from the *arangs* instead of relying on the dadni merchants. Rs. 40,000 was sent by the EEIC at Kasimbazar to be invested in *patni.*

We have no indication from the EEIC records as to whether the *dadni* merchants at Kasimbazar realised how ominous this change was to be. Under the entry of February 10th the Kasimbazar Council noted that if the *dadni* merchants learnt that the EEIC were planning to send money directly to the *arangs* they might come down to the EEIC's terms. They did not do so and in the consultation of May 6, 1754 it was reported that on being asked once again to lower their prices—the alternative being that the EEIC would buy *patni* directly from the *arangs*—the merchants replied that they had agreed to provide silk so as to continue in *dadni* and not with any view to profit. So, if the EEIC did not accept their terms 'they are glad to be excused in that business that year.'

The Calcutta Council was however apprehensive at so revolutionary a departure in investment. It urged the Kasimbazar Council to still try to persuade the merchants and procure silk by traditional means. But the consultations of May 6, 1754 noted that the Calcutta Council had changed its mind. Part of the reason was, as the entry of April 24 noted, the muster or sample of 'Guzerat' silk which the Kasimbazar factory had sent down to Calcutta. The muster had been wound off from *patni* at the factory itself and it turned out 7 annas/seer cheaper than what the merchants had asked for. The quality too, was better.

Manufactories for supervising the entire process were set up and previously independent weavers, now by virtue of the English proclamations forbidden to work for any other merchant, came in to backup the entire operation. Those *dadni* merchants that survived the transition were brought in to act as under supervisors under an English factor. Experts in silk reeling and in silk winding were brought in from as far afield as Italy and France to impart specialised knowledge. By 1758 this was a full blown operation and Wilder arrived at Kasimbazar from England to advise on matters relating to silk winding on a fairly regular basis. The Company had become the ultimate merchant. Centralised manufacture of silk arrived at Kasimbazar.

15

The Departure

It is thus clear that the Agency System was born out of an intense crisis, at least at Kasimbazar. But by 1756 the EEIC's new system was well on its way to success in Bengal. On January 16, 1756 it was noted that the company's 'own' Guzerat was good and the November Bund silk better.[1] The letter of the Court of Directors dated January 31, 1756 said, of the steps leading to the Agency System that:[2]

> The bad circumstances of the generality of the merchants employed in the providing your Investments, their many impositions and non confidence with their contracts have for a long time been so notorious that other measures were absolutely necessary to be taken, we cannot therefore but look upon their obstinacy and insolence in their treaty with you for the Investment of 1753 as the occasion of one of the luckiest incidents that could have happened to the Company, we mean the laying you under the necessity of making the Investment in a new method, which from your accounts of it and the great advance we have in its very infancy experienced by the superior quality of the goods provided under your New Regulations, has been already a great advantage in point of profit and will, we are satisfied, be productive of much greater if pursued with zeal and vigour and conducted with integrity.

The letter from the Court of Directors of January 31, 1756 (mistakenly referred to as of 1755) noted that:[3]

> As the sale of our Bengal goods is now ended, we find it necessary to confirm to you the several remarks made in the course of our list of investments on the several species of goods bought on the new plan at the Aurungs compared with the same kinds bought off or contracted for with the merchants, the sales of which have answered even beyond our

> expectation in favour of the former . . . thanks to the conduct of these merchants which has drove you to expedients which might not other ways have been thought of, you now find many sorts of goods are fabricated within our bounds, cheap and of good qualities, and may be had at the first hand as it is evidently for our interest. Therefore, to encourage not only all the weavers now in our bounds but likewise to draw as many others as possible from all countries to reside under our protection, we shall depend upon your utmost efforts to accomplish the same and shall hope the time is not far off wherein we shall find a great share of your investment made under your own eyes.

While it is obvious from the course of events narrated here that the Agency System was born out of expediency and not of any deep plot on the part of the EEIC, it should also be kept in mind that at the turn of the century the EEIC had expressed a wish to bypass the merchants and buy cheap at the *arangs.* See how the EEIC regarded its farman of 1717 as a charter for free trade in Bengal. In 1717 it was pleaded that:[4]

> In the Subahships off Bengal, Behar, and Orixa with others in ye Kingdom off Indostan; the Company have Subordinate Factory where English Men reside. There are likewise some places, & Aurungs where Englishmen cannot be sent: for which reason we make arrangements with ye Merchants off ye Country, giving impress money; with which they go to ye Aurungs and buy Goods. In some places ye Kings Officers molest & hinder ye buying off Such goods. Wherefore we humbly petition, That Pursuant to ye Dustick off ye Chief of that Factory, the Merchants may be permitted to trade as Englishmen, and enjoy their privileges without hindrance.

The Agency System was therefore not just all about the replacement of the *dadni* merchant by subordinate *gomasthas.* It was also all about facilitating unrestricted European entry into the mart towns and manufactories of the interior. It was the *dadni* merchant who was the obstacle to this expansion.

Born in the trade and tutored in its ways from a very early age, it was the merchants who while 'still very young—begin to be trained as merchants (and) made to pretend to engage in trade while playing, first buying *cauris,* followed by silver and gold. In this training as money changers, they acquire(d) the capability of engaging in large scale trade. They are always sober, modest, thrifty and cunning—They have the exceptional capability of discovering the humour of those who are in a position to help or hurt them,' as the Dutch document of 1687 noted.[5] The K.F.R. echoed this; the merchants had been 'bred in this business (that is, supplying silk) since childhood'.[6] This group had deeply entrenched interests in the silk business. In truth, the *dadni* merchant was not just an intermediary in trade; he was the instrument through which trade was conducted in pre-British Bengal. Operating with a certain amount of court sanction, and in his role as supplier and purchaser, he was not only the agent through whom specie was brought into the country; he was also the device through which the political economy of Bengal expressed itself. The *dadni* merchant therefore had to go and a class of subordinate merchant-officials had to be created. This was the *gomastha* in the Agency System.

The expedient of going directly to the *arangs* was not novel, nor was it an English discovery. The Dutch were already trying it out in Shantipur. Likewise the Gujarati merchants were following the practice of going directly to the *arangs* and buying up the *patni.* In 1755 a board for *arang* management was formed with Drake, Manningham, Becher and Frankland as supervisors.[7] Until 1770 the *arangs* were placed under the Committee of Arangs under the charge of the President of the Calcutta Council.[8] Thereafter, from 1774, the Board of Trade administered the *arangs.* In the 1780s all the silk *arangs* were put in charge of agents and the cotton *arangs* in Patna, Dhaka, Shantipur and Lakhipur were also put under the Agency System.[9] But along with the Agency System another system, known as the Contract System, also operated at this time. The Agency System was not universal.

It is also generally accepted that the changeover of 1754 signalled the end of the *dadni* system in RS, SPG, G&D, Kumarkhali and Rangpur investments. This also is far from the truth, for Kasimbazar at least, because the K.F. R. entries of February 13, April 21 and October 24, 1755 show that the EEIC was still toying with the idea of *dadni* for the raw silk investment. Only the 'mean circumstances' of the merchants and the fact that the merchants complained that they had suffered by the contracts of 1753 and 1754 and that the EEIC had brought them to ruin through the *dadni* system deterred the EEIC from reintroducing the *dadni* system at Kasimbazar.[10] We also get the names of at least two independent EEIC merchants: Heli Chowdhury and Nando Chowdhury in the K.F.R. Consultation of October 24, 1755.

Silk piece goods, *garas* and the Kumarkhali silks were provided by the old method. In 1755 Warren Hastings, then a subordinate factor at Kasimbazar, was despatched to the Kumarkhali *arangs* to explore new ways of procuring silk. Chyton Podar and Cossenaut Surma provided the bulk of the SPG investment in 1755.[11] As did Rada Kissen Sircar, a merchant who, the Kasimbazar Council felt, had served the EEIC well. More importantly for the

EEIC, he had not joined the other merchants in the complaint to the durbar in 1754.[12] Bridgoo Coveraje, Bullub Biswass, and Ramsurn Gose also provided SPG in 1755. Other merchants supplying SPG in 1755 were Alamchand Gainchand, Manikchand, Myachand, Radhamohan, Nandadulal Surma, Nusseray, Ramdulal Conjoo, Radhakissen, Niti Katma, Kisenchand Surma and Bistum Charan Addy. The securities were Motichand, Kisseninder, Morley Poddar, Chand Sircar, Jiban Babu, Nimo Sen, Ramsaran Ghosh, Ballabh Biswas, Dulal Sircar, Shibnath Toppull, Kishanchand Katma, Kushal Sow, Onup Kapri, Pran Kapri, Briju Poddar, Udaychand (K.F.R., June 2, 1755).

This continued until 1756 when Kissen Inda Surma was appointed *gomastha* for SPG and *garas*, Monickchand and Nirsing Taggoor were appointed as *gomasthas* to Paddapar (Padmar Paar) and Morley Chatigee (Murali Chatterjee) as *gomastha* at Kumarkhali.[13] 'Sunmatoon' (Sanatan) was appointed *gomastha* at Rangpur only in 1758.[14] Other *dadni* merchants providing *patni* under the new system were 'Morley Podar, Becul Tagggoor, Gocul Gose, Chyton Podar (also SPG), Radakissen Sircar (also SPG), Bridgoo Coveraje (also SPG), Chand Sircar, Jibbon Bobboo, Beharry Sing, Nihal Shaw and Rogonaut Biswass'.[15]

But the old system also survived because we get the names of old *dadni* merchants such as AllumchundGainchund, Monick-chund, Cossenaut Surma, Myachund, Radamohun Surma, Luckicundgose, Nemosene, Bullub Biswass, Bistumchurndee, Chyton Podar, Chand Sircar, and Ramdoolol Conjoo.[16] Some, such as Chyton Podar and Monickchund obviously wore two hats. The survival of the *dadni* merchant is corroborated by the FEIC records for 1768. On August 20, 1768 Lacheney of Kasimbazar wrote to Chandernagore that the silk merchants were creating difficulties in procurement. They insisted that the FEIC pass through their intermediaries. Under such circumstances the French at Kasimbazar asked the Chandernagore Council to request Fort William not to indulge the merchants at Kasimbazar.[17]

On Becher's recommendation the *dadni* system was resumed in Kasimbazar from 1769 once again.[18] One reason was the oppression caused by the Company *gomasthas* who, along with a servant of the EEIC, would get the goods from the *arangs*. In 1760 it had been noted that chiefs at subordinate factories gained at least 20% profit in the goods they sold private traders.[19] In other words Company servants had become *dadni* merchants!

Under the new *dadni* system on Becher's recommendation Kisseninda (Surma?), Nundoolol Surma (the Nundoolol Surma of the SPG contract for 1749?), Kissenchurndutt, Baidya Nath, Ramkissen, Radha Modhab, Onoop Chund, Indra Naraindutt, Ramkissendass, Jagat Kundu, Krishna Kanta

(Krishna Kanta Nandy?), Bijoyram, Nityananda, Jaggernaut Dass and Gour Chowdree were advanced money for SPG contracts.[20] Note that all these are new names except perhaps that of Nandalal Surma.

But the Calcutta Council voted against the reintroduction of the *dadni* system and by 1771 *gomasthas* and *pykars* were at work, supplying cocoons to Kasimbazar.[21] This became known as the *pykari* system and the new generation of men and women who were the protagonists of the system in the silk filatures of Bengal came from a very different background than those of the *dadni* merchants. After the Board of Trade was established in 1774 both this system and the agency system became official. Prices rose and the quality deteriorated, especially in the case of raw silk.[22] In 1776 the Board observed that there remained hardly any substantial 'country' merchants who could supply goods to the EEIC.[23] Actually after 1757 it did not matter to the Indian merchant whether the Agency or the Contract System was followed. Contracts always fell into Europeans hands and the *gomastha* had to work under them.

16

The End of the Eighteenth Century World at Kasimbazar

After the famine of 1770, when the economic decline of Bengal became evident, the Court wanted to go back to the old *dadni* system. By then of course it was too late because the protagonists of the booming trade in silk in the 1730s at Kasimbazar had disappeared. Sadanand Bandyopadhyaya's report before the Board of Trade in 1791[1] and Taylor's report on the decline of trade at Dhaka[2] paint a dismal picture of the once flourishing trade in textiles.

A document dated 1752 from Kasimbazar highlights the trajectory of decline of the *dadni* merchant of Kasimbazar.[3] It detailed the state of the *dadni* merchants owing money to the EEIC between 1741 and 1746. This is what it says:

> Coosalchund being called on acknowledges our Demand on him to be just, but says he is intirely ruined, Not to be able to pay any part thereof being reduced to serve as a gomastha for his maintenances, Rogonaut (Biswas) being asked of the balance due from him to the Honble Company agreed with his Account. Acknowledging the same, but says he is quite incapacitated to Discharge it being intirely ruined from the Morattoes entering the Province and plundering the Aurungs where he had very Considerable Effects Together with the Prodigious Loss sustained by Sir Francis Russell and other misfortunes and that is now reduced to live on the Charity and Benevolence of his friends.
>
> The Biswasses and Kissenpersaud, son to Narran Biswass, Reply that they are in no ways capable to Discharge any part of their Debts. That the Considerable Losses by Sir Francis Russell together with what they have suffered from the Morattoes plundering them of their Money and Goods at the several Aurungs and the Oppressions of the Government intirely

puts it out of their Power to pay us. And that they have before given this Answer in much the same manner to former Chiefs Who after Confining them some months believed them again, On finding them totally ruined.

Annunderam Surma his Servant being summoned says his Master is at Hugley and intirely ruined being obliged to serve as an under Banian for his Livelihood.

Coolean Biswass his ready to pay part of his debt But cannot possibly discharge the Whole He says that Sir Francis Russell is indebted to him considerably more than he owes the Hon'ble Company.

Ram Tagoo He says he is incapable to Discharge his Balance And that he is a great Sufferer by Sir Francis Russell.

Bissenaut and Cossenaut being present alledge that their father and family are totally Ruined from the heavy Losses they have met with from the Morattoes, the Large Debt owing them from Sir Francis Russell and the Governemnt's oppression, that they have a House and Compound made over to the Hon'ble Company which is all they are Worth.

Bistumchurn he offers to pay DM Rs 2000 for his Debt on our forgiving the Interest on his balance and on our delivering him an Acquittance from any future Debt.

Nunderam Sircar who is now a Dutch Dadni merchant being himself Indisposed Sent his Gomastha Modon Sing to answer in his behalf Who says his Master owes nothing on Balance being transferred his Debt to the Hon'ble Company by Delivering to Sir Francis Russell his Note of hand.

Bridjukissore Surma Who Stands indebted to the Hon'ble Company anno 1746 being called on for his Ballance, Acknowledges his Debt of Rs. 1474-9-9 but adds he is not Able to pay it by reason of his being Ruined and at present out of all manner of Employment.

Gosseram being Dead his Gomastha Seabouray (Shibu Rai) appearing Says his Master was ruined and his House and effects seized by the Nabob's order after his Death, that the Morattoes in the Year 1745 and 1746 plundered him at the aurungs to a Considerable amount in silk and silk piece goods designed for the Hon'ble Company That as there now remains in the Cottahs (kuthis?) a Small Bale Containing Different Sortements of piece goods belonging to the said Gosseram His Gomastha desires We would sell them at Publick Outcry and bring their produce to the Hon'ble Copmany's credit adding that this his all we can expect for the debt.

Maudeb appearing before us Acknowledges his Ballance of DM Rs. 1018-15-9 he says it arrives from Dadney money Stopt by Sir Francis

Russell and insists on transferring it with Honble Company. He likewise adds that Sir Francis Russells Estate owes him Considerably more.

Radamohoon his Gomastha Lahoon being called Acknowledges his Debt, but says his Master is incapable of paying any part, being ruined from the Morattoes plundering to a considerable amount at the Aurungs, That his Master and his Son are now Prisoners for Debt at Muxadabad at Newroulecawn's suit.

Obviously, along with the Marathas, Francis Russell was in no small way responsible for the plight of these merchants. Russell was in charge of the Kasimbazar Factory from April 1, 1741 until February 26, 1743 when he died of dropsy and jaundice. During this period he did not settle the debts of the *dadni* merchants and four of them (unnamed) applied after his death to the EEIC for Rs. 14,000 which Russell had promised to pay up. Russell had also borrowed, on his personal account, Rs. 25,000 off Fatehchand who now demanded repayment.[4] The Company did not honour Russell's debts.

The Kasimbazar factory consultations of March 8 and 19, 1753 noted that 'Ruggonaut' and Narran Biswas were financially ruined and that Jagoorjee Achargee, one of the prominent *dadni* merchants, was throwing up service.[5]

On September 22, 1755 another 'State of the Merchants' Ballances' was prepared once again at Kasimbazar. This document detailed the final and effective removal of the middle man in the textile trade. It ran as follows:

State of the Merchants' Ballances
List of Debts Contracted by our Dadney Merchants
in the Year 1753 and 1754

1753	
Hurris Chowdree from 1745 to 1753	2005-12-3
Jettoo Surma from 1748 to 1753 (These merchants promise (to pay) Expect they will pay their Debts in a few days).	575-5
Davypursaud Gose from 1751 to 1753 (Has made over a House in Calcutta in part Ballance. We shall endeavour to get the Remainder from security).	8494-13-6
Narran Surma from 1750 to 1753 (We are largely indebted to Sevepursaud Surma his Security therefore when we pay him we deduct this Balance).	3006-14-9
Rs. 14082-13-0	

1754	
Chyton Podar from 1745 to 1754	531-15
Jogram Louchand from 1751 to 1754 (He has promised to discharge his Balance in a few days of this Merchant and also promises to pay his Ballance).	829-4-3
Rudachurn Surma from 1753 to 1754 (Mortgages some possessions instead).	2212-1-6
Rojchund Surma from 1753 to 1754 (Promises to discharge Debt or pay in ready money goods).	1131-8-9
Odit Burral from 1746 to 1754 (Promises to pay. Kasimbazar is assured that he will).	12058-2-6
Ramsurn Surma from 1747 to 1754 (The recovery of this Debt is very Doubtful).	20689-6-3
Podolochund Surma from 1753 to 1754 (Not sure)	8443-3-3
Gopee Tagoor from 1747 to 1754 (Kasimbazar expresses apprehensions).	3122-12-6
Gettoo Telly from 1745 to 1754 (This merchant is under confinement and there is little hope of recovering his Debt. A part has been recovered by selling his house and garden estimated together at Rs. 2000).	7284-1-6
Sam Mohun Surmah from 1750 to 1754	3307-9
Coosal Surma from 1751 to 1754	2429-2
Kirtee Surmah from 1750 to 1754 (These three merchants expected to pay up).	2606-3-9
Chyton Bridgoo Mohun from 1751 to 1754 (Under confinement. Circumstances same as Gettoo Telly).	11004-11-9
Sutchee Burrall (This merchant has been greatly distressed by the Government's People. He has delivered in gurrahs to the amount upwards of Rs. 3000 and the remainder of his Balance he promises to pay as he collects in the several sums owing him).	10739-1-6
Jagoordasdur and Moorley Burrall from 1747 To 1754 (We expect payment of Ballance soon).	2614-6-6

Ramsurn Surma whose Debt is the largest has been many years a Company Merchant always behaved honestly and his circumstances were never suspected'.[6]

We see therefore that by 1754 the dadni merchants were some SR 90 000 in debt. Once again, on November 13, 1756, the EEIC at Kasimbazar made a list of those merchants who owed them money. This list gives no names but mentions that the *dadni* merchants owed some Rs. 77042-12-3.

But some merchants made the transition, albeit as dependents of the EEIC; Murali Poddar, Manickchund and Narasingha (Nirsing Taggoor) became salaried servants at Kasimbazar, as did Kissen Inda Surma. By 1756 the Company's new system was well under way and successful. *Patni* was bought at the *arangs* and wound off at the Kasimbazar factory. This new system needed supervisors and 'Morley Poder', previously a *dadni* merchant, now undertook the responsibility of supervising the winding off of the silk.[7] Experts in silk reeling and in silk winding were brought in from as far afield as Italy and France to impart specialised knowledge. By 1758 this was a full blown operation and Wilder arrived from England to advise on matters relating to silk winding on a fairly regular basis.

But it is noticeable that as bankruptcies occurred progressively at Kasimbazar, the EEIC was forced to revise its list of 'substantial merchants'. On February 28, 1741 the 'best and most substantial merchants' were Naran Biswas, Gobardhan Biswas and Raghunath Biswas of the Biswas clan, Mahadeb and Kablaram of the Surmas, Ram Thakur and Kushalchand.[8] Note that this fits in with our depiction of the coterie, except for one significant fact. The Katmas, obviously in disgrace, are excluded from this list.

Once these were ruined, and in 1752, the Kasimbazar Council named as its four principal merchants 'Kissenundee, Maudeb Sircar, Hurris Chowdree and Morley Podar.'[9] These were lesser merchants (other than Harish Chowdhury) and in no way comparable to the original coterie. In turn these merchants ceded way to 'Chyton Podar, AllumchundGainchund, Cossenaut Surma, Monickchund and Myachund' in 1755.[10] It is noteworthy that only one name stands out from the coterie of the 1740s-that of Surma. Evidently these few merchants had weathered the transition of 1754.

17

The Arakan Connection and the East

If events at Kasimbazar were ruled by Murshidabad and Calcutta, Jugdia was influenced in history by events at Chattagram, Dhaka and Arakan. Contacts between Arakan and Bengal are significant for the history of Bengal because much of medieval Bengal, namely the Chattagram-Jugdia area, lay within Arakanese territory for much of their histories. Shihabuddin Talish described Arakan as a land of mystery; one bound by deep rivers and wide sea on the west, a land of marshes and jungles, irregular creeks and crocodile infested rivers that served as a warning to any invader.[1] Arakan was accessible only from the 'Far East' of Bengal.

Bengal had cultural ties with the Buddhist world of the north Bay, an area which comprised Arakan. Arakan however is not explicitly mentioned in the early annals. The Arakan connection first comes to the fore in the history of Bengal when we are told that the eleventh century Chandra kings of Eastern Bengal claimed Arakanese descent, issued silver coins from their capital at Bikrampur at a time when the Palas in Western Bengal had reverted back to a natural economy, and carried on a brisk trade with the countries of Arakan and beyond in the north Bay. Much later, in the thirteenth century, this region splintered into small states ruled by offshoots of the Mongol clans. As we saw from the section on silk, this area was an important conduit for both overland and overseas trade with Mongolia and China.

The early history of Arakan itself is obscure. It comes to the forefront of Bay history with the rise of the Chandra dynasty there around the fifth century. It becomes more defined after the collapse of the Pagan kingdom at the end of the thirteenth century. In the fifteenth century it became a political ally of the Ilyas Shahis in Bengal; and from then on Arakan-Bengal relations come to the fore in our history. Relations between Arakan and Bengal were cordial; Bengal seems to have been a favourite place of refuge for Arakanese kings. In the early part of the fifteenth century the Arakanese king Narameikhla spent his exile from Arakan at Gaur and later regained his throne with the help of the Bengal sultan. Narameikhla's successors used Muslim designations and titles and issued Islamic style coins.[2] Under Husain Shahi expansion Arakan came into the political and cultural fold of Bengal. Islamic influence from Husain Shahi Bengal permeated the Arakan court in the sixteenth century. Islamic-Bengali litterateurs flourished at the Arakanese court. In the post-Husain Shahi period the Arakan rejected the Muslim names earlier kings had adopted, and they also stopped the older practice of inscribing coins with the Bengali along with the Arakanese script.[3]

Relations soured between the two countries when the Mughals conquered Bengal. The Arakanese claimed succession to the rulers of Gaur (possibly through their ancient lineage from the Chandras), expanded into south eastern Bengal and developed the port of Mrauk U in the Arakan to rival Chattagram. Slave raids were carried out in southeast Bengal. The Mughals continued to politicize the Arakan issue. Matak Rai was given asylum at Dhaka following a succession dispute.[4] The Portuguese presence complicated matters further.

While Mughal-Arakan relations soured at this time, another external factor disturbed Arakan. Burma (Pegu) now rose as its political other. The Toungoo dynasty built up a strong maritime state with Pegu (and then Syriam) as rivals to Arakan which was then the strongest maritime state in the north Bay. The Toungoos wished to capture Siam and thereby control the ports of Martaban, Moulmein, Tavoy, Mergui and Tenasserim. The last three ports lay in the hazy frontier area between Burma and Siam and both countries sought to control them as a pathway to maritime wealth. These ports were traditional trading partners of Bengal merchants and Bengal cottons were much in demand here.

Campaigns undertaken by Burma towards Siam produced no permanent results; on the contrary, the Thai offensive against Pegu at the end of the sixteenth century, combined with the Arakanese-Portuguese assault upon Burma at the same time, left the Irrawady delta in ruins. At the start of the seventeenth century, new power relations emerged in the area. De Brito founded a maritime state based on Syriam in 1600 while King Naresuen of Siam annexed southern Burma upto Martaban. So things changed once again; by the end of the sixteenth century. Burma was destroyed, to the advantage of Arakan.

But in the seventeenth century there was a brief revival in the Irrawady delta under the leadership of Burma and Arakan was attacked repeatedly.[5] This southern offensive against Arakan impacted on the history of Bengal since the only alternative open to Arakan, in the face of a political reassertion by Burma, was an westward expansion into Bengal through Chattagram-Jugdia.

Moreover, with a treasury exhausted by the campaigns against Burma, and with an abortive commercialization of agriculture, Arakan now had to seek more profitable items with which to participate in the maritime trade of the Bay of Bengal. It had an uncertain rice harvest, good timber and elephants, but these were not enough to generate the kind of commercial revenue that the Arakan ruling elite needed to pay for the arms and luxury goods that it imported increasingly throughout the seventeenth century.[6] Therefore a port became crucial for Arakan. Hence the importance of Chattagram.

The commercial promise of the Irrawady delta was illusory. Between 1629 and 1648, the period coinciding with Manrique's visit to Bengal and Arakan, King Thalun abandoned Pegu and concentrated on inland Ava instead. Manrique's Portuguese policy for Arakan, and the latter's dreams of a commercial empire in the Bay, has to be seen in the light of the breakdown of Arakanese-Portuguese relations in the early seventeenth century, the gradual expansion of Mughal power in the east, the frustration of the Portuguese after being chased off Dianga in 1607 by the Arakanese and from Hugli in 1632 by the Mughals, and the gradual development of a Thai commercial policy along the ports of the isthmus under kings Naresuen, Songtham and Prasart Thong from the 1590s to the 1650s which effectively challenged Arakan's commercial domination of the north Bay.

What were the territorial boundaries of the state of Arakan, a state that emerged as Bengal's political monster for much of the seventeenth century? At that time Arakan's north-western frontier terminated at Chattagram-Jugdia, its northern frontier at Tripura, and its southern frontier at Pegu under the King of Burma and Syriam under the Portuguese. Its eastern frontier was Siam.

Just as the political history of the Irrawady delta is chaotic, so is the history of the southeast at this time. The hazy boundaries to Arakan's north-west comprise today's Bangladesh, the part of Bengal that withstood Arakanese territorial ambitions through the sixteenth and seventeenth centuries. Between the fifteenth and eighteenth centuries the Chattagram-Jugdia area was fought over by the kings of Arakan, Tripura and Bengal. Bhalwa (in Noakhali district in Bangladesh) was the shadowy area through which Arakanese forces approached Bengal. Bhalwa or Bhulua became a bargaining counter in the Mughal-Arakan struggle for sovereignty over the southeast when the Mughals made Bengal a Mughal province. Ananta Manik of Bhalwa frequently enlisted Arakanese help to retain his *zamindari* in the face of the Mughal threat emanating from Bengal. Bhalwa was culturally akin to Tripura and Arakan; and Bhalwa's ruler in the early seventeenth century, Ananta Manik, shared a surname with the kings of Tripura and Arakan. Manik was a honorific title frequently bestowed on the these royals. Politics was complicated by the Portuguese presence in the area. The latter frequently acted as mercenaries in the countries of the Bay and were utilized as such by local rulers in their wars against each other.

The early history of Chattagram is therefore sketchy despite Bengali historiography to the contrary. This is the political chronology that we have been able to piece together for Chattagram and its environs: In the fourteenth century Chattagram was under Fakhruddin Mubarak and did not form a part of Bengal according to Ibn Batutah's testimony. In the fifteenth century (between 1459 and 1482) King Basawpyn (Kalim Shah) occupied Chattagram. In the sixteenth century, in 1516, Ala ud Din Husain Shah captured Chattagram from Tripura. This was a triumph for Ala-ud-Din Husain Shah because Bengal now had a sea port on the east coast. Obviously the Arakanese had lost Chattagram to Tripura in the interim. In the 1540s Arakan reconquered Chattagram. With the fall of Gaur to Sher Shah's army in 1538, south eastern Bengal and Tripura and the area upto the Meghna—especially the Chattagram area—fell prey to conflicts between the Arakanese and the Portuguese. For much of the sixteenth and seventeenth centuries Chattagram lay at the heart of that disputed area in Harikela to which both Bengal and Arakan laid claims. Finally Chattagram fell to Arakan and was lost to Bengal for much of the sixteenth century. The Portuguese were expelled from Chattagram soon after 1540. They relocated themselves in western Bengal. Most of southeastern Bengal was overtaken over by Minbin's armies and Arakanese influence extended as far west as Dhaka and the Sunderbans in the seventeenth century. Qasim Khan led an expedition against Arakan in the early seventeenth century. This was a failure and Chattagram did not become a part of Bengal.[7] The Arakanese held on to Chattagram until 1666 when the Mughals (under Shaista Khan) conquered Chattagram. In 1729, the Bengal Nawabs reconquered Chattagram. Therefore, in the interim period Chattagram may have been regained by Arakan.

Chattagram, regarded as the economic nerve-centre of medieval Bengal was, we thus see, only notionally a part of Bengal: for a short while during the Ilyas Shahi period, then again from 1516 to 1538 in the Husain Shahi period, for some time after 1666 and then again after 1729.

Chattagram was the solution to Arakan's tactical interest in littoral South Asia since it was frequently attacked by its immediate southern neighbour, the king of Barhama (Burmah or Burma).[8] These attacks foretell the rise of Arakan's political other, Pegu, as we just saw. The only solution, for Arakan, was to go west. Arakan was a militarized country with a strong navy. Mirza Nathan noted the military might of Arakan: it had 10,000 war boats, 1500 elephants and 1,000,000 infantry.[9] But it had no comparable deep water port. It is here that Chattagram assumed significance for the Arakanese.The Arakanese kept 2,000 *jaliyas* there against the Mughals' 30 or so war boats.[10] These *naos* led effective raids into the Mughal's territory throughout the seventeenth century.

Chattagram therefore became a lifeline for Arakan. Shihabuddin Talish noted that the King of Arakan maintained a viceroy/governor there.[11] This post was entrusted to a relative. Fortifications were erected at Chattagram and the governor issued gold coins from Chattgram in the King's name. The Arakanese king also sent to Chattagram each year a hundred boats full of soldiers and artillery. When Qasim Khan attacked Arakan the Arakanese built a new fort at Kathghar/Sitakunda (in Bangladesh) in the Chattagram district. The Arakanese also sent a 100,000 infantry, 1,000 war boats and 400 elephants to Kathgarh. Chattagram and Kathgarh were strategic points in the Arakanese defence against Bengal. Indeed the western frontier was so important to Arakan that the king himself came to Chattagram with 10,000 horsemen, 300,000 infantry and a great number of elephants and boats to repel Qasim Khan. Cannons, guns, rockets, stones and bows and arrows were used against the Mughal army[12] . In the face of this aggression Arakan entered into an uneasy alliance with the Portuguese and employed them as mercenaries in return for which the Portuguese were allowed to live and trade from Chattagram and Dianga.

This Arakanese-Portuguese entente was soon shattered; and the policy doomed, for the Portuguese were massacred and expelled from Dianga in 1607. King Thiri Thudhamma thereafter sent Shah Jahan a mission at Dhaka during the latter's revolt in Bengal in the 1620s. The mission presented Shah Jahan with gifts worth Rs. 100,000 in return for which Shah Jahan recognized Arakan's sovereignty.[13] The Portuguese also abandoned their imperial ambitions in Arakan; after the grant of 'Portuguese' Sandwip (under Gonzales) as jagir by Islam Khan to King Salim of Arakan they either lived as Arakanese subjects or relocated their commercial operations to the west to Hugli. It is to be noted that the Mughals used the Arakanese to break the Portuguese starnglehold in east Bengal; this was achieved again through the expulsion of the Portuguese from Hugli in 1632.

Manrique was instrumental in forging another Portuguese-Arakan alliance in the 1630s; after the expulsion of the Portuguese from Hugli in 1632 he advised Thiri Thudamma, the King of Arakan, as part of official Portuguese policy, to enlist Portuguese aid once again to repel Mughal expansion in the east. But it was too late; the days of glory for both the Arakanese and the Portuguese on the coast were over. Henceforth Mughal policy determined the politics of the eastern frontier. But the Arakanese reacted by turning southeast Bengal into a slave raiding zone. This ultimately destroyed the economy of the region. The politics of Arakan's transformation into a slave raiding society has been discussed in *Strange Riches op. cit.*

Chattagram was also the key to Arakan's commercial dominance on the coast. We do not know much about Arakan-Bengal trade in history; however we do know that the Arakanese traded almost exclusively through Chattagram until the rise of Mrauk-U in the fifteenth century. The Arakanese sought to develop their own port of Mrauk-U after their failure to hold permanently onto Chattagram. This was a short-lived port in history; its trade and traffic was soon eclipsed by Pegu. Elephants and teak from Arakan, goods from the southern ports of Cosmin, Dagon, Martaban, Syriam and Pegu were sent to Bengal in exchange for grains and cotton.

In the seventeenth century the most profitable commodity was slaves. This was a three-way trade. The Arakanese brought in their prisoners to be sold as slaves to the Portuguese at Hugli in the seventeenth century. Moreover they conducted slave-hunting raids along the coast in Chattagram, Jessore, Bakla, Bakergunge, Hijli and Orissa and sold their booty at the principal slave marts of Hugli, Saptagram, Pipli, St.Thome, Goa, Surat and Ceylon [14] so much so that deltaic Sunderbans was depopulated in the seventeenth century.[15] The Arakanese also imported slaves from Bengal. Manrique tells us that in the middle of the seventeenth century the Arakanese brought 18,000 slaves in five years from Bengal to Arakan (Dianga and Angarcale).

Jugdia was next in importance to Chattagram for Arakanese strategy. It seems to have been of considerable political importance in late medieval Arakan and Bengal. Lying on the banks of the Feni which formed the boundary of Bengal and Arakan, situated opposite the seventeenth century Portuguese stronghold of Sandwip and located partly within the rebel province of Bhalwa (Noakhali) which was Arakan's gateway to Bengal[16] Jugdia's place in history was due initially more to strategic reasons than commerce.

Jugdia is first mentioned in Husain Shahi annals as a Husain Shahi outpost against attacks by Tripura. Later in the same century Jugdia and its environs were fought over by the Bengal Sultanate, the Portuguese and the Arakanese. In the seventeenth century Arakan captured Sandwip from the Portuguese and both the Mughals and the Arakanese established border outposts at Jugdia on the Feni river and strong fortifications on the river of Chattagram, the Karnaphuli. We know that during Islam Khan's *subahdari* Jugdia had a Mughal *thanadar*, Sanjar Tar Khan, who was asked by Islam Khan to render help to the fugitive Arakan king Matak Rai, previously Arakanese governor of Chattagram.[17]

The subjugation of Arakan was determined by three factors operating in the Bay. First, the 'rebel' border country of Anant Manik's Bhalwa was secured (by Islam Khan and Qasim Khan) and hostile Tripura was conquered (by Mirza Nathan by order of Ibrahim Khan Fath Jang) during the first phase of Mughal expansion in the east in the early seventeenth century. This meant that Arakan's north-west border was sealed against further expansion. Second, Pegu and Ava began to assert themselves poltically from the beginning of the seventeenth century. These two were constantly at war. Mirza Nathan tells us that the Raja of Burmah sent Salim, the Arakan Raja, two embassies requesting his aid against the Raja of Pegu.[18] This alliance was not long lived and soon after, the Raja of Burmah attacked Arakan. These attacks posed an actual threat to the territorial ambitions of Arakan and effectively sealed off the southern corridor against further expansion on the part of Arakan.[19] Finally, the rise of Pegu, Syriam, Mergui and Tenasserim in commercial importance gradually eclipsed the commercial importance of the Arakanese ports. Pegu and its sister port Syriam challenged the commercial prominence of the Arakan ports of Akyab and Mrohaung. Trade was diverted to these ports and Arakan lost much of its revenue. In the 1660s the attempt to retake Syriam, which it had controlled along with Pegu in the sixteenth century, was disastrous for Arakan.[20]

Arakan lost much of its political significance after Shaista Khan firmly secured the eastern frontier at Chattagram in 1666. Political events also combined to decimate Arakan's mastery over the Bay. Pegu's commercial importance eclipsed that of Arakan in the eighteenth century. Since Jugdia lies within this fluid area between Chattagram and Arakan, let us now see what we can glean about the geopolitics of the Jugdia area.

Chattagram/Jugdia was a part of both Tripura and Bengal in the fifteenth-sixteenth centuries. Jugdia's status is difficult to establish as it is first mentioned in Husain Shahi annals as a Husain Shahi outpost against attacks by Tripura. In 1516 Chattagram was regained from Tripura by Ala ud Din Husain Shah and in 1521 an anonymous Portuguese mission passed by Jugdia and mentioned it as a mart town producing cotton cloth.[21]

The *Ain-i-Akbari*, in the same century, referred to Jugdia as a port. This may have been due to the fact that it was situated opposite Sandwip which Kedar Rai granted to Carvalho as *jagir* in 1602. Sandwip has been taken to be the famous Samandar of the medieval age by Mohar Ali.[22] It was an important port in medieval Bengal and various travelers passed through it. Cesare Frederici visited Sandwip in 1569.[23] Lahori tells us that there was a substantial Portuguese colony there during the seventeenth century.[24]

After the Mughals conquered the area and 'pacified' the local rulers,

Sandwip was given over to Raja Salim of Arakan as *jagir* by Islam Khan. The Portuguese were expelled from Chattagram in 1540. Early in the seventeenth century the Arakanese prince Matak Rai was offered shelter in Bengal following succession disputes in Arakan. Yet the Mughal policy toward Arakan was uncertain as we know that Qasim Khan also attacked Arakan. When Shah Jahan was at Dhaka the Arakanese came to pay their respects, declaring themselves vassals of the Mughal; this was also the time when Arakan was attacked by Burma and Manrique went to Arakan to negotiate a new Arakanese-Portuguese alliance.

The areal extent of the conflicts is uncertain, the politics of the seventeenth century very fluid. Jugdia takes shape once again as a part of Mughal Bengal only toward the end of the seventeenth century.

18

The East: The Dhaka Region

Mirza Nathan's *Baharistan-I-Ghaybi* tells the story of the Mughal 'pacification' of Bengal in the first half of the seventeenth century. He wrote, '. . . the men of the enemy's boats . . . were pushed back to their boats and the market of the angel of death was made very brisk.'[1] Spanning the *subahdaris* of Islam Khan, Qasim Khan and Ibrahim Khan in Bengal, Mirza Nathan ends his tale with the story of Shah Jahan's revolt in the 1620s and its implications for Bengal.

The narrative of *Baharistan-I-Ghaybi* is essentially situated in eastern Bengal (*samatata* and *harikela*) and is 'a history of the Mughal wars in Assam, Cooch Behar, Bengal, Bihar and Orissa during the reigns of Jahangir and Shah Jahan', as the title page informs us. More interesting to the student of Bengal's medieval history, however, is the story of the Mughal take-over of Bengal starting with the arrival of Islam Khan in 1608 in Bengal as narrated in the *Baharistan-I-Ghaybi*; the furious *putsch* of the Mughal forces to the east, the dispossession of the *Baro Bhuyias* or the independent kings of deltaic *samatata*, marginalisation of the Afghans, encounters with the frontier 'kingdoms' of Bhalwa, Bhusna and Tripura and finally the Mughal confrontation with medieval Bengal's political other-Arakan. Surprisisngly, Nathan makes no mention of Portuguese expansion in the region.

The *Baharistan-I-Ghaybi* is a valuable source material for the history of medieval east Bengal. It seems that while Dhaka had long existed in history it had done so more as a suburb or adjunct of Suvarnagram. It was only in the seventeenth century that it arose to prominence as a city, and a Mughal provincial capital with a mint, when Islam Khan transferred his capital there. Except for some years under Shuja (1639–60) when he transferred the capital back to the north in Rajmahal, Dhaka was the Mughal capital of seventeenth century Bengal. Both Mir Jumla and Shaista Khan ruled from there. Azim-us-Shan, the last *subahdar* of Mughal Bengal and Aurangzeb's grandson, started his tenure from Dhaka. So did Murshid Quli Khan, the future *subahdar* of Bengal. After Murshid Quli moved to Murshidabad to lay the foundations of what would ultimately become the independent *nizamat* of Bengal, Azim-us-Shan shifted his capital to Patna. There his career petered out. So did Dhaka's position as a 'Mughal' capital.

Under the Nawabs of Bengal Dhaka was retained as a secondary capital as seat of the Naib Nazim or 'Chhota Nawab' as he was called by the English factors. The Naib Nazim was an important court official and usually a relative of the ruling nawab. The rulers of the Dhaka *niabat* were, in 1717, Khan Muhammad Ali Khan and I'tisam Khan from 1723 to 1726. Between 1728–1734 Mirza Lutfullah, known in history as Murshid Quli II, became naib nazim of Dhaka.

The second Murshid Quli, Mirza Lutfullah of Tabriz, then became governor of Orissa during Nawab Shuja's reign in Bengal. Sanjay Subrahmanyam claims that the second Murshud Quli weathered the storm of the 1739–40 succession dispute and was appointed Naib-Nazim (what the English refer to as the 'Chhota Nawab') of Dhaka during Alivardi's reign.[2] This is not right.[3] Dhaka came before Orissa. The second Murshid Quli was a favourite of Shuja and wielded considerable power at Murshidabad prior to the takeover by Alivardi Khan. He was the naib nazim of Dhaka from 1728 to 1734 and not after 1739–40. This second Murshid Quli and his associates Mir Habibullah of Shiraz and Mir Razi of Shustar appear to have practised state mercantilism from Dhaka[4] and in the process built up a powerful clique of Iranian and Central Asian traders in Bengal. They had links with the EEIC at Dhaka. This group also maintained close links with Surat and Basra and there is every likelihood that a major portion of Bengal's westward trade was monopolized by this Iranian group. After Murshid Quli II Sarfaraz Khan, future Nawab and grandson of Murshid Quli Khan who was deposed by Alivardi's *putsch* from Bihar, ruled at Dhaka through deputies in the period 1734–39. Between 1740 and 1754 the post was held by Nawazish Muhammad Khan through deputies. He was the son-in-law of Nawab Alivardi Khan and a very important personage who terrorized the European companies at Dhaka. Nawazish Muhammad Khan played an important part in palace intrigues at Murshidabad. He spent most of his time in Murshidabad and ruled through deputies.

Nawazish Muhammad Khan was appointed Diwan of Bengal by Alivardi which gave him enormous financial powers in Bengal. If we see the affair of Husain Quli, his *diwan* and deputy *naib nazim* at Dhaka who was plotted against by Gokul Chand during the period 1740–44, we find the extent of his power. Gokul Chand, formerly Husain Quli's deputy, got Husain Quli dismissed on his election to the post of deputy. Finally Nawazish Khan's wife, Ghasiti Begum, appealed to her father Alivardi Khan to have Husain Quli reinstated.

Why was there this palace revolution in Dhaka? Was it a mere political affair or was there a conflict of trade interests? Note that this is probably the same Gokul Chand (as mentioned by Om Prakash[5]) who was financially ruined in 1744 and to whom no banker would extend a guarantee. Note too that 1744 was the year Husain Quli got himself re-instated as deputy through the efforts of Ghasiti Begum. Did Gokul Chand then fall out of favour?

That Gokul Chand played a dangerous game seems evident. It also seems that his career as merchant was ruined after this episode.[6] Gokul Chand was referred to as 'a financier of eminence who was now audited to the extent that he was financially bankrupt and lost his office.[7]' Husain Quli appointed Raj Ballav as his *diwan*. This marks the rise of Raj Ballav.[8]

Jesarat Khan was the next *naib nazim*. He ruled between 1755 and 1762 and established markets in Dhaka which were held in his name and that of his family. Jesarat Khan tried to corner the trade in eastern goods. The last *naib nazim* who concerns us here is Muhammad Reza Khan. He was a famous official indeed who oversaw the transition to Diwani. He ruled from 1763 to 1765.

What was the jurisdiction of the Dhaka *niabat*? When Dhaka had been the seat of Mughal presence in Bengal in the seventeenth century, it was an imperial capital, a Mughal mint town, a Mughal port and a centre of Islamic scholarship. Its architecture was a tribute to Mughal presence in the area. Its port, administered by the Shah Bandar, oversaw the *sair* duties of Mughal Bengal, and through its mint Dhaka remitted taxes to the Imperial government at Delhi. Its *subahdars*, even Islam Khan the first Mughal *subahdar* who brought peace to the region,[9] and subsequently Mir Jumla[10] and Shaista Khan, ruled fairly independently much to the chagrin of the Mughal at Delhi. It was a Mughal capital, but it was also independent. It presaged the rise of Murshidabad in the eighteenth century.

While Dhaka's political importance declined after the transfer of capital to Murshidabad, its economic importance continued as Dhaka controlled one half of Bengal politically and economically. The establishment of the Dhaka *niabat* coincided with the revenue reforms introduced by Murshid Quli Khan. The new system regrouped the original *sarkars* of the *Ain* into thirteen *chaklas* in Bengal and Dhaka was put in charge of three *chaklas*-Jahangirnagar (Dhaka), Sylhet and Islamabad (Chattagram). In 1728 when Mir Habib conquered Tripura (during Mirza Lutfulla's *niabat*) it too was placed under the Dhaka *niabat's* administration as Chakla Raushanabad. Dhaka therefore administered four *chaklas* or districts.

The *niabat* paid a total revenue of Rs. 2,729,437 of which Jahangirnagar paid Rs. 1,928,194, Sylhet paid Rs. 531,455, Islamabad paid Rs. 176,795 and Raushanabad paid Rs. 92,993. Note that Chattagram paid only a marginal revenue. This contrasts with Husain Shahi times when Chattagram was the chief revenue earner of the province. When District Chittagong passed under the Company's administration it paid Rs. 443,918. This rise in figure from Rs. 176,795 is explained by the fact that the additional sum represents the exactions of the *faujdars* levied without knowledge of the Nawabs. This additional figure may be taken as a pointer to the flourishing state of commerce in this part of the world. Interestingly the Company regularised the illegal exaction and carried it over to the Company's account.[11] But by 1772–73 Chattagram paid only Rs. 7250 as export-import and town duties.

Apart from the major expenses of maintaining the old Mughal style provinicial administrative and revenue machinery (albeit on a reduced scale as befitting Dhaka's status as *niabat*) the chief expense was the maintenance of the *amla-I-nawwara* or *nawara* fleet with 768 war boats stationed at Dhaka at an annual cost of Rs. 843,452. Dhaka also maintained the *amla-I-asham* or 8112 artillery troops for guarding the eastern frontier through forts in *samatata* and on the sea coast. These expenses were offset by the capture of elephants from Sylhet and Tripura (*kheda*) and the muslins of Dhaka which were exported to Delhi and indeed all over the subcontinent. A Mughal *karkhana* (manufactory) was set up for Dhaka muslins which continued manufacturing into the eighteenth century. Dhaka's royal mint issued its first coins from 1617 and the mint was used to remit revenues first to Delhi and then to Murshidabad. Its port was one of three within Bengal and was administered through the Shah Bandar. Dhaka port controlled the commerce of the easternmost parts of the province. All eastern goods passed through it.

European presence in the Dhaka region rose considerably in the eighteenth century and continued to rise until mid century. We have these figures for the English East India Company and private English trade in cottons.[12]

Table 20
English Trade in Cotton Textiles at Dhaka

Year	Company Trade	Private Trade
1736–37	Rs. 222,366-3-3	Rs. 59,009-10-6
1737–38	Rs. 348,962-15-6	Rs. 212,437-5-9
1743–44	Rs. 567,791-3-0	Rs. 206,822-7-9
1744–45	Rs. 566,627-14-0	Rs. 133,068-6-9

We know the breakdown of the export trade at Dhaka in 1747.[13]

Table 21
Export Trade From Dhaka: 1747

For the Emperor	Rs. 100,000
For the Nawab at Murshidabad	Rs. 300,000
Jagat Seth	Rs. 150,000
Turani merchants for trade in north India	Rs. 150,000
Armenian merchants for Basra, Mocha and Jedda	Rs. 500,000
Mughal merchants for the same and home consumption	Rs. 400,000
'Hindus' for internal market	Rs. 200,000
English Company for Europe	Rs. 350,000
English Private Trade	Rs. 200,000
French Company for Europe	Rs. 250,000
French Private Trade	Rs. 50,000
Dutch Company for Europe	Rs. 100,000

Note from Table 20 that the stabilised figures for 1743–44 and 1744–45, after the spectacular rise in both Company and private trade in the 1736–1738 period, correspond to the falling figures in silk investment from Kasimbazar in the same years when the 'crisis' showed its face. The figures of 1744–45 for private trade show, moreover, a decline in investment.

Tables 20 and 21 give a clear picture of the trade of the east. Jugdia lay in the territory administered by the *niabat.* This administration, we shall see however, was only notional. We see from Table 21 that the French trade interest in Dhaka (and its environs) was quite considerable and their investment close to that of the English Company—a fact that has its bearing on French attempts to open (and sustain) the trade at Jugdia even as late as in the 1780s.

19

Trade in the 'Far East' – Jugdia and Lakhipur

Jugdia, we noted, lies in the borderlands of Bengal. Situated in a shadow area bound by the warring medieval kingdoms of Tripura (Tipperah), Bengal and Arakan, the early history of Jugdia is shrouded in mystery. In the early sixteenth century Jugdia lay in that area that was fought over by Tripura and Bengal. Close to Chattagram and linked to it by the Karnaphuli-Feni waterway, Jugdia is first mentioned in medieval history as a Husain Shahi outpost against attacks by Tripura. Jugdia and its environs were fought over by the Bengal Sultanate, the Portuguese and the Arakanese. After the Husain Shahis, both the Mughals and the Arakanese established border outposts at Jugdia on the Feni river and strong fortifications on the river of Chattagram, the Karnaphuli. In 1521 Jugdia lay on the route of a Portuguese mission from Chattagram to Gaur. The next reference we get to Jugdia is in de Barros' largely inaccurate map of Bengal drawn in 1550. It is then mentioned in the *A'in* of 1598.

Although shrouded in mystery as to its orgins, Jugdia seems to have been of considerable political importance in late medieval Bengal. Lying on the banks of the Feni which formed the boundary of Bengal and the Arakan, opposite Sandwip and situated partly within the rebel province of Bhalwa (Noakhali) which was Arakan's gateway to Bengal[1] Jugdia's place in history was due initially more to strategic reasons rather than for any kind of metropolitan magnificence. We have already read that during Islam Khan's *subahdari* Jugdia had a Mughal thanadar, Sanjar Tar Khan, who was asked by Islam Khan to render help to the fugitive Arakan king Matak Rai.[2]

Lying halfway between Dhaka and Chattagram, Jugdia, it appears, was seen culturally as a part of the Chattagram, and not the Dhaka, complex.[3] Chattagram was 'annexed' to Bengal *subah* by Shaista Khan in 1666 but its fuzzy political status was never established and we are told that the Bengal Nawabs 'recovered' Chattagram from the Arakanese again in 1729. This suggests that Chattagram had been lost to Bengal at some point in the interim. It was understandable under these circumstances that the Bengal Nawabs maintained a strict vigilance at Jugdia. While the strategic importance was due to its proximity to Chattagram and Arakan[4] Jugdia's economic importance in eighteenth century Bengal's commercial history would be due to its proximity to the Tipperah Hills which grew the cottons that provided Jugdia's market with *baftas*.

Jugdia was strategically placed for commerce as well. Its lifeline, the Feni, is actually two rivers. Both rise in the Tipperah hills; the little Feni or the Dakatiya, scene of countless bloody encounters between 'maghs', Ananta Manik of Bhalwa and the Mughals in the seventeenth century, connects with the Brahmaputra and washes west Noakhali district while the big Feni flows through eastern Noakhali (Jugdia) and forms the principal waterway to the Arakan. This, we shall see later, greatly enhanced Jugdia's commercial importance in the eighteenth century. Chattagram's river, the Karnaphuli, linked Jugdia and Dhaka with Chattagram and the resultant Padma-Feni-Meghna-Brahmaputra waterway brought to Chattagram, the only proper sea port of Bengal, the produce of the interior.[5] But in the period under review here, that is the sixteenth to the eighteenth centuries, Arakan controlled Chattagram both politically and economically. Jugdia, lying within the Chattagram area, probably had as its chief trading partner Arakan and not Bengal. The Dhaka *niabat* had no jurisdiction over Jugdia in real terms. This fact should be borne in mind when we discuss the lack of a central authority in Jugdia in the middle of the eighteenth century.

French and English company records mention Dhaka, Suvarnagram and Jugdia as important textile weaving centres.[6] French company factors noted that in Jugdia, unlike other parts of Bengal which traded in luxury items, trade in articles of everyday necessity was the norm. For this reason, the French felt they could overthrow all other commerce in Bengal and concentrate exclusively on Jugdia.[7]

However indigenous historical records are silent about the commercial potential of Jugdia which leads us to surmise (1) that Jugdia either may not have been as important a textile producing area as company records lead us to suppose, or (2) that while it was an important production centre it was never regarded as a part of Bengal even after it was conquered from Tripura or even (3) that its production base and commerce was so oriented towards Arakan that it was deemed a part of the last. The last two suppositions seem probable; in the course of the EEIC's revenue administration of Chattagram during 1761–85 it was noted that the Naaf, and not *chakla* Ramu, was the dividing line between Bengal and Arakan. The Mughals had proceeded only upto the Ramu wherein flowed the Feni, and Rennell correspondingly marked Ramu as the frontier between Bengal and Arakan. But Jugdia lay beyond; it was situated in the area between Ramu and the Naaf, and the Company surveys of 1790 and then the researches of Blochmann proved that it was the Naaf and not the Feni that was the true divider between Bengal and Arakan.[8] Jugdia was truly a frontier land and Hameeda Hossain's pioneering study of weavers in the eastern region devotes only one cursory mention to Jugdia on page 184.[9]

Mughal and eighteenth century Indian sources mention other textile towns in this part of the world: Narayanpur, Jangalbari, Bazitpur, Chandpur, Srirampur, Dhamrai and Titbari which made up the Dhaka production area named 'Dacca Aurungs'. Jugdia, however, does not seem to be a part of this complex. Yet it is not clear as to whose *arang* it was. There is no mention of a large town in the area to which Jugdia could be deemed a satellite or *arang*; like Dhaka metropolis for its *arangs*. This reinforces our assumption that Jugdia was part of the shadowy Chattagram commercial space within the borderlands of Bengal.

More than the EEIC, it was the FEIC that concentrated on this area. Chevalier's efforts, in the 1750s, at opening up the Franco-Assam trade hinged upon Dupleix's dream of the 1730s of creating a huge Bay of Bengal trade zone centering on Chattagram and connecting Arakan, Ava and Pegu through the Brahmaputra, the Meghna and the Bay.[10] Between 1750 and 1751, at the time the Jugdia-Chandernagore letters were written, Dupleix still considered an alliance with Pegu against Burma to reinforce the FEIC presence at Syriam and thereby regain the FEIC's lost position in the eastern seas.[11] This notion continued in later years. Cordier noted in 1823[12] that while Chattagram did not produce any articles of trade by itself its proximity to the kingdoms of Ava, Arakan and Pegu, as well as its deep water port, provided great opportunities for trade in eastern India. Chattagram received wood for building works from Pegu and Arakan and communicated directly by sea with Jugdia, Srirampur, Dhaka, Sylhet and Goalpara; these factors contributed to the richness of the area. Therefore Jugdia was crucial to FEIC possessions in Bengal.

Like its own history, the history of the English and French companies in Jugdia is obscure. There is some confusion as to when the English East India Company founded its factory there. Hunter claimed that the Jugdia factory was opened in 1756.[13] This is wrong. The confusion may be due to the fact that the EEIC's relationship with Jugdia was murky beyween 1752 and 1755.[14] For, as early as in 1748, the Calcutta Council of the EEIC noted the following figues for investment at Kasimbazar (SR 568 400), Dhaka (SR 840 390) and Jugdia (SR 252 880).[15]

There is a similar error regarding the date of the French presence in Jugdia. One contemporary document claims that Jugdia was given (cede) to the French in 1710[16] but another contemporary document claims that the French factory in Jugdia was established by Dupleix in 1735.[17]

Joseph Cordier noted:[18]

> La loge de Jougdya fut batie en (1735) a deux lieues loin de la mer, dans un pays plat, mais, lorsequ'en 1756, les Francais quitterent le Bengale, elle n'en etait plus qu'a trois quarts de lieue; en 1765, lorseque nous en reprimes possession, la mer baignait les murs de loge (qui) fut submergee quelque tems après . . . En 1785, l'ancien Jougdya etait alors a plus de quatre lieues dans la mer. (The Jugdia factory was built in 1735 two leagues away from the sea, on flat countryside, but when the French left Bengal in 1756 the sea had moved closer and Jugdia was only three quarters of a league away from the sea. In 1765 when the French repossessed their territory in Bengal the sea was close to the walls of the factory and submerged them soon after. In 1785 the old Jugdia was over four leagues in the sea-*my translation*).

The French had a chequered history at Jugdia.[19] Moreover English plans in that region firmly precluded any lasting French presence in that region. That Jugdia may literally have been the last commercial frontier of Bengal is reinforced by the fact that the Jagat Seths had no branch there despite Manickchand, the founder, having started his career from Dhaka in the seventeenth century when it was a Mughal capital. The D.F.R of 12th November, 1750, mentions the following financial firms in Dhaka with eastern offices: Seat Martabray (Mahtab Rai), Seat Syroopchund (Swarupchand), Coshaulchund (Kushalchand), Allumchund Nimchund (Alamchand Nimchand), Onoopchund Kissenchund (Anupchand Kissenchand or Krishna Chandra), Bularamray (Balaram Ray) and Anunderam (Anandaram). Alam Chand was the Rai-Rayan (chief minister) of Bengal in Shuja's time, and his son Raja Kriti Chand had considerable financial interests in Azimabad (Patna). Alam Chand's agent Chain Ray was appointed Ray-Rayan of Bengal by Alivardi Khan. Alam Chand was reputed to have controlled the finances of Bengal before Alivardi's dynasty grasped power. The firm/combine of Allumchund Gainchund figures prominently in investment lists of the EEIC from Kasimbazar, as we have seen. Many of the other names figure in the K.F.R. lists as well as either merchants or as bankers. The presence of these banking firms at Kasimbazar, Patna and Dhaka indicates that an integrated financial market was coming into existence in Bengal in the eighteenth century.

It is therefore all the more striking that none of these firms were to be found at Jugdia, considering its reputation as a textile centre. European companies faced difficulties trading there as they could not change the money they brought in in Arcots rupees to buy textiles for investment. In 1752 the English Company thought of shifting to Kalindi, five hours from Jugdia and a big mart for *baftas*, for the former had the advantage of being 'under Juggut Seat'.[20]

Given this financial marginality, trade in Jugdia was 'unregulated'. Unlike in Dhaka or in western marts of Bengal such as Kasimbazar, trade at Jugdia was constantly fraught with difficulties for the EICs. It was mentioned that there was no central authority there, implying that the administration of the Dhaka *niabat* did not extend upto Jugdia.[21] This meant that company investments suffered as there was no rule of law. That company authority did not count for much there was evident by the flourishing trade European private traders such as Jambon of the FEIC were carrying on there.[22] This brings us back to the point made earlier; that trade in Jugdia was conducted on open market lines with ready money sales. This was a system that was anathema to companies used to preferential treatment at the hands of a government they affected to despise.

The EEIC was particularly against such sales. In 1748 the Calcutta Council noted that it spent SR 352 054 on ready money goods as against SR 10 53 756 on *dadni*.[23] Credit was essential to all EICs. They did not want to tie up their own money in commercial transactions. A large part of the Bengal-Europe trade was financed through Asian money, as we saw in the case of Kasimbazar.

To overcome this problem the EEIC decided in 1752 to move to Kalindi. In 1753 the EEIC abandoned its Jugdia factory.[24] But the EEIC did not move to Kalindi as decided previously but favoured Lakhipur instead. Lakhipur was some distance from Jugdia and had the advantage of being much closer to Dhaka. The factors asked the Kasimbazar factors to obtain a *parwana* from the Nawab to that end.[25] We are told that the EEIC had abandoned the Jugdia factory in June 1753; that this was not voluntary was indicated by an entry in the K.F.R. noting that the local authorities there had put peons on the EEIC's *dalal's gomastha*. This had effectively stopped all EEIC business at Jugdia. The K.F.R. factors were asked to obtain a *parwana* from Murshidabad for the shift to Lakhipur.[26] The French noted on February 16, 1753 that the affair of the Jugdia dalals would not be soon resolved.[27] The *parwana* for the EEIC was effected in 1755 but the Jugdia *dalals* still opposed the move and it was evident that they had now secured the support of the Dhaka *niabat*.[28] The FEIC feared that their business at Jugdia would come to a standstill as well.[29]

In 1755 the EEIC shifted to Lakhipur but the Jugdia *dalals* had still not accepted defeat. In July 1755 it was noted that the Lakhipur factors had informed Kasimbazar that the *parwana* from Murshidabad had been effective in enabling the EEIC to set up operations in Lakhipur but that the Jugdia *dalals* were trying to get the *parwana* revoked so that they could again be employed by the EEIC. The Kasimbazar factors were asked by Lakhipur to prevent this at any cost. The matter was serious enough for Kasimbazar to send a *vakil* to investigate the case of the Jugdia *dalals*.[30] By August 1755 the matter had not been resolved; Kasimbazar wrote to Baillie that they would use their influence with Diwan Rajballav to stop the Jugdia *dalals'* petition at the Murshidabad durbar.[31]

Given the previous neglect of Jugdia in both Asian and company annals this sudden interest of all parties in Jugdia in the mid-eighteenth century comes as a surprise. The amount of trade carried on at Jugdia might provide us a clue:[32]

Table 22
Trade at Jugdia

	French Francs	Sicca Rupees
EEIC	2,000,000	1,000,000
FEIC	1,500,000	750,000
Danish Company	800,000	400,000
European Traders	2,000,000	1,000,000
Indian Traders	3,000,000 or more	1,500, 000

Compare these figures with the ones for Dhaka (in sicca rupees).[33]

Table 23
Trade at Dhaka

	EEIC	Private Trade	FEIC	French Private Trade	Dutch Co.
1736–37	2 22 366-3-3	59 009-10-6	-	-	-
1737–38	3 48 962-15-6	2 12 437-5-9	-	-	-
1743–44	5 67 791-3-0	2 06 822-7-9	-	-	-
1744–45	5 66 627-14-0	1 33 068-6-9	-	-	-
1747	Rs. 350,000	Rs. 200,000	Rs. 250,000	Rs. 50,000	Rs. 100,000

Now compare the figures for Jugdia and Dhaka (in Sicca Rupees)[34]

Table 24
Trade at Jugdia and Dhaka

	Jugdia	Dhaka
EEIC	1,000,000	400,000
FEIC	750,000	280,000
European Traders	1,000,000	230,000
Indian Traders	1,500,000	1,800,000

We see that in all respects French and English company and private trade was far far higher in Jugdia than at Dhaka. Only in the matter of internal and caravan trade as carried on by Mughal, Armenian, Turani and local merchants is the figure for Dhaka higher. Note however that the Armenians contributed Rs. 500,000 worth of trade to the figure of 18,00,000 at Dhaka. We have no comparable records for Armenian trade at Jugdia.

While the French AE BIII 459 is quite clear about the magnitude of European investment at Jugdia we have, unfortunately, no such English documents. Writing in the nineteenth century Hunter put the EEIC investment in *baftas* at Jugdia at Sicca Rupees (S.R.) 1,200,000. This corroborates the figure of 1,000,000 given for the EEIC in AE BIII 459. The magnitude of the European investment at Jugdia is apparent when we note that English estimates of the value of English exports from Dhaka was S.R. 350 000 annually and that of the French S.R. 280,000.[35] The only other investment figures comparable to those for Jugdia are the EEIC's figures for their silk investment at Kasimbazar. Between 1733 and 1750 the average spending on different grades of silk was S.R. 772 060; in 1745 as much as S.R. 1 594 780 was spent. Moneys spent for 1733 and 1744 came close to this figure.[36]

We have already noted that the French rated commerce at Jugdia higher than that anywhere else in Bengal.[37] In a letter dated April 9, 1786, Dangereux the French chief at Chandernagore, placed Jugdia fourth in importance after Patna, Kasimbazar and Balasore. Dhaka was fifth in importance and was followed by the subordinate French settlements at Khirpaye, Karicola, Supur and Monipur (Mohanpur/Midnapore?).[38] Jugdia's commercial potential was deemed supreme by the FEIC because it produced *baftas* (ordinary plain cotton), its labour was plentiful and cheap,[39] its abundant water offered tremendous advantages for washing the textiles[40] and moreover because its chief trading partner was the east-Achin, Malacca, Pegu and Manila-Jugdia's position in the 'Far Eastern' trade conducted from Bengal was deemed unassailable. But Jugdia also had the distinction of providing cargo for Basra, Mocha and Jedda.[41] Note that Dupleix dreamed of a grand French trading complex which would extend from Chattagram upto Pegu.[42] Jugdia fell within this area; moreover its strongly east-oriented commercial links ensured it would play a prominent part in this French design. Following the EEIC takeover in the west after 1765 the French thought of withdrawing from Chandernagore and establishing their HQ in Chattagram.[43]

Jugdia's fleeting celebrity as production centre, its gigantic leap into commercial prominence in the middle of the eighteenth century had but one reason: it wove *baftas. Baftas* formed the singlemost important item in the East India trade of the European companies in India. *Baftas* were initially produced in Gujarat, chiefly in Bharuch, Baroda, Navsari and Surat; they were referred to as Gujarat calico in two varieties—broad and narrow, two qualities—coarse and fine, and two chief colour schemes—white (for Europe) or dyed (red, blue and black for Asian markets). *Baftas* were the staple commodity in the Surat trade where even the Chinese seem to have participated.[44] *Baftas* were in great demand in England: it has been estimated that between 1677 and 1680 textiles worth between 200 000 and 300 000 pounds sterling was exported through Surat to England. Of these *baftas* accounted for between 150 000 to 160 000 pounds sterling.[45]

The manufacture of *baftas*—probably the item most in demand in Europe apart from chintzes—soon spread beyond Gujarat. They were equally in demand throughout the Asian world: *baftas* were an important item in India's external trade with Iran, Turan and Rus.

But how did *baftas* come to be manufactured in Jugdia? We are told that after the famine of 1630 in Surat *baftas* became scarce there. They were then manufactured in other parts of India, notably at Burhanpur[46] and soon Jugdia, with its abundant source of cotton from the Tipperah Hills, began to specialise in this item.

The documents on European trade at Jugdia throw up the different attitudes of the English and the French to Jugdia. The EEIC obviously saw Jugdia as far more important to their private trade while the FEIC displayed more of an 'official' interest in Jugdia as part of their plans to establish a 'Far Eastern' empire centering on Jugdia, Chattagram and Pegu. This is understandable in view of the fact that by mid-century the EEIC were firmly entrenched in the western part of Bengal and squeezing out rival European companies. The only alternative for other Europeans, as had been the case before with Indians, was to 'go east'. The last commercial frontier of

Bengal—Jugdia—with its open market policy was therefore attractive at a time when the EEIC was cornering the trade everywhere else.

Bedier took up the story of Jugdia after Cordier and added in 1838:[47]

> Aucun agent francais n'ayant ete a Jougdya depuis 1817, nous ne pouvons que rapporter ici la note y relative qui se trouve dans les archives de Chandernagor.
>
> The loge de Jougdya ayant ete enlevee par les eaux de la mer, M. Chevalier obtint en 1767 un paravana du Nabab du Bengale pour faire l'acquisition d'un nouveau terrain a Jougdya et y batir une loge.
>
> Les Anglais ayant force le nabab a retracer ce paravana, ce ne fut qu'a la reprise de possession, en 1785, que M.Joseph Dayot fut envoye a Jougdya pour y faire l'acquisition d'un nouveau terrain. Le territoire de Chandella . . . fut achete par Mr.Joseph Dayot. Le contrat de ce terrain ne fut regularise qu'en 1790 par les soins de M.Gilliot, chef de la loge de Jougdya, qui obtint un patta original au nom du Roi de France, a la charge d'une redevance de 558 f.9 et 1626 f. de salamy. Le contrat de ce terrain se trouve au controle de Chandernagor.

These lines prove that Jugdia remained important to the French even at the end of the eighteenth century despite the difficulties they faced in the procurement of *baftas* there.[48] Moreover, they indicate that a tussle was going on between the French and the English as regards European expansion into the 'Far East' of Bengal; while the EEIC had forsaken Jugdia for Lakhipur they had made equally certain that no other European, except under English aegis, should function in the region.

The EEIC's trade at Lakhipur seems to have had more of an 'official' blessing to it. Because the EEIC shifted to Lakhipur in 1755 we have more information on Lakhipur. Lakhipur was equally profitable, it was also a large mart for *baftas* and as at Jugdia private Europeans made a killing there. Lakhipur assortments formed the largest proportion of the private merchants' trade.[49] See this table for private investment there (in sicca rupees).[50]

Table 25
Private Trade at Different Arangs in Bengal Including Lakhipur at the End of the Eighteenth Century

Arang	1795–96	1796–97	1797–98	1798–99	1800–01
Dhaka	879,829	-	777,504	577,910	602,565
Malda	208,071	-	179,595	138,061	152,186
Lakhipur	1,659,996	416,811	561,585	667,162	1,226,453

EEIC trade there flourished as well. See Table 26 (in sicca rupees).[51]

Table 26
EEIC Trade at Different Arangs Including Lakhipur 1754–1800

Arang	1754–55	1758–59	1761–62	1771–72	1791–92	1794–95	1799–1800
Chattagram	-	-	-	100,000	102,850	121,117	18,179
Dhaka	168,000	134,067	546,000	1,177,607	966,000	543,380	197,009
Malda	194,620	296,088	-	360,000	538,326	469,692	179,595
Lakhipur	-	139,596	168,000	700,000	898,338	545,128	567,585

Arangs such as Harial, Haripal and Santipur were far behind Lakhipur in investment in both private and company trade. The average annual circulation of EEIC capital at *arangs* between 1795 and 1800 is shown in Table 27.[52]

Table 27
The Circulation of English Capital at Arangs

Factory Arang	Private English Trade	EEIC	Total
Dhaka	709,452	370,194	1,079,646
Malda	169,478	324,778	494,256
Lakhipur	906,401	556,356	1,462,757

Because of the enormous profitability of trade at Lakhipur as we see in the above three tables it is not surprising to see that private trade flourished at Lakhipur. Commercial Residents downwards everybody had a stake in the Lakhipur trade in a private capacity. In 1770, Brajaballabh, zamindar of Lakhipur and also the Company's *dalal* at Lakhipur were found in arrears of a sum of Rs. 2,493 but the Chittagong Committee advised Calcutta that:[53]

> The importance of this man's employ at the aurung mentioned, made me think it expedient to observe a greater degree of delicacy towards him than would otherwise have been requisite, lest calling him hither in person might in any degree have impeded or proved detrimental to the prosecution of the investment provision there.

Everybody, therefore, had a stake in the Lakhipur trade. English officials not only carried on this lucrative trade but also acted for European companies which did not have a commercial presence in the area. Companies with their HQ at Calcutta became active in supplying Lakhipur goods; for example Palmer and Co. supplied Lakhipur goods to the Danish Company.[54]

It seems that while private trade also flourished in the west the magnitude of private trade in the east was far larger. Central authority—either official as in the case of Dhaka or informal as in the case of company mandate—did not extend to the easternmost parts of Bengal.

20

The Market at Jugdia – Textiles, Merchants and Companies

Jugdia produced 'cossaes' (khas), 'hammams', 'sanas', garas, 'romalls', 'baffetas' and 'doreas'. The *doreas* were deemed as fine as the *malmal* and the organdies of the Coromandel.[1] It produced also '*les toiles a quatre fils, les bazins communs, les nappes, les serviettes, coutant 5 a 30 Francs la piece*',[2] which the FEIC invested in. According to Hunter Jugdia's *baftas,* woven from cotton from the Tipperah Hills, formed the singlemost important item in the EEIC's trade there. This trade was estimated by him to be worth Sicca Rupees 1,200,000 annually.[3] The Jugdia factory was fourth in importance to FEIC factories in Patna, Kasimbazar and Balasore. Dhaka was fifth in importance to the FEIC. As in the case of its political fortunes, Jugdia's economic fortunes too rose and fell with that of Chattagram. Jugdia's importance declined when the Karnaphuli started to become unnavigable from mid-eighteenth century onwards. In the eighteenth century Chattagram's revenue assessment was only Rs. 176,795, as compared with Jahangirnagar's (Rs. 1,928,194), Sylhet's (Rs. 531,455) and Raushanabad's (Rs. 92,993); a far cry from former days indeed!

Jugdia had a cost advantage because, as we have noted, labour there was plentiful and cheap. But this cost advantage was cancelled out by the fact that Jugdia provided 'ready money' goods (that is against cash purchase) as opposed to other parts of Bengal where advance (*dadan* in the west and *pattan* in the east) was the norm. This was anathema to the European companies as heavy demand in any one year pushed up prices. They therefore moved for a more regulated market with state intervention in their favour. Their failure to establish a 'regulated' market in Jugdia and the EEIC shift to Lakhipur forms the story of this chapter.

The textile market in Bengal came into being through trader and buyer combines and was hierarchically organized. Markets in Bengal were divided into the following categories. At the very bottom lay the primary markets. These were *arangs* or permanent producing centers. These were serviced by weavers who supplied seasonal and periodic markets. The produce of the *arangs* fed the secondary markets of *haats*/ *melas*/fairs and festivals and were serviced by *pykars* and *dalals* who bought goods for ready money and supplied the merchants. Permanent procuring markets found expression in market-towns[4] such as Patna, Rajmahal, Hugli, Kasimbazar, Malda, and Dhaka where wealthy Asian and European merchants were to be found increasingly from the seventeenth century on. All market towns were, of necessity, either riverine ports or close to waterways.

The commerce at these market towns was well-lubricated by the presence of big financial firms such as those of 'AllumChundGainchund' or 'CoosalChund' at Kasimbazar or of 'AllumChundNimchund' or 'Coshaulchund' at Dhaka. The financial markets in their turn were controlled by the great financial firm of the Jagat Seth. The firm of Jagat Seth, in its capacity of Treasurer-General of Bengal, oversaw the finances of Bengal.[5] The fact that Jugdia's market was not under the control of the Jagat Seth posed problems for the East India Companies[6] although this seems to have posed no such problems for the Indian traders judging by the volume of trade they carried on at Jugdia.[7]

The European settlements along the Bhagirathi (Chandernagore, Srirampur, Bankibazar, Chunchura, to name a few) can be seen as European attempts to introduce alternative market-towns. Their settlements in the interior such as at Patna in the north, Malda in the west, Rangpur in the north and Harial, Jugdia and Lakhipur in the east served as subsidiary market towns. Here finances were a perennial problem; European imports of specie were continually frustrated by the Jagat Seth's control over the mints in Bengal. European shortfalls in specie had to be made up by short term loans from local merchants. There were no merchants in Jugdia comparable to the merchants of Kasimbazar who could supply short term loans to the EICs.

How was the market organized in Jugdia? We know that Dhaka functioned as the market-town for the *arangs* of Titbari, Dhamrai, Jangalbari, Narayanpur, Bazitpur, Chandpur and Srirampur. As market town Dhaka had developed a sophisticated system of procurement with a hierarchy of agents—the 'Dacca Dellols'—in place. Moreover, financial firms vetted by the chief financier, the Jagat Seth, were also active in Dhaka in the eighteenth century. An integrated north-west-east financial market, running in an arc from Patna-Murshidabad-Dhaka, made commercial policy easier. This financial market oversaw all transactions in Bengal.

But Dhaka's jurisdiction (both political and financial) did not continue as far as Jugdia. The FEIC rued the fact that there was no central authority there.[8] This made their procurement difficult. Agents in place were hard to find. Moreover, the European companies at Jugdia were confronted with the practice of ready money sales at a time when the rest of Bengal had switched to procurement on the basis of advances.[9] Generally speaking a ready money sale was an unacceptable practice for permanent trading. It had the effect of pushing up prices in the market. This mosaic of trade practices at Jugdia confirms our view that trade there was mainly localized; Jugdia had not been integrated into either one of the three main phases of commerce that we noted earlier: the Mongol caravan trade order emanating from China which had links with Ilyas Shahi Bengal, the Husain Shahi Islamic order or the Mughal Middle East order.

The absence of political and financial authority at Jugdia comes as a surprise given its prolific production and the prodigious quantity of trade carried on there. It is yet to be explored whether Jugdia formed a part of even older commercial networks such as the Buddhist. This seems likely as Jugdia lay at the heart of that religious area in Bengal.

By the middle of the eighteenth century, however, sources inform us that the 'Dacca Dellols' were moving in to regulate the market in Jugdia. An EEIC letter of October 23, 1752 mentions that they had applied to Murshidabad for a *parwana* allowing them to control the cloth business of Jugdia as well as all the Dhaka arangs. They had obtained such a *parwana*.[10]

Who were these 'Dacca Dellols'? The first mention that we get of them is in the late seventeenth century. William Hedge's Diary notes on July 25, 1684: 'This day five Dellols or Brokers of Dacca . . . went to Mr. Beard's Chamber'.[11] Taylor writing in 1800–01 mentions two such *dalals:* Royjee and Bandoo Singh.[12] 'Rotonne Monique' (Ratan Manik) referred to in the FEIC letters 5, 6 and 8[13] was probably one of the 'Dacca Dellols' for he is referred to as the chief of the *dalals* in Jugdia and trusted by the EEIC (Letter no. 5). The 'Dacca Dellols' were therefore a distinct group of merchants who worked with political back-up from Dhaka. They furnished the company investments and in the comparative absence of mart-towns in the east their area of operations was probably very wide. This absence of mart-towns gave the 'Dacca Dellols' enormous power; it was noted by the French that 'Rotonne Monique's' *dalals* operated as far away as at Srirampur (one of the Dhaka arangs).[14] The FEIC were, consequently, unwilling to upset him (Letter no. 5).

The Dhaka *dalal* mishap of the 1740s leads one to speculate that there may have been a major change in the composition of the *dalals* with the upheaval following what the EEIC termed the 'revolution of 1739–40'. A set of merchants described by Om Prakash went bankrupt in 1746. In '*Trade and Politics in Eighteenth Century Bengal*' Om Prakash notes:[15]

> 'In 1744 . . . it was believed that the fortunes of several of the merchants supplying textiles to the Dutch Company were under strain. These suspicions were confirmed in 1746 when it was learnt that four important merchants operating in the major textile centre of Shantipur near Dhaka-Hinkar Chaudhary, Jag Bhusan, Gokul Chand and Bhagwan Gopi Chand, together with their associates, Radhamohun Chaudhary and Radhakant Chand, had been financially ruined. The Company suffered considerable losses . . . But the local sarrafs and bankers, who would have been acceptable to the Company as guarantors, flatly refused, saying it (providing the merchants' sureties) was too risky a proposition'.

Shantipur like Jugdia was not a part of the Dhaka arangs. But here too *dalals* had been operating with official sanction from Dhaka since the 1740s. Many, we have seen, had strong political connections at both Dhaka and Murshidabad. The changeover from Murshid Quli Khan's dynasty to that of the Bihar based one of Alivardi Khan brought many changes in its wake; not least among them was the rise of new interest groups.

The Dhaka *naib nazim* from 1740–54 was Nawazish Muhammad Khan. We saw that Nawazish Muhammad Khan played great part in palace intrigues at Murshidabad and was appointed Diwan of Bengal by Alivardi. This gave him enormous financial power in Bengal. Son-in-law of Nawab Alivardi Khan and a man who terrorized the European companies at Dhaka, he spent most of his time at court in Murshidabad and ruled Dhaka through deputies. One such was Husain Quli. Husain Quli was previously Nawazish Khan's diwan. He was now appointed deputy *naib nazim* at Dhaka. Gokul Chand, formerly Husain Quli's deputy, got Husain Quli dismissed on his election to the post of deputy.

We have already noted this palace revolution in Dhaka and speculated as to whether it was a mere political affair or a conflict of trade interests. We saw that this is the same Gokul Chand as mentioned by Om Prakash[16] who was financially ruined in 1744 and to whom no banker would extend a guarantee. Note too that 1744 was the year Husain Quli got himself re-instated as deputy through the efforts of Ghasiti Begum who was Nawazish Muhammad Khan's wife and Nawab Alivardi Khan's daughter. Gokul Chand was referred to as 'a financier of eminence who was now audited to the extent that he was financially bankrupt and lost his office[17] and Gokul Chand's career as merchant was ruined thereafter.[18]

By mid-century we are told of a second group of *dalals*-a ring of five 'Dacca Dellols'—who had cornered the procurement for European companies and that, as the sources from Calcutta and Chandernagore[19] tell us, these Dhaka dalals were moving onto the Jugdia textile trade with sanction from Murshidabad by 1752. In the same year the EEIC at Dhaka decided to abandon Jugdia.[20] They decided to move to Kalindi, five hours distance from Dhaka, a big mart for *baftas* and possessing the advantage of being 'under Juggut Seat'.[21] Was this a mere coincidence? It is obvious that Dhaka and Murshidabad had separate jurisdictions in the 'far east'. Kalindi and Lakhipur were obviously under the jurisdiction of Murshidabad; Jugdia occupied an intermediate space that Dhaka was trying to bring under its control.

In 1753 the Kalindi project was abandoned; in February the Jugdia factors decided on Lakhipur and requested Kasimbazar to get a parwana from Murshidabad sanctioning the move.[22] But the Lakhipur move had not been effected in June 1753. We find an entry in the K.F.R. noting that the EEIC's business at Jugdia was stopped as the local authorities there (the Dhaka *niabat*) had put peons on the EEIC's dalals' gomastha. The Jugdia factors of the EEIC urged Kasimbazar once again to get the *parwana* immediately.[23]

In 1754 the Dhaka *niabat* entered officially into the picture. Supporting the 'Dacca Dellols', it opposed officially the EEIC shift from Jugdia to Lakhipur. And the *parwana* was still to come.[24] In 1755 the EEIC shifted to Lakhipur but the Jugdia dalals had still not accepted defeat; they were now trying to get the parwana revoked at Murshidabad. The Kasimbazar factors sent a *vakil* to Jugdia to investigate.[25] In August Kasimbazar wrote that they would try and stop the Jugdia dalals at Murshidabad through Diwan Raj Ballabh.[26] Soon after the matter died down and the EEIC did not returm to Jugdia.

The French, on the other hand, decided to remain back at Jugdia. This decision not to incur additional expense was wise, in hindsight, as the Anglo-French wars meant that all French territories in Bengal were taken over by the English in 1756 and only returned to the French in 1765. Moreover the FEIC had one advantage over the EEIC: their Jugdia trade was tied to their factory at Dhaka and not independent as was the case with the EEIC. This meant that troubles, such as those the EEIC faced with the 'Dacca Dellols', could be solved on the spot, and without involving Murshidabad. Cordier wrote in 1823:[27]

> Jougdya dependait du chef de Dacca . . . Sa situation n'etant pas proper aux debouches des marchandises d'Europe, la Compagnie n'en envoyait d'aucune espece. Les produits de cette loge etaient envoyes a Dacca, d'ou on les expediait a Chandernagor.

Why was the second set of Jugdia *dalals*, obviously the Dhaka *dalals*, so opposed to the move? These *dalals*, backed by the local court and financial interests from Dhaka, clubbed together to monopolise the entire cloth trade of the region from 1752. Lakhipur was obviously outside their sphere of influence; hence their opposition to the English move there. The question that arises is: which set of *dalals* controlled the Lakhipur trade? If not the older Dhaka agents or the Dacca Dellols was there a third set of *dalals* backed by Murshidabad operating in Lakhipur?

It seems quite clear from the French and English accounts used here that there were at least two sets of *dalals* operating in Jugdia—local and the Dhaka *dalals*. Of these the 'Dacca Dellols' were obviously more powerful as a bloc, backed as they were by the *niabat*. The EEIC move to bypass them, sanctioned by the Murshidabad Durbar, frustrated the efforts of the *dalals* and the Dhaka *niabat* to corner the lucrative *bafta* trade at Jugdia. The lack of coordination between the Murshidabad and Dhaka *durbars* as regards Jugdia was an indication that the western part of Bengal did not take this eastern trading region seriously; for the court at Murshidabad the last frontier terminated at Dhaka and not beyond.

21

The Mid Century Textile Crisis at Jugdia

In the previous chapter we mentioned the goods produced at Jugdia. Of these *baftas* formed the single most important item in the FEIC's and the EEIC's investments at Jugdia. The French noted that an added advantage at Jugdia was that labour was plentiful and cheap at Jugdia.[1] Yet by 1751 Jugdia no longer produced *baftas*. Textile production there was seriously disturbed. Why was this so?

The disappearance of *baftas* from company investment lists is symptomatic of the disjunction that company trade had introduced into the commercial landscape of eighteenth century Bengal. Moreover, the decline in production of *sanas* in Jugdia was indicative of the extent by which production at Jugdia had turned away from traditional markets by mid century. Mughal political economy envisaged a mercantile terrain within which manufacturing centres and mart towns maintained the delicate balance between poltical authority and economic activity. Strung out on the Mughal economic map of South Asia were hundreds of such centres controlling production which were in turn regulated by the economies of the emporia towns of Dhaka, Hugli, Rajmahal and Patna in the east, Burhanpur in the centre, Masulipatam in the south, Surat in the west, and Agra in the north.

The Mughal political economy was a liberal one that envisaged a spontaneous economic system and a market without undue regulation by political authority. The European intrusion into this landscape introduced an alien note. English and French political economy, with their emphasis on state intervention and regulation of markets, were products of a system that had already seen a reordering of the economy and market in their respective countries. Social relationships had been slaughtered and then forged too in their markets at home by the eighteenth century. Now the imposition of such ideas in Bengal under the aegis of foreign capital dictated new relations here too: these new relations were both physical and social.

The EICs introduced a different ordering into the Mughal commercial landscape. EIC urbanization in Bengal, as in other parts of South Asia, was inherently economic in nature. All EIC centres were essentially procurement points; by virtue of this the EICs introduced a three tiered mart-town system whereby all traditional Mughal centres—emporia, town or *arang*—were viewed by the Europeans as mere procurement areas. The vitality of Mughal urbanization was therefore subordinated to the notion of towns as industrial zones. Be they Jugdia, Dhaka or Lakhipur in the east or Kasimbazar, Murshidabad and Malda in the west, all Mughal trading towns were deemed secondary to the main EIC mart town of the region: be it Chandernagore, Calcutta or Chunchura (Chinsurah). In its turn, the regional EIC mart town was subject to the political and economic compulsions of its HQ in South Asia: in the case of the French it was Pondichery and, in the case of the Dutch still more distant, Batavia. This meant in its turn that the economic activity of the EICs spanned a physical area distinctly different from the Mughal political arena; for example by linking their procurement at Jugdia to the sailing time table from Chandernagore to Pondichery the French introduced a note of externality into the traditional commercial landscape.

The manufacturing centres generally determined the production process from start to finish; rarely do we find instances of production being farmed out between centres. Now by linking the production of one centre to the finishing process of another, the EICs introduced a discordant note into the rhythm of production, fragmented the production process and introduced a new division of labour within the conventional manufacturing paradigm. Cloth that could not be washed or otherwise 'finished' at Jugdia was sent to Chandernagore to be finished so as to fit into the sailing schedules of the FEIC.[2]

By mid-century textile production in all centres in Bengal was almost exclusively re-oriented towards the European market. The *dadni* merchants', the *dalals*' and *pykars*' fortunes were closely linked to the investment demands of the European companies. Of the European investments it was most of all towards English investment that textile production at Jugdia re-oriented itself. This was because the English were the largest buyer among European nations in Bengal by mid-century and could dictate terms by virtue of the sheer magnitude of their company and private investments. This meant that the investments of the Asian merchants and other European companies such as the French and Danes who had interests at Jugdia were affected.

This chapter looks at the textile crisis at Jugdia on the basis of the letters exchanged between Chandernagore and Jugdia. The letters have been numbered serially from 1 to 26[3] and cover the period running from

September 21, 1750 to December 17, 1753. All of them are from Duval de Leyrit in council at Chandernagore to the FEIC's agent in Jugdia; we have unfortunately no letters from Jugdia to Chandernagore. In the absence of a Jugdia-Chandernagore correspondance we have no record of the assessment of the man on the spot, only Chandernagore's assessments of the same. We also have no similar records of private transactions in Jugdia except for a mention of the FEIC's M.Jambon's private trade at Jugdia in Letter 7 of April 16, 1751. However we know from Table 22 that private investment in Jugdia was as high as the company trade of both the French and the English put together. Nevertheless, a continuous record of the FEIC's transactions in Jugdia helps us to piece together a picture of the commercial landscape in Jugdia in mid-century even as Bengal began the journey from autonomy to subjection. Moreover, this French documentation of a little known place in the commercial history of Bengal is invaluable, enabling us as it does in putting together a picture of an alternative commercial space, and of European presence in the region.

Jugdia traditionally was a producer of *baftas* of various grades but it also produced *khas, sana, gara, rumals,* serviettes, 'bazins communs' which I have been unable to identify, chintzes and a cloth with four threads[4] (as opposed to *dusutty*) whose actual name is not mentioned in the records.

Compulsions rising from this almost total linkage of the production sector at Jugdia with English demand now resulted in Jugdia becoming increasingly disassociated from the internal/home market. This disjunction from the home market meant that certain varieties of cloth were no longer produced such as *baftas* of the B.2 variety and *sanas.*[5] Moreover during this period of readjustment of the production process some items were discontinued in full such as the *sanas.*

On August 31, 1751 Duval de Leyrit wrote from Chandernagore to Albert at Jugdia (Letter no. 10) that the *baftas* sent from Jugdia were too expensive and that the lower category of *baftas* known as B.2 was no longer made at the *arangs.* On March 25, 1752 (Letter no. 12) it was noted that Nicholas had written in from Jugdia that the only *baftas* available were of the expensive silk kind. On February 16, 1753 (Letter no. 19) it was noted that since the *EEIC did not take baftas any more at Jugdia they were no longer produced and that this had resulted in a great inconvenience for the French.* (My emphasis).

As for the *sanas* we have the following details: On May 3, 1752 (Letter no. 13) it was noted that *sanas* were no longer produced. Nicolas was instructed to get production going once again in this item. He was even asked to offer extra money to the *dalals* as incentive to furnish *sanas.* Despite this,

Nicolas informed Duval de Leyrit from Jugdia on July 10, 1752 that it was impossible to procure *sanas* at Jugdia anymore. They were no longer produced. (mentioned in Letter 14 of Duval de Leyrit to Nicolas of August 5, 1752).

During this time prices continued to rise for all items. Letter 10 of Duval de Leyrit to Albert dated August 31, 1751 mentioned that the *baftas* and *hammams* were too expensive. The FEIC decided not to invest in *hammams* that year. Letter 12 of March 25, 1752 reiterated again that *hammams* were too expensive.

Similarly, there was a deterioration of quality. Letter 1 of September 21, 1750 mentioned the bad quality of goods. This was ascribed to excessive rains. Letter 3 of November 17, 1750 mentioned the bad quality of *garas.* Letter 4 of December 18, 1750 made this point again. Letter 11 of December 16, 1751 mentioned that the goods (quantity and variety not specified) were of inferior quality. Letter 13 of May 3, 1752 said that the *baftas* sent from Jugdia were of poor quality so much so that Nicolas was instructed not to contract for them at Jugdia.

There was also a shortfall in supplies. Letter 10 of August 31, 1751 mentioned that there was a shortfall of *bafta* supplies from Jugdia. Out of the 3,000 demanded there was a shortfall of 30% (or about 800 pieces plus). Letter 12 of March 25, 1752 mentioned that Nicolas could get only 200 of the 1000 *baftas* demanded (i.e. a shortfall of 80%) and that it was impossible to get *hammams* in the quantities the FEIC demanded. Letter 13 of May 3, 1752 emphasised again the shortfall in *bafta* investment.

The goods also arrived late at Chandernagore. Letter 1 of September 21, 1750 spoke of late deliveries due to rains. Letter 4 of 1750 said that the late arrival of *garas* delayed the sailing schedule from Chandernagore to Pondichery. Letter 9 of July 26, 1751 mentioned that *bafta* deliveries had been late in 1750 and 1751. Letter 11 of December 16, 1751 mentioned that all deliveries had been sent late to Chandernagore.

Inadequate finishing was another cause for concern. The traditional practice at Jugdia, as at all producing centres in Bengal, was to undertake all aspects of production at one centre. Now, however, letter 3 of November 17, 1750 noted that the rates of the washers at Jugdia were too expensive. The goods were, therefore, to be sent to Chandernagore in an unfinished state. This comes as a surprise since labour was supposed to be cheap and plentiful in Jugdia, a fact that made the Jugdia goods' prices attractive. Letter 9 of July 26, 1751 instructed Jugdia to send *unfinished* baftas to Pondichery.

Alternative centres to Jugdia now rose, fragmenting both the production process and facilitating the rise of alternative production. We have already noted that some of the Jugdia goods were being 'finished' in Chandernagore, despite the fact that one of Jugdia's claims to production advantage was its proximity to plentiful and clean waters.[6] Now it was suggested that the FEIC would procure *baftas* at Chandernagore (Letter 13 May 3, 1752).

There was also the disturbing news that the *dalals* had gone bankrupt. Letters until the very end reiterate the themes of insolvency and bankruptcy of the Jugdia *dalals*. Indeed the bankruptcy angle saw the FEIC sending three agents to Jugdia in the space of three years; Albert, Nicolas and Caillot. Letter 5 of January 13, 1751 instructs Albert to ensure that 'Rotonne Monique'pays back his dues to the FEIC before he is discharged, while however cautioning Albert that Ratan Manik, the chief of the *dalals* at Jugdia, was trusted by the EEIC. The FEIC was diffident in sacking Ratan Manik from its investment and Albert was asked to ensure that his removal did not cause any problems for the FEIC there. Letter 6 of February 27, 1751 empowered Albert to remove Ratan Manik while Letter 7 of April 16, 1751 exhorted Albert to 'control' the *dalals* and try to recover dues from the bankrupt *dalals*. These dues were estimated at Rs. 8045 in Letter 8 of May 5, 1751. Letter 9 of July 26, 1751 emphasised that Albert had not yet succeeded in recovering dues from the *dalals*. Letter 10 of August 31, 1751 emphasised this once again.

Between December 1751 and March 1752 Albert was removed from his post and Nicolas appointed the FEIC chief at Jugdia. We do not know if Albert was removed because of his failure to recover the money from the *dalals*. There is a faint hint in the Chandernagore letters that Albert was suspected of carrying on private trade in Jugdia and being in collusion with the *dalals* there; however Letter 19 of February 16, 1753 urged the new agent Nicolas as well to recover dues from the dalals which makes it likely that the bankruptcy was genuine.

Letter 16 dated November 5, 1752 refers to the *dalals* refusing to furnish the investment unless chintzes ('chitties') were included. This was an understandable tactic of the merchants; to slip in more expensive items into the investment at a time of recession but it was noted, in the same letter, that the *chintzes were expensive and not more than the baftas previously provided* (emphasis mine).

Letter 20 of March 20, 1753 brought to light the serious news that the *dalals* had not acquitted their debts since Albert's departure; more grave was the fact that they had also not fulfilled their engagements to the FEIC since that time (shortfalls seems the likely explanation). Nicolas was instructed to stop all advances until the dues/shortfalls were cleared. Letter 21 of April 17, 1753 noted that the debts of the Jugdia *dalals* escalated each year; Nicolas was urged yet again to recover dues and was reprimanded for advancing Rs. 1000 to the *dalals* despite the FEIC's decree to the contrary. Letter 22 of May 20, 1753 insisted that all debts were to be recovered and that no new advances were to be given. Letter 23 was more sombre. On June 20, 1753 the FEIC noted that unless all debts were recovered the FEIC would have to abandon the Jugdia factory like the English had done (obviously a reference to the Lakhipur affair). Another option was to engage a new set of *dalals* as the letter instructed Nicolas; this however was impossible as we have seen from the EEIC letters. Letter 24 of July 15, 1753 urged recovery of debts but noted optimistically that despite Nicolas acting against orders in advancing money to the *dalals* the latter had kept their word and furnished the FEIC investment for Jugdia in full.

Under these circumstances letters 25 (July 16, 1753) and 26 (December 17, 1753) come as a surprise. Nicolas was threatened with replacement by Caillot unless he persuaded the *dalals* to make good the debts in the letter of July 16. On December 17 he was given his marching orders and told to start for Chandernagore as soon as he managed to recover the dues from the *dalals*.

Letters from the beginning of 1752 introduce other themes following upon the *dalals'* bankruptcy. Bad quality goods, shortfalls in deliveries, insolvency and financial straits are not emphasized; instead letters from February 1753 speak of the 'complicated affair of the *dalals* of Jugdia', the imbroglio with the EEIC and express the apprehension that the FEIC would have to abandon Jugdia.

But trade continued at Jugdia and as late as on May 27, 1767 Dangereuex, the French chief at Dhaka, borrowed SR 7000 from Haji Muhammad at Dhaka for Jugdia @ 12%.[7] Entries 3149 of May 1, 1767, 3150 of May 21, 1767, and 3151 of June 6, 1767, all from 22 MIOM 46 at C.A.O.M. in Aix, continue to speak of the difficulties of trade at Jugdia. The French also considered a move like the EEIC. On June 19, 1767 Manohargunge was deemed as suitable by the FEIC. It was located in the 'Pargana of Umabat' on the banks of the Dakatiya river. It was half a days route from Jugdia and was better situated. As its name suggests it was a mart town.

On October 12, 1768, the French took account of their trading operations in India. French commerce at Kasimbazar, Balasore, Patna, Dhaka, and Jugdia were in decline. It was noted that the sea was eating away at Jugdia.[8] Therefore, all through 1767 and 1768 the FEIC considered moving to 'Manorgonge'.[9] On June 15, 1768 Nicolas de Forency was sent to Jugdia.[10] On October 20, 1768 Chandola was suggested as an alternative to Manohargunge. The FEIC noted that it was to be a subordinate factory, two days' route from Jugdia.[11] The shift was never effected although Chandola was 'bought' by the FEIC.

We do not know Nicolas de Forency's antecedents but an entry of January 26, 1769 speaks of the reception of M. Nicolas at Chandernagore on July 22, 1767.[12] Trade continued at Jugdia in the meanwhile.[13] But trade was impeded through Magh raids, rising expenses and finding cash to pay the money owed to the *dalals*.[14]

On May 28, 1774 Desgranges was relieved of his post as chief of the Dhaka factory and sent to take over the FEIC factory at Jugdia.[15] On October 28, 1785 Fouquet de Champigny was in charge at Jugdia for we find in an entry that he informed Dangereux, the chief of the FEIC factory at Dhaka, that the EEIC was building a bazaar at Srirampur next to the French factory and the problems this would entail for French trade there.[16] In July 1786 Dayot was sent to Jugdia to 'settle the Jugdia affair'.[17] In August the FEIC noted that he had done so.[18]

But problems continued to plague the FEIC at Jugdia.[19] On July 1, 1787 the FEIC noted that the hut used by Roche at Jugdia was so primitive that Dayot had been obliged to rent a boat at Rs. 50 a month for his residence.[20] Complaints continued to come from Jugdia for the rest of the eighteenth century. The need to build a new factory, the shortage of money and the sea washing away the factory were themes that were reiterated. More significant were the themes of the EEIC entering this last frontier in a big way, stopping trade, attacking FEIC personnel and denying them customs rights.[21]

Domination of foreign capital, subversion of the production process, infighting between at least two groups of *dalals*, diminishing inland trade, decay of traditional production centres and the rise of new centres are the sub-themes that underscore the Chandernagore-Jugdia letters of the FEIC of the 1750s. Most important of all is the evidence that by mid-century the English were entering into *arangs* in the east (Lakhipur) as they were in the west (Kumarkhali). New mart towns were established by them at Lakhipur and Srirampur.

The story of Jugdia that we have managed to reconstruct from the archives at Aix continues this theme from the 1760s but the emphasis now moves on to English attempts to regulate the last frontier of Bengal. The story of FEIC trade at Jugdia at the end of the eighteenth century is a story of commercial decline of a once booming economy.

Overshadowing these themes is the blatant emergence of two trends that mark the history of the eighteenth century in Bengal hereafter: the weakness of local mercantile orgnisation and the inefficacy of the political authorities to combat growing European influence in the economic realm. None could face up to the challenge to local political authority.

Finally, the Jugdia documents are testimony to a relatively unstudied phenomenon in eighteenth century South Asia; the making and unmaking of commercial 'places' due to investment demands of the East India companies: we know accordingly that Kalindi, Manohargunj and Srirampur were well-established mart towns, Jugdia a production centre and Lakhipur an *arang* town that blossomed briefly in mid century.

At the beginning of the nineteenth century Cordier noted that the Jugdia factory was abandoned by the French; there was practically no commerce and only modest huts there.[22] Bedier noted in 1838 that no FEIC agent had been sent to Jugdia since 1817.[23] So the French, too, had pulled out of Jugdia.

At the end of the nineteenth century Hunter mentioned that only Kalindi merited a mention on the maps.[24] The commercial map that the English East India Company made and unmade in its first phase of trading in South Asia was manifest in the rise of Lakhipur and the decline of Jugdia. Lakhipur and Jugdia now passed into oblivion; their brief moment of glory eclipsed by the needs of foreign merchant capital at its most vicious in South Asia.

22

The End of the Economic World of the Mughal

But indebtedness and EEIC policy were not the only reasons for the disappearance of the merchants of Kasimbazar and Jugdia. The systemic crises within the political economy of the Mughal were responsible in no small way for their disappearance as well.

For the Mughals, the free and adequate flow of specie was necessary to maintain equilibrium in the realm, much as proper blood circulation maintains the health of the human body. The Mughals conceived of the state as an organism where any disturbance—such as the circulation of too much of or too little specie—could trigger off decline. The Mughal notion of the economy, where foreign trade conducted on Mughal soil on equal terms with other Asian merchants was seen as beneficial to the agrarian, commercial and financial realms, contrasted sharply with the aggressive mercantilism of Europe.

The circulation of specie was impeded in mid eighteenth century Bengal for two reasons. One was external. All of us know about the Maratha invasions and how they harmed the economy of the western part of Bengal. From 1742 to 1751 the Marathas pillaged Bardhaman, Medinipur and Orissa as far as Balasore. The areas around Candrakona, Dignagar, Khirpai, Nimgachi, and Palasi were particularly affected. The Katwah subdivision of Bardhaman district was ruined.[1] Note that the areas pillaged by the Marathas were mainly the raw silk and *gara* producing areas.[2] These were the items that showed a prolonged crisis in production and supply at Kasimbazar. This resulted in late deliveries, shortfalls in supply, problems associated with procurement, deterioration in quality and deviation from samples, as we saw. The English records are not alone in pointing out the dimension of the Maratha invasions. The French records from 1744 emphasise the dislocation in production and trade in western Bengal. Maratha attacks at Ganjam and Balasore were noted.[3] On January 3, 1746 Fournier wrote to Chandernagore that the Marathas had pillaged Kasimbazar.[4] On December 28, 1746 the news of the Maratha arrival near Kasimbazar provoked villagers and Muslim administrators to take shelter within the factories of the English, the Dutch and the French.[5] The FEIC entries emphasise this theme of invasion throughout the 40s for western Bengal.

The second external cause was the Afghan revolt in Bihar in 1747–48. Between February 1745 and November 1748 the Afghan insurrection against Alivardi's government caused much plunder and ruin in Bihar. Merchants and shroffs were looted of their effects. Shamsher Khan, the leader, attacked the DEIC at Fatwa, plundered cloth worth SR 65 000, hampered European trade, and plundered the EICs in the shape of a general tax. The Afghans captured Patna, the key to Bengal's trade with North India and beyond, for three months. Patna was plundered, and Alivardi's brother, Haji Ahmad, and his son (Alivardi's nephew) were killed.[6] Bengal's trade with the Gangetic plain came to a standstill.

Alivardi quelled the revolt in November 1748 but the Afghan revolt, much more than the Maratha invasions, was a challenge to the legitimacy of his rule. Between 1742 and 1748, then, Bengal was attacked both from the south west and the west. And the south east was not free from invasions as well; the FEIC letters from Jugdia reveal daily French apprehensions of Magh raids in 1750–51. Dhaka was attacked in 1748.[7] Thus trade was hampered in the east as well.

The money for the campaigns against the Afghans and the Marathas was raised by the nawab through three expedients. One was by raising the taxation of mulberry lands. We have seen before that the Bengal nawabs encouraged mulberry cultivation because such lands were taxed more. Murshid Quli Khan realized in 1706 that mulberry cultivation had to be promoted as mulberry lands were taxed at Rs. 3 per bigha while rice lands and land for pulses were taxed at Rs. 0.75 and 0.37 per bigha respectively.[8] The benefits accruing to the treasury from mulberry cultivation were immense. Revenue from silk production and trade became a cash cow to be milked by the state in the 1740s.

The second expedient was to raise money through the financiers and merchants. The Seths financed some of Alivardi's campaigns against the Marathas. More significantly, *dadni* merchants were asked to contribute to the cost: in 1744 Preet Katma, an EEIC merchant, was arrested and bought his release for SR 135 000 with a promise to pay another SR 300 000.

Nursing Das, Bally Katma and Keblaram Surma were also asked to pay up.[9] The third expedient was to raise money from the EICs, something that Alivardi did successfully through the 1740s.

All the three means of raising money ultimately caused a glitch in the circulation of finance in Bengal. Jagat Seth's house was robbed by the Marathas, rents on their way to the Murshidabad Treasury were taken by the Maratha bands, markets were looted, local merchants and companies had to pay protection tax to the state and the common people were forced to pay the same to Maratha freebooters. Credit therefore was in short supply. The Calcutta Council wrote as early as on February 3, 1743: 'no vend for silver at Calcutta though Morattoes withdrawn, Mint shut up'.[10]

Neither state nor merchant nor company could function under such circumstances. Moreover with increased taxation there was a consequent rise in production costs at a time when the English were attempting to keep prices at the 1730s level by increasing the dependence of the merchants on the English Company. This led to the bankruptcy of the merchants at both Kasimbazar and Jugdia.

In the wake of the financial (revenue) and commercial chaos after the English take-over of Bengal, Muhammad Reza Khan, the Naib-Subahdar of Bengal who had been installed in that post by the EEIC and entrusted with the economic management of post-Plassey Bengal, commented:[11]

> Formerly this country was the principal resort of foreign merchants who brought hither considerable sums to purchase its commodities. I am well informed that in the time of Aly Verdy Cawn the merchants of Akbarabad (Agra), Lahore, Multan, Gegerat (Gujarat), Ferkabad, Hyderabad and the port of Surat reckoning the Mahometans and Hindows only, exclusive of Europeans, purchased cloth and silks to the amount of Seventy Lacks of rupees, and from this source the Ryots were maintained, the native merchants enriched and the revenues supplied. Now every branch of foreign commerce is ruined. Men of credit and large capital are retired and the merchants who still retain a connection with these provinces scarcely purchase to the amount of Seven Lacks in the year. This sudden failure of the usual supplies of specie is already felt to such a degree that business is almost to a total stand. The revenues are extorted rather than collected and the country thereby subjected to a variety of evils destructive to good order and population.

Muhammad Reza Khan therefore drew a direct connection between the import of specie into a country and its health. Moreover, he emphasised the close connection between trade and the well being of the body politic. He commented:[12]

> the true spirit of trade is the mutual satisfaction of the buyer and seller. There are nevertheless . . . Gomastahs (who) under the sanction of that name carry on an *illegal* and oppressive trade which in its effect depopulate the country by causing general distress . . . (italics mine).

The solution was to throw trade open to all as had been previously the case in Bengal, Reza Khan felt. Then:[13]

> The merchants would then find an advantage as formerly, in importing specie and renewing the commerce . . . By these means (open and free trade) manufactures of all kinds will be increased (;) cultivation become the care as it is the interest of the Ryot . . . (who) will be enabled to live comfortably(;) a spirit of improvement would prevail throughout the country and the revenues would be collected with ease and without having recourse to rigorous methods.

But this was not done because after the grant of Diwani the Bengal sultans were not in a position to do anything so radical. Between 1766 and 1769 the EEIC used its newly acquired position to stop all trade except its own. The FEIC noted on January 10, 1766 that the Nawab (Naib Nazim) of Dhaka had assembled all the *dalals* of Dhaka and forbade them to work for Muslim and Armenian merchants.[14] Both overland and sea borne trade of the Asian and Armenian merchants was affected. EICs other than the English were similarly affected. On November 17, 1768 the FEIC noted:[15]

> Un Parawana de Moxoudabad avait prescript au Nabab de Dacca de faire verifier si a la loge francaise on n'aurait pas recu des armes et des munitions en grande quantite. Ce Nabab avait envoye plusiers de ces agents pour faire une perquisition. Dangereux avait voulu tout absolute s'opposer a une operation aussi deshonorante. . . .

Patna was in bad straits. On May 27, 1767 Dangereux reported to Chandernagore that the army of Mir Kasim had ravaged Patna and burnt all European factories. The EEIC lost SR 12 00 000.[16] On January 15, 1769 Carvalho of the FEIC wrote in from Patna that the local government there (Sitab Rai, see entry 2483 of February 6, 1769, 22 MI 41) had stopped all French commerce on orders of Murshidabad. Sepoys had been put on the French factory there. Further commerce in salt petre and textiles was not possible.[17] The situation was similar at Kasimbazar where the EEIC created difficulties in silk procurement.[18] On January 26, 1769 the FEIC noted that the Nawab at Murshidabad had outlawed French trade in Bengal and had forbidden all merchants to trade with them.[19] On January 31 it was noted that the weavers too were prohibited from working with the FEIC. They were stopped from delivering cloth to the factory despite having received advances. Saltpetre was held up on boats and exposed to the weather. There was a total breakdown of trade.[20] The situation was aggravated by the famine of 1769–1770. Entry No. 2507 of December 31, 1769 (22MI41) noted that at Patna at least sixty people were dying each day and that all the EICs were helping in the relief work by donating Rs. 10 per day to the poor. As late as on September 25, 1774, the effects of the famine were still visible.[21] A once flourishing economy had broken down irrevocably.

As for silk, the EEIC resumed the exclusive right to trade in silk after 1785. Although the Court of Directors of the EEIC pointed out to the Governor and Council at Fort William in 1785 that the price of Bengal silk was exceeding that of Italian silk,[22] it was generally recognised that the EEIC investment was procured at a 'considerable reduction of the former price'.[23] It was also pointed out that the reduction in prices was possible because of the cessation of the FEIC and DEIC investments.[24]

But silk and cotton were not the protagonists of this phase of our history. By the 1780s the old world was shattered, a new one was yet to emerge. And land revenue from Bengal powered the next phase of EEIC expansion in South Asia.

23

Conclusion

A specific development—the change in methods of procuring silk and cotton cloth—in two places, one each in west and south east Bengal: Kasimbazar and Jugdia – was used in this volume to illustrate the big themes of the 1750s in Bengal's commercial history. These are (1) the diversity of Bengal in this period between west and east, (2) the somewhat limited nature of the commercial and political order that grew up in Bengal under the Mughals, (3) the disruption of that order by the activities of the Europeans, and (4) the failure of the inland Indian merchants to maintain their role in both places. Both the *dadni* merchants at Kasimbazar and the *dalals* at Jugdia failed *before* the European take-over. They could not cope with the increase in demand by their methods of procurement without having to charge ever rising prices and delivering shoddy quality of goods. They could not influence the production sphere or maintain and continue production in traditional textile goods. Nor could they cope with the political turmoil of the Marathas or the rising taxation of the nawabs. But their failure was not merely due to external causes or internal factors. The failure lay in differing notions of economic governance. These differing notions ruled interactions between company and Indian merchants and decided the outcome in favour of the EEIC ultimately.

The EICs introduced a new notion of the economy into eighteenth century Bengal. There was, if I may put it so, a clash between two widely divergent notions of how to control and direct the economy. Trade and tribute were still intertwined for the Mughal. This was not the case for the EICs in Bengal in the eighteenth century which clearly differentiated between economic activity versus political expediency and allegiance. For the EICs, unlike the Mughals, the two were not similar.

The Europeans were therefore forced, in a sense, into getting more directly involved in Bengal for reasons of trade and for meeting the demands of the Court of Directors in London. This comes out clearly in case of Kasimbazar, and less so perhaps Jugdia. The EEIC could not take control at Jugdia as they had done at Kasimbazar. The fact that it could, and did so, at Kasimbazar-a place close to the political nerve centre of Bengal-shows the fragility of Mughal governance even in the heartland of empire. In the case of Jugdia, the EEIC went on to other places where it could impose economic control. The FEIC tried as well, but ultimately failed. The big growth in population and cultivation in the east, probably ensuring that prices and labour costs were lower there, made the 'far east' a very attractive proposition for both the EEIC and the FEIC. These points have been emphasized consistently in this volume.

But there are other, smaller, themes in the volume as well. One such is the making and unmaking of commercial places in Bengal due to the demands of merchant capital, yet another is the making of the last commercial frontier, be it land or sea based, in Bengal. Both were interlinked. The introduction of new market places, new production centres and new commercial routes went together. The reordering of the commercial space of the Bay world under EEIC aegis was evident by the 1790s, as we shall see from the affair of Lourant Severin.

Yet more sub themes-the social relations that permeated the economic world of the Mughal, and the social mobility visible in medieval Bengal-have been discussed in the sections on *bazaars* and on the caste affiliations of the *dadni* merchants of Kasimbazar earlier on in the volume. Economic and social mobility were not attendant upon British rule, as a whole generation of sociologists in independent India believed. Contrary to all historical experience, it was present throughout South Asian history. The fifth *varna*-the original dumping ground of the caste system-witnessed unprecedented mobility from the very start as more and more *jatis* were created (through job specialization) and absorbed within the four fold *varna* system.[1]

But most important of all the themes introduced here is the continuation of the Mughal notion of economic activity even after almost three centuries of exposure to the demands of European expansion and trade. Khan's testimony in post-1760s Bengal, two hundred and seventy years after the first Europeans set foot in South Asia, and soon after the take-over of internal commerce in Bengal, is illustrative of the fascination with the Mughal notion of the state as an organic microcosm of the greater cosmos in the eighteenth century South Asian official mind. Why the South Asian mind was so tardy in responding to new changes, despite the issues of attitude and technological stagnation[2] is something that only further research can bring about.

This volume makes no claims to do this, it only reiterates the point that the Mughal ideal of political economy was essentially medieval in nature. It was thus fundamentally opposed to the notions of state, merchants, companies, fiscal bodies, financial management and monetary realms that were in vogue in seventeenth century Europe. In Europe the economic determined the social, in Mughal South Asia the contrary was the case.

The Mughals did not combine mercantilist practices with protection to a particular group of merchants. For the Mughal all merchants were equal, and all were welcome as long as they brought specie into the country. Any kind of protectionism, apart from royal monopolies – which they regarded as one of the perquisites of office – and restrictions on free movement of Europeans in the interior, was anathema to the Mughal economic order.

The restriction on free movement hinged on the right to enter the mart towns and manufactories in the interior. The Mughal prohibition of foreign entry into the *arang* was inherently monopolistic in nature as it sought to control both the volume of goods for sale as well as protect the textile workers against price variations. The entry into the *arang* was a right that had been systematically denied to the EICs by the Mughals. After them the Bengal nawabs reserved this right only for Asian merchants.[3] We saw that the EEIC had pleaded that it might be allowed to enter the interior marts and *arangs* on par with Asian merchants from the time it sent the Surman Embassy to Farruksiyar to obtain trading privileges and customs rights in 1717. By denying the EICs entry into the *arangs* the Mughal economic system sought to keep supply always one rung lower than demand. The prohibition on entry was designed to safeguard both the indigenous merchant and the fiscal interests of the Mughal.

But the perceived equality of all merchants stopped once the EEIC entered the *arangs* from 1754. This right was affirmed when the English decided on a different method of procurement of textiles and thereby asserted their right to enter the *arangs* through the Agency System. The change in procurement, decided at and by Kasimbazar in the western part of the province, showed that the EEIC were making independent economic decisions even prior to 1757.[4] In 1755 Warren Hastings, then a subordinate factor at Kasimbazar, was despatched to the Kumarkhali *arangs* to explore new ways of procuring silk.[5] Palashi, or Plassey, was therefore also a culmination of earlier events, and not just the inaugurator of new, dependent, social relations in Bengal. It was the grant of Diwani after 1765 that definitively laid the new patterns of a dependent relationship once and for all time in Bengal. These patterns peaked by the time the famine took place in 1770.

The changeover in the system of procurement and the entry into the *arangs* also signified the ultimate commodification of goods, at least in eighteenth century Bengal. By the late 1730s, in western Bengal at least, although demand still outpaced production, there were indications that the productive sphere had become almost completely geared to the EIC demands. This was less easy to do in the east, as the market there was 'unregulated', as we saw. Therefore we can assume that Mughal regulation of the economic sphere worked for the Europeans and the non regulation of the market worked for Asian merchants and against EIC interests. Chronic shortages of liquid cash, the absence of financial houses at Jugdia and consequent difficulties of trade, the non availability of mint facilities, Jugdia's distance from Dhaka as well as from Calcutta and Chandernagore led both the English and French companies to decide on shifting out of Jugdia and establishing bases elsewhere in the neighbourhood. Infighting between various groups of *dalals* who tried to corner the trade in cottons, the deterioration in textile quality and the indebtedness of local merchants were other factors that decided the move away from Jugdia. The 'regulation' was attempted somewhat only from the 1750s in south eastern Bengal and we see that it was from this time that trade at Jugdia entered a phase of crisis. It seems that by the early 1750s, EEIC control over production was complete all over Bengal. There is deep significance in the often voiced FEIC complaint that many categories of textiles were no longer manufactured at Jugdia in the 1750s because the EEIC did not order them.[6]

When, at the turn of the eighteenth century, the East India Companies bought goods against ready money in western Bengal, the production sphere was more or less independent of EIC dictates. When, later in the same century, the East India Companies tied production through the mechanism of *dadan* (or cash advance), this independence was curbed to a great extent. When, by the 1750s, the EEIC entered the *arang*, production was made completely subordinate to its demand. The entry therefore represented the ultimate commodification of goods for trade in Bengal. The moment the EEIC entered into the *arangs* of Bengal it dealt a death blow to the mercantile – indeed the entire economic – organisation of the Mughals. And, as noted, this entry declared the supremacy of the EEIC over other East India companies.

The entry into the *arangs* was achieved with force. Between 1766 and 1769 the EEIC used its newly acquired position in Bengal to stop all trade except its own. The FEIC noted on January 10, 1766 that the Nawab (Naib Nazim) of Dhaka had assembled all the *dalals* of Dhaka and forbidden them to work for Muslim and Armenian merchants.[7] Both overland and sea borne trade of the Asian and Armenian merchants were affected. EICs other than the English were similarly affected. The handful of Bengali letters in the archives at Aix[8] testify to a similarly lawless situation at the *arangs* in western Bengal. These letters were written in January-February 1768. The letter of January 27, written by a FEIC *gomastha* named Gobindaram Ghosh, testified by a weaver named Jagannath Das, as well as a Mukundabikramdas Ghosh and a Ram Biswas (unidentified) from Amarpur in Burdwan district, mentions harassment by the EEIC *tagidigar* in furnishing goods for the FEIC at nearby Golyhata. This area produced cotton cloths, mainly *garas* and *dusutties.* Weavers' depositions showed that their cloths had been seized by the EEIC *peada.* These weavers were also weaving cloth for other companies; and the depositions from Amarpur mention clearly that the cloths for the Dutch and the French were destroyed by the EEIC *peada.* When the French took the weavers to task for not supplying the goods, they also started a process against Ghosh and the EEIC *tagidigar* at the same time. Hence the letters kept among the Chandernagore Council's papers now in the archives in Aix en Provence. A year later, on January 26, 1769, the FEIC noted that the Nawab at Murshidabad had outlawed French trade in Bengal and had forbidden all merchants to trade with them.[9] On January 31 it was noted that the weavers too were prohibited from working with the FEIC.[10] The Bengali letters in the French archives are significant therefore in that they hint at events that were to follow in Bengal.

The changeover in procurement meant that the *dadni* merchant and *dalal* as middleman were now bypassed. We have seen, in the case of Kasimbazar, how some weathered the transition and became servants of the EEIC there. The EEIC now bought goods directly. There were prohibitions on the weavers, and the *sirdars* or the heads of the silk winders, to work for any merchant organisation other than the English, or to supply textiles to them. The regulation of the availability and control over *patni,* or the raw filaments of silk, was the next step. *Patni* was confiscated from the houses of the weavers and winders. The Kasimbazar Council decided that no *patni* should be found at the houses of the *sirdars* after a stipulated number of days. The agreement was signed by the DEIC as well and the news was read out to the accompaniment of drum beats.[11] The Gujarati, Armenian and the French merchants did not sign. The EEIC went ahead anyway, the terms were announced and all *patni* was to be delivered up in five days on pain of confiscation.[12] In 1758 Marriott was appointed as *gomastha* to buy *patni* around Kasimbazar.[13]

How was such a radical change possible? It was possible because the inherent instability of a mercantile economy, made more so by way of its dependence on monoculture, cannot sustain itself for too long and it soon shows its vulnerability. In Bengal the boom lasted less than a century. In the eighteenth century demand from Europe fuelled textile production to an extraordinary degree in Bengal, so much so that production turned away from supplying the older Asian markets. This ultimately caused a shortfall in the regional and Asian markets. The silk trade became so profitable under the aegis of western capital and demand that (1) the domestic textile market became totally separated from this booming trade in textiles and finally languished for lack of demand and want of commodities specific to the domestic market and (2) the presence of European joint stock companies with their ever expanding volume of trade helped reorient production towards the west as before but to a different world system, one with its core in north west Europe.

These changes have been well documented by a generation of historians from N.K. Sinha onwards. Other than the change in procurement, the prohibition on the primary producers on supplying raw materials and goods to other merchants too has been documented.[14] We see that European companies, initially drawn into the system through the demands of capital and the driving need for profits, now profited from the situation. The EEIC was the winner. Once it was embedded in the system, the final positioning was accomplished through brute force whereby a once flourishing independent economy was made a subject one.

By the 1750s the EEIC's mercantile domination over Bengal was complete and it emerged as the foremost economic power in Bengal. All trade in textiles was more or less controlled by it. But by 1770 the world of famine in Bengal and Bihar put paid to this new system once and for all.

After 1770 radical readjustments had to be made by the EEIC not only in the matter of revenue, currency and trade within Bengal but also in its relations with other East India Companies. In the mercantile and fiscal spheres there was now an unabashed fight to establish new mart towns, levy customs duties, and deny others trading privileges; and the fights were particularly vicious in Bengal's south cast in the area that I term the borderlands of Bengal. This was the last commercial frontier of Bengal that had to be annexed to EEIC interests. And this was the area that saw the commercial map of Bengal completely overturned.

Between 1752 and 1770, therefore, the trade of the East India companies in Bengal entered a new phase. This period has received less attention than the East India trade in earlier decades, largely because the trends visible from the beginning of the eighteenth century had already climaxed by this time and the English East India Company's (EEIC) rule in Bengal had become a foregone conclusion. This volume has attempted, in a small way, to correct this imbalance.

Yet another change took place at this time: this was a vigorous attempt by all the companies from the 1750s to change the urban map of Bengal by establishing new mart towns. This endeavour, largely successful, meant that production and marketing were now delinked from hitherto established mart-towns with their own chains of procurement and distribution. While this trend was also visible in the western part of Bengal it was most marked in eastern Bengal. Bazaars and market towns established by the Mughals and the Bengal Nawabs[15] were now bypassed systematically and hitherto marginal towns were brought into the economic map through their transformation into production centres. New water routes were explored to bring commodities from these marginal areas to European headquarters such as Calcutta or Chandernagore. It is no accident that James Rennell's hydrographic survey of Bengal took place at this time.[16] Revenue assessment by the EEIC was also undertaken in these 'newly acquired' areas.[17] The mercantile map of Bengal was completely overturned. I call this phenomenon the 'making and remaking of commercial places in Bengal'.

This attempt to bypass the traditional mart towns of *Nawabi* Bengal and establish bases at other, smaller, mart towns such as at Kalindi, Lakhipur, Srirampur, Manohargunj and Chandola was necessary for the East India Companies. The companies wished to do away with all manner of 'interference' at the established mart towns. By establishing new markets they tried to draw in all trade at their new *bazaar* or mart towns. It should be noted that both Jean Baptiste Gentil and James Rennell mark Kalindi, Lakhipur, Srirampur and Manohargunj on their maps. I have not been able to locate Chandola on any map but we know that as early as in 1768 the FEIC had toyed with the idea of Chandola when Nicolas de Forency was sent to Jugdia. For some reason the move to Manohargunj was dropped and an alternative – Chandola – was suggested on October 20, 1768. The FEIC noted that it was to be a subordinate factory, two day's route from Jugdia.[18] It was bought by the FEIC in 1785. Bedier wrote in 1838 that:[19]

> en 1785, (que) M.Joseph Dayot fut envoye a Jougdya pour y faire l'acquisition d'un nouveau terrain. Le territoire de Chandella . . . fut achete par Mr.Joseph Dayot. Le contrat de ce terrain ne fut regularise qu'en 1790 par les soins de M.Gilliot, chef de la loge de Jougdya, qui obtint un *patta* original au nom du Roi de France, a la charge d'une redevance de 558 f.9 et 1626 f. de salamy. Le contrat de ce terrain se trouve au controle de Chandernagor.
>
> (In 1785 Mr. Joseph Dayot was sent to Jugdia to buy new territory. Chandella was bought by Mr. Joseph Dayot. The contract for this was regularized only in 1790 by Mr. Gilliot, chief of Jugdia, who managed to obtain a *patta* in the name of the King of France, by paying 558 FF and 1626 FF of tribute. This contract is under Chandernagore-*my translation*).

It seems therefore, from the passage quoted here, that the shift to Chandola had not been effected as late as in 1790.

What were the implications of dropping the Kalindi and Manohargunj shifts? No records have come to light regarding this but we can assume that entrenched interests at some of these places opposed the shift at courts at both Dhaka and Murshidabad. Additional evidence comes to us from cartography and allied sources. We see that only Kalindi and Manohargunj (places that were initially considered by the EEIC and the FEIC) continued to be marked on maps in the nineteenth century; this supports our view that these towns had survived company onslaughts because they were established mart towns and not ephemeral townships like Lakhipur and Chandola that could not survive into the nineteenth century.

In the 1760s a new trend emerged; the EEIC now used its newly acquired power to stop, or at least impede, the trade of the other European companies in Bengal. It stopped other East India Companies from establishing smaller subsidiary bases at secondary mart towns even as it moved on to establish bases at similar market towns for itself. This latter process obviously threatened, in many cases, the continued existence of many small towns in Bengal. The result was a complete reordering of our urban map at the end of the eighteenth century. I have no doubts that the process continued into the nineteenth and twentieth centuries as well, but my researches stop short of this era.

At the same time the EEIC attempted, in the marginal areas, to establish and administer tolls, and deny customs rights to other companies. The EEIC was now entering this last frontier in a big way, stopping trade, attacking FEIC personnel and denying them customs rights.[20] This was easy as *nawabi* authority did not always extend to the far east of Bengal. There are ample testimonies to this trend in the French and English documents. Overshadowing these themes is, of course, the unabashed emergence of two trends that mark the history of the eighteenth century in Bengal: the weakness of local mercantile organisation and the inefficacy of the political authorities to combat growing European influence in the economic realm. None could face up to the challenge to local political authority. We read that the Nawab at Murshidabad, and the Chhota Nawab at Dhaka were used by the EEIC to prohibit trade of the other European nations. The result was a complete rewriting of the economic map of the Mughal by the 1760s.

This was also the period when FEIC trade suffered in western Bengal due to a lack of funds. As per the Sykes-Chevalier agreement,[21] Sykes gave the FEIC SR 10 000 on July 18, 1768 and an additional SR 100 000 on August 18.[22] On January 26, 1769, the FEIC noted that the Nawab at Murshidabad had outlawed French trade in Bengal and had forbidden all merchants from trading with them.[23] On January 31 it was noted that the weavers too were prohibited from working with the FEIC. They were stopped from delivering cloth to the factory despite having received advances. Saltpetre was held up on boats and exposed to the weather. There was a total breakdown of trade.[24] The situation was aggravated by the famine of 1769–1770. On August 22, 1771 the Chandernagore Council wrote to the Pondichery Council that the commercial situation was so bad in Bengal that it was impossible to find credit.[25] As late as on September 25, 1774, the effects of the famine were still visible.[26]

If Jugdia was the last commercial frontier on land, the expanding maritime world of the Bay offered the last maritime frontier for trading, privateering, piracy and smuggling. Historically it was the FEIC, far more than the EEIC, that had concentrated on this area, as we have seen. Chevalier's efforts, in the 1750s, at opening up a Franco-Assam trade was essentially a continuation of Dupleix's dream of the 1730s. This envisaged the creation of a huge Bay of Bengal trade zone centreing on Chattagram and connecting Arakan, Ava and Pegu through the Brahmaputra, the Meghna and the Bay.[27] Dupleix had dreamed of a great commercial complex, centreing on Chattagram and stretching from Chandernagore in the west to Arakan, Pegu, and Ava in the east. The transport network for this grand project envisaged a melange of existing river routes, coastal sailings as well as the utilisation of the grand Brahmaputra-Meghna water route.

Between 1750 and 1751, at the time the Jugdia-Chandernagore letters were written, Dupleix still considered an alliance with Pegu against Burma vital to reinforce the FEIC presence at Syriam and thereby regain the FEIC's lost position in the eastern seas.[28] Chevalier partook of the same vision as Dupleix during these same years but he took it even further. In Chevalier's vision Chattagram was to be at the centre of a great maritime and strategic bloc linking the eighteenth century kingdoms of Bengal, Assam, Tripura, Ava, Arakan, Pegu, Mergui, Ile de Roy (situated off the coast of Mergui. It was ceded to the French in Louis XIV's time), the Andaman and Nicobar islands and southern China.[29]

We see therefore that while the original French vision stopped at Arakan, Ava and Pegu, the renewed vision extended it to China. China was the principal object of Chevalier's missions between 1752 and 1765 and he tried twice to go there (once from Katha and once from Tibet) but he failed. Access to China through Tibet and Katha was known as the Southern Silk Route that connected Yunnan and Szechwan with the Bay of Bengal ports. 'Catta' (Katha) in Burma on the western bank of the Irrawady was the key to

Chevalier's dream.[30] This was because Katha granted an easy access to China through river routes: it was bounded on the north by Szechwan province and on the south by Yunnan, China's gateway to South Asia. It is therefore no accident that Anquetil Duperron mapped the northern course of the Ganga and the Ghagra at this time while seeking a route from north Bengal into China.[31] We should note that this is the same vision that is driving the move for Bengal-South China cooperation in the twenty first century, now dubbed as the Kunming initiative.

But this cartography was land based. But now the French were exploring alternative routes to hang onto the Bay world. In 1777 Gregoire Lafitte de Brassier was sent out from Pondichery on a cartographic trip in the Bay of Bengal covering Pegu, Sumatra and Nicobar.[32] In other words, in the last commercial *maritime* frontier, the FEIC were doing precisely what the EEIC were doing on land with Rennell. The difference lay in the vision. For the English the last frontier lay on land, while for the French this was an expanding maritime space. The EEIC were obsessed with borders that denoted their zone of control; the French dreamt of borders that could be constantly expanded as ever newer spaces were brought under their control. Their notions of frontier were fundamentally different.

This French notion of the commercial frontier continued in later years. Cordier noted in 1823[33] that while Chattagram did not produce any articles of trade by itself, its proximity to the kingdoms of Ava, Arakan and Pegu, as well as its deep water port, provided great opportunities for trade in eastern India. Chattagram received wood for building works from Pegu and Arakan and communicated directly by sea with Jugdia, Srirampur, Dhaka, Sylhet and Goalpara; these factors contributed to the richness of the area, and explained the French fascination with the area as late as in the nineteenth century. Now Chattagram lies within Bangladesh, a country with its own notions of its strengths and failures, and current geopolitical considerations make it, willy nilly, a major player in the world of the Bay.

This was an area where the French were particularly active throughout the eighteenth century, as private individuals, as company traders, private traders or as pirates. On January 11, 1766 the FEIC noted that there were reports of trouble in the Chattagram area and that the EEIC were just about managing to contain by force.[34] A day earlier the Chhota Nawab (Naib Nazim) had assembled all the *dalals* of Dhaka and forbidden them to work for the Muslim and Armenian merchants.[35] Note that these were big merchants and prominent shipowners, whose trade could easily give competition to the EEIC. Now the EEIC was using its newly acquired power to persuade the *nizamat* to marginalise other merchants. This was clearly illegal as long as the *nizamat* was in power, however notionally. On January 26, 1769 the FEIC noted that the Nawab at Murshidabad had outlawed French trade in Bengal and had forbidden all merchants to trade with them.[36] But the Nawab's edicts did not hold for much in this area. Consequently, the whole area had become lawless.

And the lawlessness extended beyond the confines of south eastern Bengal. On February 25, 1768 the FEIC at Chandernagore reported that four Frenchmen had been released from Pegu. One of them had stayed back in Ava as trader and renegade.[37]

As late as in 1793 'l'affaire Abdullah', as entered in the French records, showed that the FEIC was still active in this maritime area. On February 2, 1793 a so called 'Malay' pirate attacked a French ship sailing the Bengal-Bhimlipattinam-Pedir route. On closer inspection the 'Malay' who ran amok (!) with his knife and musket on the crewmen was deemed to be no other than a Frenchman named Lourant Severin who had part Malay parentage and who had settled in the area. Lourant Severin was part corsair, part brigand, part pirate and part trader. We know that in the pre modern age identities frequently coalesced in this part of the world as Europeans expanded the theatre of their activities. Lourant Severin thereby carried forward a long and distinguished tradition of buccaneering in the eastern seas, much as the Portuguese had done before him.

But this cosmopolitan world of the Bay too was coming to an end. Privateering was no longer permitted as the EEIC sought to regulate all sea traffic in the region. As the ship contained a motley crew consisting of English, French and Portuguese sailors, the EEIC put pressure on the Pondichery Council of the FEIC to institute proceedings against Lourant Severin. On May 8, 1793 a *process verbaux* started at Pondichery[38] whereby this style of functioning was condemned. A 'permanent settlement' of the maritime space was thereby effected in 1793 even as the EEIC introduced land reforms in the shape of the Permanent Settlement of Bengal in the same year.

This brings me to the last sub theme of the volume – the importance of the eastern Indian Ocean in history. A large part of the success of the EICs was effected in *this* maritime space, contrary to the emphasis on the western Indian Ocean in history. The statement of Auguste Toussaint, a pioneer in Indian Ocean studies, is symptomatic of the overemphasis on the western Indian Ocean:[39]

> La rive orientale du golfe du Bengale, de Chittagong jusqu'a l'extremite de la peninsule malaise, n'offrait, du point de vue commercial, rien de

> comparable aux productions de la cote de Coromnadel ou a celles du Bengale, ni 'denrees coloniales' d'interet majeur, ni articles 'nobles'.

Towards the end of his life in 1992, at one of the very last public lectures that he gave, Ashin Dasgupta stressed the importance of the eastern Indian Ocean: 'There has been an unnecessary crowding of the western Indian Ocean, and the east has been neglected.'[40]

As European companies widened their capital base and gained economic power, they challenged the Mughal routes through the cost advantages of the Cape route. This was evident from the fifteenth century when the *Estado da India* rooted itself in South Asia. They could also take over successfully the older Ilyas Shahi commercial networks in the eastern Indian Ocean, once the Chinese and then the Portuguese were removed from this area. More important, the DEIC and the EEIC extended this network up to Japan, something that had not been tried previously. The FEIC concentrated on Siam, and this explains their obsession with the immediate world of the Bay. By the eighteenth century an interdependent trading network emanating from Europe and encompassing the sea lanes and commercial networks from east Africa to Japan spelt the end for older routes and commodities.

1757 and 1765 were landmark years in Bengal for the English East India Company in its long journey from an insecure commercial beginning to triumphant economic control by mid century. The 1740s and the 1750s saw the entry of the English East India Company into the villages of the interior; into the *arangs* where it could undertake its investment without fear of harassment either by local political authorities or by recalcitrant merchants. This entry into the *arang* marked the final chapter in the initial commercial undertakings of the English East India Company in South Asia. Thus Peter Marshall could write, and with justification, that 'By the end of the eighteenth century Britain was a world power on a scale that none of her European rivals could match. Not only did she rule a great empire . . . Britain's overseas trade had developed a strongly global orientation . . . (and) Britain was at the centre of intercontinental movements of people . . .'[41]. The roots of this global hegemony, in which scheme South Asia was reduced to a minor player, go back to the events described here.

A Note on the Archival Sources Used

The Factory Records Series at London are the G series, numbered according to the factory (for example, number 15 for Dhaka and 23 for Kasimbazar) and then divided into volumes. For Kasimbazar I consulted volumes 1 to 16; this number may have been changed as more and more archives turn to microfilms. The factory records contain entries much like a diary and are of immense value in reconstructing the micro history of a particular region, as all those who have worked with these series know.

The Home Miscellaneous Series are exactly that. They are a miscellaneous collection of papers and documents and some of the Bengal Public Consultations are contained therein, as is Taylor's report from Dacca, which was later printed as *A Descriptive and Historical Account of the Cotton Manufactures of Dacca.*

The C2 series at Paris (now at Aix) are similar to the HMS in that they contain reports, documents and letters which are invaluable in helping us reconstruct a macro-picture of the East India trade. The AE series is similar. By contrast, the microfilmed MIOM series at Aix are more like the EEIC factory records. Each MIOM contains upwards of some 600 entries pertaining to a particular region. I saw the Chandernagore MIOMs; there are similar MIOMs for Mahe, Karikal and of course Pondichery.

The Romain Rolland Library at Pondichery contains FEIC correspondence between Pondichery and other factories. Some of these are printed, but a large majority is as yet unprinted and unaccessed. Yet another small archive is the Institut Historique at Pondichery. Located in a former house of Dupleix, it contains some old papers and records on eighteenth century Pondichery-Chandernagore trade.

Notes

INTRODUCTION

1. Consultations of February 7, 1745 and December 1, 1746. K.F.R., I.O.L.R.
2. Risley, H.H., 1891, 1981 Reprint, *The Tribes and Castes of Bengal*, 2 vols. Calcutta, Firma Mukhopadhaya, V.II: Ethnographic Glossary: 301–3. Reed is *shana*, reed frame is *dafti* and spinning wheel is *charkha*. See p. 303.
3. Habib, I. 1982, '*Non Agricultural Production and Urban Economy*' in *The Cambridge Economic History of India*, V.I (eds.), Tapan Raychaudhuri and Irfan Habib, CUP, Orient Longman, 1982: 86.
4. Raychaudhuri, Tapan, 1982, '*Inland Trade*' in ibid.: 344–45.
5. Datta, K.K., 1963, *Alivardi and His Times*, Calcutta, The World Press Private Limited: 155.
6. See Chapter 2 '*The East India Company's 'Investment' Policy in Bengal*' in N.K. Sinha, 1965, *An Economic History of Bengal, V.1 From Plassey to the Permanent Settlement*, Calcutta, Firma K.L. Mukhopdhyay: 6–34.
7. We see therefore a changeover from trading conditions in this region in the late seventeenth century when middlemen brought goods from the interior for sale to Europeans at the emporia market at Hugli. See Manrique *The Travels of Fray Sebastian Manrique 1629–1643*, Luard, C.E. (Tr). 2 vols. London, Hakluyt Society 1926–27 (1630s and 1640s) and Challes, Robert, *Journal d'un Voyage Fait aux Indes Orientales*, 2 vols. Mercure de France, MCMLXXXIII. (1690–91). See Chaudhuri, Sushil, 1975, *Trade and Commercial Organisation in Bengal, 1650–1720*. Calcutta: Firma KLM. Luillier, who travelled in Bengal at the turn of the eighteenth century tells us that this earlier system was still in vogue at the beginning of the eighteenth century and that Hugli was the emporia market *par excellence*. See his 3 editions, *Voyage du Sieur Luillier aux Grandes Indes avec une Instruction Pour le Commerce des Indes Orientales*, Paris, Claude Cellier, MC CC V, Luillier, *Voyage du Sieur Luillier aux Indes Orientales Avec une instruction pour le commerce des Indes Orientales*, 1705, Paris, Claude Cellier, and Luillier, *Voyages du Sieur Luillier dans des Grandes Indes Orientales*, 1726, Rotterdam.
8. See later for a complete list of the Dhaka *arangs*. See Anisuzzaman, M., 1981, *Factory Correspondence and Other Bengali Documents*, London, I.O.L.R. Publications.
9. See Om Prakash, 1988 edition, *The Dutch East India Company and the Economy of Bengal 1630–1720*, Delhi, OUP for the different categories involved in the procurement of textiles: 102–7. Originally published in 1985.
10. From the 1680s Bengal emerged as the major source of raw silk for the EICs. See

Om Prakash, 1985, 1988, *The Dutch East India Company and the Economy of Bengal 1630–1720*, Delhi, OUP: 23.

11. Anisuzzaman, M., 1981, *Factory Correspondence and Other Bengali Documents*, London, I.O.L.R.
12. Manufacturing centre around which mart towns grew up. In some cases, if an *arang* was situated strategically, the *arang* evolved into a market town.
13. Chapter 2 '*The East India Company's 'Investment' Policy in Bengal*' in N.K. Sinha, 1965, *An Economic History of Bengal, V.1 From Plassey to the Permanent Settlement*, Calcutta, Firma K.L. Mukhopdhyay: 6–34.
14. *The Trading World of Asia and the English East India Company 1660–1760*, Cambridge, 1978.
15. It has been argued by Sushil Chaudhury that the idea of 'crisis' comes from an excessive dependence on Bengali and Persian sources. See Chaudhury, Sushil, 2002, '*Was There a Crisis in Mid-Eighteenth Century Bengal?*' in Barnett, R. (ed.) 2002, *Rethinking Early Modern India*, New Delhi, Manohar: 129–52.
16. K.F.R. March (undated) 1752, September 22, 1755, November 13, 1756.
17. Separate groups for the EEIC and the FEIC. 'Rotonne Monique' was common to both. See later.
18. Sinha, N.K., 1965 op. cit. Datta, K.K., 1963 op. cit.
19. See K.F.R. G Series, IOLR, London.
20. Taylor, J., 1851, *A Descriptive and Historical Account of the Cotton Manufactures of Dacca*, London and Taylor, James, 1840, *A Sketch of the Topography and Statistics of Dacca, Calcutta.* See also Mukherjee, Rila, 1990–91, '*The French East India Company's Trade in East Bengal from 1750–1753: A Look at the Chandernagor-Jugdia Letters*', *The Indian Historical Review*, 17, nos. 1–2, 1990–91.
21. Om Prakash, 2002, '*Trade and Politics in Eighteenth century Bengal*' in Alavi, Seema (ed.), 2002, *The Eighteenth Century in India*, New Delhi, OUP. See later. Also Mukherjee, Rila, 1990–91 op. cit.
22. See later.
23. As in the case of Lakhipur as shown later.
24. Quoted in Om Prakash 1988: 104–5.
25. K.F.R., February 28, 1744.
26. See Duarte Barbosa, *The Book of Duarte Barbosa*, Tr. M.L. Dames, London, Hakluyt Society, Varthema, Ludovico, *The Itinerary of*. . . (Tr. R.C. Temple), London, Hakluyt, 1928 and Mukherjee, Rila, *Strange Riches: Bengal in the Mercantile Map of South Asia* (forthcoming from Cambridge/FoundationBooks).
27. Sanyal, Hitesranjan, 1981, *Social Mobilty in Bengal*, Calcutta, Papyrus, indicates that internal trade in Bengal in the sixteenth and seventeenth centuries was in the hands of Gujaratis, many of whom had settled in Bengal. Similarly the case studies of Khemchand and Chintaman Shah by Chaudhuri, Sushil, 1975, *Trade and Commercial Organisation in Bengal, 1650–1720*. Calcutta: Firma KLM, indicate that overseas trade from Hugli was also monopolized by Gujarati merchants.
28. See Tarafdar, M.R. 1965, *Husain Shahi Bengal 1494–1538 AD: A Socio-Political Study*, Dacca: 117.
29. Portuguese 'informal rule' in Bengal was confined mainly to the deltaic region of Samatata and Harikela; nevertheless this 'rule' is significant in that many of the

smaller ports which traded with other ports across the Bay were located in this area. One such was Sandwip at the mouth of the Meghna. This island was placed under the control of the Portuguese Carvalho by Kedar Rai of Sripur in 1602. During Shah Jahan's time Sandwip was well populated by the Portuguese (see Abdul Hamid Lahori's *PadshahNama* in Elliot and Dowson's *History of India as Told by Its Own Historians*, Allahabad, 1969, Reprint, V.7). Similarly Sripur was under Portuguese control at the end of the sixteenth century (*Narrative of Ralph Fitch 1583–91* in William Foster (ed.) *Early Travels in India 1583–1619*, London, 1921, Reprint, New Delhi, 1968). For more on Portuguese adventurers in the Bay see Winius, George, 1983, '*The "Shadow Empire" of Goa in the Bay of Bengal*', *Itinerario*, v.vii (2): 83–101.

30. Around 1540 Arakanese expansion under Minbin (1531–53) extended as far as Chattagram, Dhaka and the Sundarbans. See Subrahmanyam, Sanjay, 1990, *Improvising Empire: Portuguese Trade and Settlement in the Bay of Bengal 1500–1700*, New Delhi, OUP: 120 and Mukherjee, Rila, *Strange Riches etc* op. cit.
31. See Mukherjee, Rila, *Strange Riches* op. cit.
32. See also ibid.
33. Tarafdar, M.R., 1986, *The Bengali Muslims in the Pre Colonial Period: Problems of Conversion, Class Formation and Cultural Evolution*, 92–110, in Marc Gaborieau (ed.), *Islam et Societe en Asie du Sud*, Paris, *Purusartha*, Vol. 9; Sanyal, Hiteshranjan, 1981 op. cit.
34. Risley, H.H., 1891, 1981, Reprint, *The Tribes and Castes of Bengal: Ethnographic Glossary*, Calcutta, Firma Mukhopadhyay, 2 vols. V.II: 298–9, 308.
35. Ibid. V.II: 309.
36. Ibid. V.II: 81.
37. Pearson, M.N., 1987, *The Portuguese in India, New Cambridge History of India*, 1.1, Cambridge, University Press, Indian edition, Orient Longman.
38. See Mukherjee, Rila, *Strange Riches* op. cit.
39. Subrahmanyam, S. 1990, *Improvising Empire: Portuguese Trade and Settlement in the Bay of Bengal, 1500–1700*. Delhi, Oxford Press: 113.
40. Dermigny, Louis, 1964, *La Chine et l'Occident: Le Commerce a Canton au XVIIIeme siecle, 1719–1833*, 3 vols., Paris, S.E.V.P.E.N. see Tome 1: 92–95.
41. Das Gupta, Ashin, 1987, '*Introduction II: The Story*' in A. Das Gupta and M.N. Pearson (eds.) *India and the Indian Ocean 1500–1800*, Calcutta, OUP: 25–45. See p. 36. See also *Strange Riches* op. cit.
42. John Marshall. See Shafaat Ahmad, 1927, (ed.), *John Marshall in India, Notes and Observations in Bengal 1668–1672*, London, Oxford University Press.
43. Father Georgi in Bernouilli's *L'Inde*. See Bernouilli, 1788, *L'Inde: Description Hisrorique et Geographique de l'Inde qui presente en trios volumes et enrichis de 64 cartes*, 3 vols. Berlin. Contains accounts of Tieffanthaler, Rennell, Father Georgi and Anquetil-Duperron among others. I La Geographie de l"Indoustan par le Pere Joseph Tieffanthaler, II Des Recherches Historiques et Chronologiques sur l'Inde et la description du Cours du Gange et du Gagra avec une tres grande carte par M. Anquetil Duperron, III. La Carte Generale de l'Inde, Celle du Cours du Brahmapoutre, et de la navigation interieure du Bengale, avec des Memoires Relatifs a ces cartes, par M. Jacques Rennell.

44. Federbe, Louis Laurent de, Comte de Modave, *Le Voyage en Inde de...etc. 1773–1776. Nouveaux Memoires sur l'Etat actuel du Bengale et de l''indoustan* (tr. and ed), Jean Deloche, 1971, Paris, Ecole Francaise d'Extreme Orient.
45. Ghulam Hussein Salim, *Riyas-us-Salatin,* Tr. Maulavi Abdus, 1902, Calcutta, Asiatic Society.
46. Hamilton, Walter, 1828, *East India Gazeteer*, 2 vols., London.
47. Report of Hughes and Parker 1620–25 in R.C. Temple (ed.), 1911, *The Diaries of Streynsham Master 1675–1680 And Other Contemporary Papers Relating Thereto,* London, John Murray, Indian Records Series, 2 Vols.
48. Bouchon, Genevieve and Thomaz, Luis Filipe, 1998, *Voyage dans les Deltas du Gange et l'Irraouaddy,* 1521, Fondation Calouste Gulbenkian, Paris.
49. See Mukherjee, Rila, *Strange Riches: Bengal in the Mercantile Map of South Asia* (forthcoming Cambridge/Foundation) for the historical evolution of the two Bengals.
50. Ibn Batuta, *Voyages,* 3 vols., (Tr). Defremery, E.C., Sanguinetty, B.R., 1982, Paris, Maspero and Edward Terry, *Voyage to East India,* London, T. Wilkes, MDCC LXXVIII. See too Baffins map of Bengal (1619) which marks Purb and Patan clearly.
51. For more divisions within Bengal see Paul, Pramode Lal, 1939, *The Early History of Bengal,* Calcutta, Indian Research Institute and Morrison, Barrie M., 1970, *Political Centers and Cultural Regions in Early Bengal,* The Association for Asian Studies, University of Arizona Press.
52. See Mukherjee, Rila, *Strange Riches* op. cit.
53. Lombard, Denys, 1990, *Le Carrefour Javanais: Essai d'histoire Globale,* V.III, *L'Heritage des Royaumes Concentriques*, Paris, Editions E.H.E.S.S: 15–54. See Mukherjee, Rila, 2004, '*A Rice Culture of Divine Right in a Celestially Ordered Zone: A Case Study of South Asian and South East Ideologies and Hegemonies from c. 2000 BC to c. 1800 AD with Specific Reference to Bengal', Campus Social,* Lisbon. Editor Teotonio de Sousa.
54. Ibid.
55. Thapar, Romila, 1975, *Time as a Metaphor for History,* Calcutta, K.P. Bagchi: pp. 31–33; Lombard, Denys 1990 III: 55–56; Coedes, George, 1964, *Les Etats Hindouises d'Indochine et d'Indonesie*, Paris, Boccard: 51–53.
56. See Deyell, John, 1983, '*The China Connection: Problems of Silver Supply in Medieval Bengal'* in J.F. Richards (ed.), *Precious Metals in the Later Medieval and Early Modern Worlds,* Durham, Carolina Academic Press: 207–227. Reprinted in Subrahmanyam Sanjay (ed.), 1994, *Money and the Market in India 1100–1700,* Delhi, OUP: 112–36.
57. See Ali, Muhammad Mohar, 1985, *History of the Muslims of Bengal,* 2 vols., Riyadh, Imam Muhammad Ibn Sa'ud Islamic University. V.1 B: 929–930.
58. See *Strange Riches* op. cit. Ray, Anirudda, 1997, '*Middle Bengali Literature: A Source for the Study of Bengal in the Age of Akbar'* in Habib, Irfan, *Akbar and His India,* New Delhi, OUP: 229–233 traces urbanization and trade for this neglected period of Bengal's history.
59. Ali, Muhammad Mohar, 1985 V.1 B: 956.
60. Gill, Sandrine, 1999, '*Mahasthangarh: A Riverine port in Ancient Bengal'*, in Himanshu Prabha Ray (ed.), *Archaeology of Seafaring: The Indian Ocean in the Ancient Period,* New Delhi, Pragati Publications: 154–172. See also Salles, Jean Francois, Boussac,

Marie Francoise, Breuil, Jean Yves, 2000, '*Mahasthangarh (Bangladesh) and the Ganges Valley in the Mauryan Period'* in Sengupta, Gautam and Panja, Sheena (eds.), *Archaeology of Eastern India: New Perspectives,* Calcutta, Centre for Archaeological Studies and Training, Eastern India: 527–50.

61. Srichandra's capital was Vikrampur (all four of the copper plate grants during his reign were issued from there), he ruled over samatata and harikela (possibly he ruled the whole of east Bengal and the coastal regions of south Bengal) and it is very likely that he ruled a portion of north Bengal as well, as two of the inscriptions (II and IV) mention that the lands granted were situated in Pundravardhana bhukti. But the last may not be true for Pundravardhana bhukti became an expanding territorial and sacred concept at this time. Other than at Vikrampur, Srichandra's other capital was near Comilla, at Pattikera.
62. Eaton, Richard, 1993, *The Rise of Islam and the Bengal Frontier 1204–1760,* California, Berkeley and Los Angeles.
63. Sun quoted in Frank, A.G., 1998, *ReOrient: Global Economy in the Asian Age,* University of California Press and Sage/Vistaar: 102.
64. Rila Mukherjee for Bengal, Robert Wicks for Pagan, Anthony Reid for South East Asia and Robert Marks and Bin Wong for south China in Mukherjee, Rila, *Strange Riches* op. cit.
65. Bagchi, P.C., 1945, *'Political Relations Between Bengal and China in the Pathan Period', Visva Bharati Annals,* V. 1, Cheena Bhavan.
66. Ibn Batuta, *Voyages,* 3 vols, (Tr). Defremery, E.C., Sanguinetty, B.R., 1982, Paris, Maspero. See the section on Bengal.
67. Bernier, Francois, *Travels in the Mogul Empire,* 1656–1668, revised Vincent A. Smith, Reprint, Delhi, Munshiram Manoharlal, 1992: 442.
68. Ray, Indrani, '*Journey to Cassimbazar and Murshidabad: Observations of a French Visitor to Bengal in 1743'* in Subramanian, L. (ed.), 1999, *The French East India Company and the Trade of the Indian Ocean: A Collection of Essays by Indrani Ray.* Calcutta, Centre for Studies in Social Sciences and Delhi, Munshiram Manoharlal: 144–76. See p. 162.
69. Taylor, James, 1840, *A Sketch of the Topography and Statistics of Dacca,* Calcutta.
70. In Om Prakash 1985, 1988: 25.
71. Fitch, Ralph, *Narrative of Ralph Fitch 1583–91* in William Foster (ed), *Early Travels in India 1583–1619,* London, 1921, Reprint, New Delhi, 1968.
72. Especially Bowrey, Thomas, *A Geographical account of the Countries Around the Bay of Bengal 1669–1679,* R.C. Temple (ed.), Cambridge, Hakluyt Society, M D CCCCV: 212. See also Manrique and de Gennes de la Chanceliere op. cit. For Tieffanthaler see Bernouilli, 1788, *L'Inde: Description Hisrorique et Geographique de l'Inde qui presente en trios volumes et enrichis de 64 cartes,* 3 vols. Berlin. Contains accounts of Tieffanthaler, Rennell, Father Georgi and Anquetil-Duperron among others. I La Geographie de l"Indoustan par le Pere Joseph Tieffanthaler, II Des Recherches Historiques et Chronologiques sur l'Inde et la description du Cours du Gange et du Gagra avec une tres grande carte par M. Anquetil Duperron, III. La Carte Generale de l'Inde, Celle du Cours du Brahmapoutre, et de la navigation interieure du Bengale, avec des Memoires Relatifs a ces Cartes, par M. Jacques Rennell.
73. See later.

74. Karim, Abdul, 1964, *Dacca The Mughal Capital*, Dacca, Asiatic Society of Pakistan: 112–113.
75. As in Bihar. See Muzaffar Alam's '*Aspects of Agrarian Uprisings in North India in the early Early Eighteenth Century*' reprinted in Alavi, Seema, 2002, *The Eighteenth Century in India,* New Delhi, OUP: 84–112.
76. From Karim, Abdul, 1964, *Dacca The Mughal Capital*, Dacca, Asiatic Society of Pakistan: 111–13.
77. Ibid: 111–13.
78. From Sen, Sudipta, 1998, *Empire of Free Trade, The East India Company and the Making of the Colonial Marketplace*, Philadelphia, University of Pennsylvania Press: 44.
79. The K.F.R. data contain various interdictions on European ships from carrying more grain than was strictly necessary to feed their crew. A permit stating the number of persons on each voyage had to be obtained and an official came aboard to re check prior to the ships' departure. A similar form of customs clearance had to be gone through at Hugli and at various inland ports when ships came into Bengal. The Pachotra Daroga-Hukum Beg-clashed often with the EEIC on the matter of quotas and permits (see the section on the merchants' links with court). However the increasing English control of the inland waterways in Bengal from the 1730s led to clashes between company and *nawabi* forces and soon made Nawabi attempts to regulate the internal economy of Bengal futile.
80. Master, Streynsham, *Diaries* op. cit. V.1: 37.
81. Master V.1: 99.
82. Master V.1: 44–47.
83. Bowrey: 180.
84. Bowrey, op. cit: 179.
85. Ibid.: 179–180.
86. Om Prakash 1988: Table 2.2. Pp. 30–31. Of the 50 Bengal merchants engaged in coastal and intra Asian trade between 1670 and 1718, 16 were state officials. 15 were Muslim, and I was Hindu. There were no Armenians in this category although 1 such was found among the 34 ordinary merchants from Bengal.
87. Ray, Indrani, '*India in Asian Trade in the 1730s: A Discussion by a French Trader*' in L. Subramanian (ed.), 1999 op. cit.: 177–202. See pp. 188–91.
88. Om Prakash 1988: 29. He calculates this on the basis of the Dutch shipping lists.
89. Om Prakash, 1988: 99.
90. It was frequently called the Kasimbazar river by Europeans in the eighteenth century.
91. Modave op. cit.
92. Hamilton, Walter op. cit. Also see *The Imperial Gazeteer*, 1908, vol. XI. See Hamilton, Alexander, 1727, *A New Account of the East Indies 1688–1723,* 2 vols. Edinburgh. See Bowrey op. cit.: 213.
93. Hamilton, Walter op. cit.
94. I have dealt with this point at some length in '*Marchands et Commerce autour de Kasimbazar 1704–1757*' (Dissertation presented for the award of the PhD. degree at the Ecole des Hautes Etudes en Sciences Sociales, Paris in 1985) and also in *Review* 1994.

95. The merchants would then find an advantage as formerly, in importing specie and renewing the commerce . . . By these means (open and free trade) manufactures of all kinds will be increased (;) cultivation become the care as it is the interest of the Ryot . . . (who) will be enabled to live comfortably(;) a spirit of improvement would prevail throughout the country and the revenues would be collected with ease and without having recourse to rigorous methods', Muhammad Reza Khan in Khan, Abdul, Majed, 1969, *The Transition in Bengal 1756–1775: A Study of Saiyid Muhammad Reza Khan*, Cambridge, University Press:173.
96. Om Prakash, 1988, *The Dutch East India Company* etc.: 232.
97. Bowrey, op. cit.: 225.
98. Master, Streynsham, *Diaries* op. cit. V.1: 53–54.
99. K.F.R. February 22, 1736.
100. To my knowledge there has been no substantive work on Kasimbazar except Somendra Chandra Nandy's *Like and Times of Canto Baboo: The Banyan of Warren Hastings*, 2 vols., Bombay, Allied Publishers, 1978. This is largely a family history of the Kasimbazar Raj. There has been no work done on Jugdia.

CHAPTER 1: SILK AS SYMBOL OF SUBSTANCE

1. Used here in the sense of raw silk bales as opposed to silk and cotton mixes and piece goods for which we get references from the sixteenth century. See Bagchi, P.C., 1945, (ed.), *'PoliticalRelations Between Bengal and China in the Pathan Period'*, *Visva Bharati Annals*, vol 1, Cheena Bhavan. Other silks are *eri, muga, tassar* and various such grades of raw silk as enumerated in the *Ain-i-Akbari.*
2. Moreland, W.H., 1920, 1962, *India at the Death of Akbar*, Delhi Reprint: 171–76. Sarkar, Jagadish Narayan, 1987, *Mughal Economy: Organization and Working*, Calcutta, Naya Prakash: 38–39.
3. Ibn Batuta, *Voyages*, 3 vols., (Tr). Defremery, E.C., Sanguinetty, B.R., 1982, Paris, Maspero.
4. Bagchi 1945 op. cit. Especially the *Ying Yai sheng lan*: 120.
5. Ibid: *Si Yang Ch'ao*: 126.
6. Ma Huan, Mills, J.V.G. (tr. and ed.), 1970, *The Overall Survey of the Ocean's Shores* (An Account of Ma Huan's voyage to Bengal), London, Hakluyt Society.
7. See Bagchi 1945 op. cit.
8. See Mukherjee, Rila, *Strange Riches* op. cit. (forthcoming) for more details.
9. Bagchi, P.C., 1951, *India and China: A Thousand Years of Cultural Relations*, New York, Philosophical Library and Bombay, British India Press: 90–91.
10. Ibid: 81.
11. Xinru Liu, 1996, *Silk and Religion: An exploration of the Material Life and the Thought of People*, OUP: chs. 3, 6–8.
12. Lombard, Maurice, 1971, *l'Islam dans sa Premiere Grandeur, VIIIe-XIe siecle*, Paris, Flammarion. In English as *The Golden Age Of Islam*, (Tr). J. Spencer, Amsterdam, 1975: 202.
13. Lombard, Maurice, 1971: 257.
14. Bagchi, P.C., 1951: 118.
15. Subodhan, the weaver in *Manasa-Mangal*, apparently bought even the most basic items on the market. Mentioned in Tarafdar 1965: 157.

16. Bernier's letter in *Correspendance Generale* 1666–1676 C2 Indes Orientales A.N. Paris.

CHAPTER 2: SILK AND EUROPE

1. Cipolla, Carlo M., 1976, *Before the Industrial Revolution: European Society and Economy 1000–1700*, London, Methuen: 102.
2. Dermigny, Louis, 1964, *La Chine et l'Occident: Le Commerce a Canton au XVIIIeme siecle: 1719–1833*, 3 vols. See pp. 393–94.
3. Cipolla, Carlo M., 1976: 257.
4. Ibid.: 52.
5. Ibid.: 257, 258, 260.
6. Om Prakash, 1984, (ed.), *The Dutch Factories in India 1617–1623*, New Delhi, Munshiram Manoharlal: VII.3, 197–99, VII.6, 218, V.1, 126, VIII.6, 80.
7. In Master's Diary op. cit.
8. Bernier's letter in *Correspendance Generale* 1666–1676, C2 Indes Orientales, A.N.Paris.
9. Tavernier, Jean Baptiste, *Travels in India* (Tr). Ball and Crooke, 1925, 2 vols., Oxford, University Press, 2nd edn. See also Tavernier, Jean-Baptiste, (Intr). Yerasimos, S., 1981, *Les Six Voyages en Turquie et en Perse*, 3 vols., Paris, Maspero.

CHAPTER 3: KASIMBAZAR SILK

1. Hamilton, Walter 1828 op. cit.
2. Silk cultivation started from Husain Shahi times in Bengal. The documentary evidence from the Ilyas Shahi period refers to silk mixes and not raw silk as such. See Bagchi P.C. 1945 op. cit.
3. Mohsin, K.M, 1973, *A Bengal District in Transition: Murshidabad, 1765–1793*, Dacca, Asiatic Society of Bangladesh: 9, 15.
4. Based on Mohsin 1973 and Om Prakash 1988.
5. Based on Chaudhuri, K.N., 1978, *The Trading World of Asia and the English East India Company 1660–1760*, Cambridge Press: 533.
6. Om Prakash, 1988, *The Dutch East India Company and the Economy of Bengal* etc.
7. Calculated from Chaudhuri 1978: 534–35.

CHAPTER 4: THE DADNI MERCHANT OF WESTERN BENGAL

1. Soon after the conquest of Malacca by the Portuguese in 1511 Pires noted Bengal merchants at Acheh and Pase. In the same century Barbosa referred to Bengal merchants trading with the Malabar, Cambay, Pegu, Tenasserim, Acheh, Malacca and Ceylon. In 1599 there was a settlement of Bengali merchants at Acheh. See Tome Pires, *The Suma Oriental* (ed. and tr.) E.A. Cortesao, 1944, London, Hakluyt Society: 88, 142; Varthema, Ludovico, *The Travels of Ludovico di Varthema in Egypt, Syria, Arabia Deserta and Arabia Felix, in Persia, India and Ethiopia AD*

1503–1508. (Tr). J.W. John, (ed), G.P. Badger, London, Hakluyt Society, M D CCC XIII; Varthema, Ludovico, *The Itinerary of*. . . (Tr. R.C. Temple), London, Hakluyt, 1928; Duarte Barbosa, *The Book of Duarte Barbosa,* Tr. M.L. Dames, 1921, London, Hakluyt Society. See also Raychaudhuri, Tapan, 1966, *Bengal under Akbar and Jahangir,* Delhi, Munshiram Manoharlal: 208.

2. In Datta, Kali Kinkar, 1963, *Alivardi and His Times,* Calcutta, The World Press: 149.
3. See *The Voyage of Peter Laval to the East Indies, the Maldives, the Moluccas and Brasil 1601–1611,* V.1. Tr. A. Gray, London, Hakluyt Society.
4. Arasaratnam S., 1987, '*India and the Indian Ocean in the Seventeenth Century*' in A. Das Gupta and M.N. Pearson (eds.), *India and the Indian Ocean 1500–1800,* Calcutta, OUP: 126 and Arasaratnam S., 1986, *Merchants, Companies and Commerce on the Coromandel Coast 1650–1740,* Delhi, OUP: 112, 126, 145–148; Das Gupta, A. 1987, *'India and the Indian Ocean in the Eighteenth Century'* in A. Das Gupta and M.N. Pearson (eds.), *India and the Indian Ocean 1500–1800,* Calcutta, OUP: 143–4, 147 and '*Introduction II: The Story*' in ibid: 38; Das Gupta Arun, 1987, '*The Maritime Trade of Indonesia 1500–1800*' in ibid.: 251–52; Das Gupta, A. 1967, *Malabar in Asian Trade,* Cambridge, CUP: 266; Evers, Hans Dieter, 1987, '*Trade and State Formation: Siam in the Early Bangkok Period*', *MAS,* XII, 4: 751–971.
5. See Subrahmanyam, Sanjay, 1993, *The Portuguese Empire in Asia 1500–1700: A Political and Economic History,* New York, Longman; Das Gupta, Ashin, 1987, '*India and the Indian Ocean in the Eighteenth Century*' in A. Das Gupta and M.N. Pearson (eds.), *India and the Indian Ocean 1500–1800,* Calcutta, OUP; Das Gupta, Ashin, 1967, *Malabar in Asian Trade,* Cambridge, CUP; Das Gupta, Ashin, 1987, '*Upakuler Bharatvarsha*' in A. Ray, S. Nurul Hasan, G. Bhadra and A. Das Gupta (eds.), *Madhyajuger Bharat,* Calcutta, OUP: 135–53; Das Gupta, Ashin, 1979, *Indian Merchants and The Decline of Surat, 1700–1750,* Wiesbaden, Steiner Verlag.
6. See Mukherjee, Rila, 1994, *The Story of Kasimbazar: Silk Merchants and Commerce in Eighteenth Century India*', *Review,* Fernand Braudel Centre, New York, XVII, 4, Fall: 499–554. See p. 514; see Chaudhuri, Sushil, 1971, '*Bengal Merchants and Commercial Organisation in the Second Half of the Seventeenth Century*', *Bengal Past and Present,* XC, July-December: 36–51 for the practice of freighting ships by Bengali merchants and Marshall P.J., 1976, *East Indian Fortunes,* Oxford, Oxford Press, on the development of the Calcutta Fleet.

CHAPTER 5:COMMODITIES, PRICES AND PROFIT AT KASIMBAZAR IN THE FIRST HALF OF THE EIGHTEENTH CENTURY

1. Nandy, S.C., 1981, '*Palasi Juger Aage Maphasvaler Bangali Resham Byabshahi*', *Aitihasik,* Jan-March: 72–103.
2. In Subramanian, L. (ed.), 1999, *The French East India Company and the Trade of the Indian Ocean: A Collection of Essays by Indrani Ray,* Centre for Studies in Social Science, Calcutta and Munshiram Manoharlal, New Delhi. See Chapter 7 *Journey to Cassimbazar and Murshidabad: Observations of a French Visitor to Bengal in 1743*: 155, 156, 161, 162, 170.

3. By my calculations I arrive at the figure of Rs. 2000 as profit for some individuals for raw silk alone. By 18th century standards this figure must have represented a princely sum. In comparison the annual *peshkash* the English paid for trade was Rs. 3000, usual *nazars* to the nawabs' court rarely crossed Rs. 2000, and the price of medium quality rice was Rs. 1 for 2 *mans.*
4. From K.F.R.
5. K.F.R. Consultations of February 14, 1740.

CHAPTER 6: THE DADNI MERCHANT OF KASIMBAZAR

1. Risley, H.H., 1981 reprint, *The Tribes and Castes of Bengal: Ethnographic Glossary*, Calcutta, Firma Mukhopadhyay, 2 vols. V. 1: 155–6, V. II Appendix 1: 4.
2. Ibid. V. II Appendix 1:1.
3. Ibid. V. II: 311 and Appendix 1: 6–7.
4. Ibid V. II: 37.
5. Nandy, Somendra Chandra, 1978, *Like and Times of Canto Baboo: The Banyan of Warren Hastings*, 2 vols., Bombay, Allied Publishers: 490. See also Nandy 1981.
6. Risley V.II, Appendix 1: 7.
7. Ibid. V.II, Appendix 1: 129.
8. Ibid. V.II, Appendix 1: 134.
9. Risley 1981, V.1: 66–88, 500–5 and V. II, Appendix 1: 82.
10. Risley, 1981, V.1: 66–68, 423, 500–5. V. II, Appendix 1: 137.
11. Risley V.II, Appendix 1: 78.
12. Hutton, J.H., 1961, *Caste in India: Its Nature, Function and Origins*, London, OUP. 3rd edn: 31.
13. Risley V. II, Appendix 1: 45.
14. Ibid., V. II, Appendix 1: 124.
15. Ibid., V. II, Appendix 1: 133.
16. Ibid., V. 1: 451.
17. Ibid., V. 1: 81.
18. Ibid., V. II, Appendix 1: 47.
19. Ibid., V. II, Appendix 1: 135.
20. Ibid, V. II, Appendix 1: 75.
21. Ibid., V. 1: 78–82.
22. Ibid., V. 1: 490
23. Sinha, N.K., 1965, *An Economic History of Bengal, V.1 From Plassey to the Permanent Settlement*, Calcutta, Firma K.L. Mukhopadhyay: 111.
24. Risley V. II, Appendix 1: 45.
25. Ibid., V. II, Appendix 1: 124.
26. Ibid. V. II, Appendix 1: 129–30.
27. Ibid. V. II, Appendix 1: 135.
28. Ibid. V. II, Appendix 1: 136.
29. See Risley V. II, Appendix 1: 58.
30. Ibid. Appendix 1: 60.
31. Ibid. Appendix 1: 63, 75.

32. Haraprasad Sastri situates his historical novel *Bener Meye* in late tenth century Saptagram where the king is Rupa Bagdi of the fishermen's caste. This is a direct allusion to the prevalent social trends of 'lower' castes assuming power in Bengal. Such trends were furthered in the eleventh century when three Kaivarta kings ruled Bengal. This episode, dismissed as the Kaivarta Rebellion, actually challenged the Buddhist Pala kingdom in western Bengal. Kaivartas are fishing folk. See Majumdar, R.C. (ed.), 1943, *The History of Bengal.* V.1 *Hindu Period,* Dacca, The University of Dacca: 152–55. See also Sastri, Haraprasad, 1980, *Bener Meye, Collected Works,* V.1. Calcutta, West Bengal State Book Board for the depiction of Rupa Bagdi as king. It is notable that Sastri portrays Saptagram, an ancient port that rose after the decline of Tamralipta, as a maritime city par excellence. *Strange Riches* op. cit. applies the concept of 'littoral societies', elaborated by M.N. Pearson for Indian Ocean coastal societies, to Bengal. The basic premise of littoral societies is that they are ruled by coastal imperatives in terms of material culture a la Braudel. See Pearson, M.N., Unpublishedkeynote address to the conference *'Seascapes, Littoral Cultures and Trans-oceanic Exchanges,'* sponsored by the American Historical Association, Washington DC, February 12–15, 2003 (sent by Prof. Pearson to me as an email attachment). In such a society it is but natural that coastal folk would ascend to a position of power and influence.

CHAPTER 7: THE MERCHANTS OF KASIMBAZAR IN BUSINESS

1. The investment of February 1748 of 1747/48 is included under 1748. The investment of January 1749 is included in that of 1749.
2. K.F.R. March 4, 1744

CHAPTER 8: THE RISE OF MERCHANT FAMILIES

1. See K.F.R. Consultations of July 25, 1737.
2. In 1683 two Kasimbazar merchants Chitramal and Deepchund told William Hedges that Charnock made a profit of Sicca Rupess 0.75 on every Sicca Rupees 2 thus defrauding the English Company to the tune of over 1000 pounds every year.
3. K.F.R. Consultations of December 24, 1733, February 5, 1737, April 6, 1737 and May 13, 1741. Bally (Beley) Katma who made a killing in the 1733 investment (see Table 12) and Huttoo Katma were Barker's banyans. Others were Oody Coshall, Raghunath Biswas and Kushalchand. In 1741 Nimdass was referred to as Eyre's private broker. Naran Biswass was Samuel Millechamp's banyan, Kishore Biswas and 'Otteram' provided goods to Walt Barwell. In 1737 Huttoo Katma's name was raised in connection with fraud by Barker, his patron.
4. See Mukherjee, Rila, 1994: 515.
5. K.F.R. Consultations of September 13, 1733.
6. Darrac C2, 115, Histoire des Etablissemens Francais en Asie et principalement Ceux du Bengale 1537–1822, A.N., Paris, now at C.A.O.M, Aix.
7. K.F.R. Consultations of February 14, 1740 and August 20, 1741. The buyers were Huttoo and Sautu Katma, Naran, Kalyan, Raghunath and Gobardhan Biswas, Nimo Poddar, Dayaram Dutt, and Mahadeb, Nandalal, Sabram and Kablaram Surma.

CHAPTER 10: THE WORLD OF FINANCE AT KASIMBAZAR

1. See Mukherjee, Rila 1994: 510 for more on this.
2. Master, Streynsham, R.C. Temple (ed), 1911, *The Diaries of Streynsham Master 1675–1680 And Other Contemporary Papers Relating Thereto*, London, John Murray, Indian Records Series, 2 Vols. See V.1.
3. See all three editions. Luiller, *Voyage du Sieur Luillier aux Grandes Indes avec une Instruction Pour le Commerce des Indes Orientales*, Paris, Claude Cellier, MC CC V; Luillier, *Voyage du Sieur Luillier aux Indes Orientales Avec une instruction pour le commerce des Indes Orientales*, 1705, Paris, Claude Cellier; also Luillier, *Voyages du Sieur Luillier dans des grandes Indes Orientales*, 1726, Rotterdam.
4. Ibid. Also Sushil Chaudhuri (1971, '*Bengali Merchants and Commercial Organisation in the Second Half of the Seventeenth Century*', *BPP*, XC, July-Decmber: 36–51) who notes that goods were bought by the EEIC in late seventeenth century Bengal on the basis of a half payment in ready money and a half in European goods. The practice of forcing the dadni merchants to buy European goods as part payment against EIC investments continued. The K.F.R. tells us that this was tried sometimes at Kasimbazar. The practice continued to exist in the Coromandel. See Arasaratnam, S., 1986, *Merchants, Companies and Commerce on the Coromandel Coast 1650–1740*, Delhi, OUP.
5. Chaudhuri, Sushil, 1971, '*Bengal Merchants and Commercial Organisation in the Second Half of the Seventeenth Century*', *BPP*, XC, July-Dec: 36–51.
6. Master op. cit.
7. Luiller op. cit.
8. Chaudhuri, Sushil, 1986–87, '*European Companies and Pre Modern South Asian Commercial Systems*', *The Calcutta Historical Journal*, XI, 1–2: 95–108, noted that 12% was the prevalent rate of interest in the 1730s. This is not borne out by the data in the K.F.R.
9. K.F.R. June 26, 1739.
10. Ibid August 6, 1741.
11. Ibid. January 3, 1745. 204 as noted in 1745 may be a mistake because the figure of 240 is mentioned thrice in May (May 29) and November (November 10 and 24) 1746 in the K.F.R.
12. Ibid. May 27, 1741.
13. Ibid. June 17, 1741.
14. Entry No. 2548 of that date, 22MI41, C.A.O.M, Aix.
15. Entry Nos. 2570 and 2584, 22MI41.
16. Marshall P. J, 1976, *East Indian Fortunes: The British in Bengal in the Eighteenth Century*, Oxford, OUP.
17. Little, J.H., 1920–21, *The House of Jagat Seth, BPP*, 20: 111–200 (1920) and 21: 1–119 (1921). Later as a publication of the Asiatic Society, Calcutta.
18. Figure arrived at by calculating the amounts entered in the K.F.R. consultations.
19. K.F.R. December 19, 1740.
20. Entry 3025 of July 18, 1768; Entry 3027 of August 18, 1768, 22 MIOM/45 at C.A.O.M., Aix, France.

21. Entry 3013 of April 16, 1768; Entry 3014 of April 18, 1768; Entry 3015 of April 20, 1768, 22 MIOM/45, C.A.O.M., Aix.
22. Entry 2530 of September 16, 1772, 22MI41. Entry 2567 of August 31, 1774, 22MI41, mentions Katmas as moneylenders to the FEIC. Both at C.A.O.M., Aix.
23. Entry No. 2584, 22MI41, C.A.O.M., Aix.
24. K.F.R.: 1733, 1737, 1739 and 1748.
25. Ibid. 1749.
26. Ibid. 1746.
27. Ibid. Entry of August 31, 1733.
28. Ibid. March 22, 1744; January 20, 1745.
29. Ibid. September 11, 1744; December 1, 1744.
30. Ibid. June 25, 1745; November 19, 1745; February 25, 1746; once date unknown; and once in October 1746.
31. Ibid. October 11, 1746.
32. See the section on the crisis and confrontation at Kasimbazar in 1753.
33. K.F.R., Cash Accounts, February 1744.
34. K.F.R. January 22, 1735/6; February 7, 1735/6; April 24, 1743; March 30, 1745; May 4, 1745; May 15, 1746; November 7, 1748.
35. Ibid. February 6, 1735/6; February 7, 1735/6; August 6, 1740 and once date not certain.
36. Ibid. June 25, 1745.
37. Ibid. April 1, 1746; January 1748; February 10, 1748.
38. K.F.R. April 24, 1743 and May 4, 1745.
39. For the Surmas and Tagóres see the K.F.R. entries on the dates mentioned in the text.
40. K.F.R. September 30, 1733.
41. Ibid. October 14, 1733.
42. Ibid. November 19, 1733.
43. Ibid. March 15, 1744; May 15, 1744; October 28, 1749.
44. K.F.R April 24, 1743.
45. Ibid.
46. Compiled from K.F.R.
47. K.F.R. October 28, 1732; September 30, 1733; June 28, 1736.
48. K.F.R. September 20, 1733.
49. Ibid. March 6, 1740.
50. Figure calculated from entries in the K.F.R. taking both Katma moneylenders and merchant-moneylenders.
51. Entry of September 16, 1772 at Chandernagore, No. 2530, 22MI41 at CAOM, Aix. Here they are referred to correctly as Katma. The names mentioned are Baburam, Boubon, Panchou and Poran. The Katmas, without individual names, are mentioned once again as money lenders to the FEIC in the entry no. 2567 of August 31, 1774, 22MI41, Aix. Same with entry no. 2570 of September 7, 1774, 22M141, Aix.
52. K.F.R. March 27, 1741.
53. Ibid. July 1746.
54. Ibid. March 15, 1744.

55. Ibid. May 7, 1745.
56. Ibid. May 19, 1737.
57. Ibid. May 5, 1738.
58. Ibid. January 31, 1738/9.
59. Ibid. September 10, 1733.
60. Ibid. October 13, 1733.
61. Ibid.
62. Ibid.
63. Ibid. March 27, 1741.
64. K.F.R. Consultations.
65. K.F.R. Letter Generall of August 16, 1738.
66. See K.F.R. Consultations of July 25, 1737.
67. K.F.R. April 6, 1737.
68. The Katmas, the favoured merchants of the English made the shift as early as in the1740s (Source K.F.R.)

CHAPTER 11: THE MERCHANT'S WORLD AT KASIMBAZAR

1. Datta, Kali Kinkar, 1963: 15.
2. KFR as before and Dacca Factory Records dated 12th November1750.
3. Datta, K.K. 1963: 132.
4. Ibid: 25–26.
5. Chaudhuri, Sushil, 1986–87, '*European Companies and Pre Modern South Asian Commercial Systems*', *The Calcutta Historical Journal*, XI, 1–2: 95–108.
6. K.F.R. January 29, 1756.
7. Nandy, S.C. 1981, '*Palasi Juddher Aage MaphasvalerBangali Resam Byabsai*', *Oitihasik*, January-March. In Bengali.
8. HMS 804, Fort William, dated October 30, 1752.
9. Ibid. See Mukherjee, Rila 1994, op. cit. for details.
10. K.F.R. February 19, 1741.
11. For more details see Mukherjee, Rila 1994 op. cit.
12. K.F.R. November 17, 1739 mentioned the fact that this northern invasion had caused the prices of Bengal silk to shoot up.
13. Ibid. December 4, 1740.
14. Ibid. March 4, 1744.
15. K.F.R. Consultations of January 27, 1740.
16. Ibid.
17. Ibid.
18. K.F.R. July 27, 1741.
19. Ibid. December 9, 1741.

CHAPTER 12: THE CRISIS

1. Chaudhuri, K.N., 1978, *The Trading World of Asia and the English East India Company 1660–1760.* Cambridge: University Press: 311–12.
2. Sinha, N.K., 1965: 10.

3. Eaton, Richard, 1993, *The Rise of Islam and the Bengal Frontier 1204–1760,* California, Berkeley and L.A; Chaudhuri, Sushil,1995, *From Prosperity to Decline, Bengal in the Eighteenth Century,* New Delhi, Manohar.
4. Chaudhury, Sushil, 1995: 102–7.
5. K.F. R. December 4, 1740.
6. K.F.R. Ibid.
7. K.F.R. March 6, 1740
8. Ibid. January 20, 1741.
9. Ibid. April 6, 27, 29, 1741;
10. Ibid. December 9, 1741.
11. Ibid. January 31, 1742.
12. Ibid. March 22, 1744.
13. January 27, 1748.
14. Ibid.
15. K.F.R. March 30 and April 18, 1748.
16. Datta, K.K. 1963: 163–64.
17. Ibid: 164.

CHAPTER 13: THE CRASH AT KASIMBAZAR

1. K.F.R. April 13, 1741; March 22, 1744.
2. K.F.R. March 19, 1753.
3. K.F.R. For 1750: January 20, February 8, 14, June 10, June 23, October 29; for 1751: February 12, 22, March 7, 31, April 23, May 8, 11, September 13, 25, December 29; for 1752: February 20, March 27, April 5, August 20; for 1753: January 7, March 8, 19, 23, May 4, June 2, August 5, September 19, November 19 as regards high prices and inferior quality of silk; for more strict sorting at the company warehouse see February 8, 1750, December 29, 1751, March 9, 1752, August 5, September 12, 19, 1753.
4. K.F.R. For 1750 see January 20, June 23, July 19, December 18; for 1752 see March 6, 27, October 1. See also Chaudhuri, K.N. (1978: 308–9). This seems to be the general situation not only at Kasimbazar but for the whole of the western part of Bengal (Chaudhuri, K.N. 1978: 311).
5. From Table 7 we have the following information for Debi Prasad. In 1733 he supplied SPG. In 1737 he supplied both RS and the G&D investments. In 1738 he took care of the RS, SPG and G&D investments. In 1739 he supplied RS, G and MB to the EEIC. In 1744 he supplied SPG twice in March and May. In 1745 he supplied SPG. In 1746 he supplied RS. There are no further entries against his name.
6. There is a also likelihood that he may have been a Ghosh. See the 1755 State of the Merchants' Ballances mentioned later on in this volume.
7. See the section on moneylenders before.

CHAPTER 14: THE PARTING OF WAYS

1. K.F.R. Consultations of March 25, May 22, 1754.
2. Ibid. March 10, 12 and 25, 1754.

CHAPTER 15: THE DEPARTURE

1. K.F.R. Consultations.
2. Fort William Correspondence, HMS 804, containing BPC February 25, 1747/48 to December 9, 1761, I.O.L.R., (now British Library) London. Henceforth HMS 804.
3. In Datta, K.K., 1963: Appendix E, pp. 217–8.
4. Wilson, C.R., 1911 (1963, 1967), *The Early Annals of the English in Bengal.* Surman's Diary, Calcutta, Asiatic Society, 2 vols. V.1: 76.
5. Quoted in Om Prakash 1985, 1988: 104–5.
6. K.F.R., February 28, 1744.
7. Datta, K.K., 1963: 156.
8. Sinha, N.K. 1965: 16.
9. Ibid: 24.
10. K.F.R. March 17 and October 24, 1755.
11. Ibid. May 12, 1755.
12. Ibid. March 28, 1754.
13. K.F.R. August 24, December 23 and December 30, 1756).
14. Ibid. January 7, 1758.
15. K.F.R. March 4, April 10, 1754; March 26, April 11, April 21, May 9, 1755; January 18, March 12, 1758.
16. Ibid. March 25, 1754; April 10, May 12, May 20, and September 23, 1755.
17. Entry No. 3028 of August 20, 1768, 22MIOM/45, C.A.O.M., Aix.
18. Sinha 1965: 17–27, highlights the fact that many systems of contracting for were tried out during this period.
19. Ibid: 21.
20. BPC, RI, V.44, August 14, 1769.
21. Mohsin, K.M. 1973: 68.
22. Sinha 1965: 22.
23. Mohsin 1973: 69–70.

CHAPTER 16: THE END OF THE EIGHTEENTH CENTURY WORLD AT KASIMBAZAR

1. Proceedings June 25, 1791 in Sinha 1965: 111–12. Bandyopadhyaya was a silk supplier at Kumarkhali who worked as gomastha for Girdhar Doss, the Gujarati merchant of Kasimbazar.
2. See Taylor, James, 1851, *A Descriptive and Historical Account of the Cotton Manufactures of Dacca,* London and also Taylor, James, 1840, *A Sketch of the Topography and Statistics of Dacca,* Calcutta.
3. The 1752 State of the Merchants' Ballances (Source K.F.R. undated)
4. In Datta, K.K. 1963: 165–66.
5. See also K.F.R. September 6 and 23, 1752.
6. K.F.R. G23/12 October (undated) 1754.
7. K.F.R. January 27, 1756.
8. See K.F.R. consultations of that date.
9. K.F.R. November 12, 1752.
10. K.F.R. May 12 and 20, 1755.

CHAPTER 17: THE ARAKAN CONNECTION AND THE EAST

1. *Fathiya-I-Ibriya* (or Tarikh-I-Mulki-Asham) of Ibn Muhammad Wali, Known popularly as Shihabuddin Talish. Tr. By Blochmann, Journal of the Asiatic Society of Bengal, 1872.
2. In Tarafdar 1965: 122.
3. *Strange Riches* op. cit.
4. See later.
5. *Baharistan-I-Ghaybi* by Mirza Nathan. 2 Vols. Tr. M.I. Borah, Government of Assam Publication, Guwahati 1936.
6. Subrahmanyam, Sanjay, 2005,'*Dutch Tribulations in Seventeenth century Mrauk-U*' in Subrahmanyam, Sanjay, 2005, *Explorations in Connected History; From The Tagus to The Ganges*, New Delhi, OUP.
7. Mirza Nathan, V.I: 404–08.
8. Mirza Nathan, V.II: 641.
9. Ibid. V.II: 710. Talish also speaks of the might of the Arakanese navy which he deemed superior to that of the Mughals in *Fathiya-I-Ibriya.*
10. Mirza Nathan. V. II: 629–30
11. *Fathiya-I-Ibriya.*
12. Mirza Nathan, V.I: 405–08.
13. For opinions on this controversial mission see Karim, Kondkar Mahbubul, 1974, *The Provinces of Bihar and Bengal under Shahjahan*, Dacca, The Asiatic Society of Bangladesh: 114–15 and Mirza Nathan, V. II: 710–11.
14. Barbosa, op. cit: 363; Francois Pyrard de Laval, 1887–1890, *The Voyage of... to the East Indies, the Maldives, the Moluccas and Brazil 1601–1611*, 3 vols. (Tr). Albert Gray, London, Hakluyt Society. See V. I: 322 and *Ain-i- Akbari*, V. II: 122 (Jarrett, Account of Bengal).
15. Shah Jahan retaliated by sending the entire Portuguese population of Hugli as slaves to Agra in 1629.
16. *Baharistan-I-Ghaybi*, Vol. 2.
17. Karim, K.M., 1974: 116–117.
18. Mirza Nathan, *Baharistan-i-Ghaybi*, V. II: 816.
19. Ibid. V. I: 383, V.II: 641.
20. Dasgupta, Ashin '*Introduction II: The Story*' in Ashin Das Gupta and M.N. Pearson (eds.)., 1987, *India and the Indian Ocean 1500–1800*, Delhi, OUP: 31–32, 36–38.
21. Bouchon, Genevieve and Thomaz, Luis Filipe, 1998, *Voyage dans les Deltas du Gange et l'Irraouaddy*, 1521, Fondation Calouste Gulbenkian, Paris.
22. Ali, M.M., 1985, *History of the Muslims of Bengal*, 2 vols, Riyadh, Imam Muhammad Ibn Sa'ud Islamic University Press. See V.1.
23. Cesare Frederici's *Travels* in Purchas, Samuel, *His Pilgrimages*, Glasgow, 1905.
24. Abdul Hamid Lahori's *Padshah Nama* in Elliot and Dowson's *History of India as Told by Its Own Historians*, V.7, Allahabad, Kitab Mahal. Reprint 1969; Abdul Hamid Lahori, *Padshah Nama* in Elliot and Dowson, *History of India as Told By its Own Historians*, V.7, L.P.P. Reprint, 1990, Delhi.

CHAPTER 18: THE EAST: THE DHAKA REGION

1. Mirza Nathan, on Musa Khan's battle with the approaching Mughal army in *Baharistan-I-Ghaybi*, V.1: 58.
2. Subrahmanyam, S., 1992, '*Iranians Abroad: Intra-Asian Elite Migration and Early Modern State Formation*' in *The Journal of Asian Studies*, 51, 2, May: 340–63.
3. Karim, Abdul, 1964, *Dacca The Mughal Capital*, Dacca, Asiatic Society of Pakistan however puts his tenure at Dhaka as Naib Nazim from 1728–1734 (p. 26) that is before his governorship of Orissa and not during Alivardi's reign which lasted from 1740 to 1756. This is borne out by *Seir Mutaqherin* (Seid Gholam Hossein Khan, *Seir Mutaqherin or View of Modern Times*, (Tr). Nota Manus, Calcutta, T.D. Chatterjee, 4 vols.) V. 1: 349–355 which notes that Alivardi subdued Murshid Quli in Orissa and left Orissa in charge of his grandson (1740–1741). Murshid Quli fled to Masulipatam where there was a substantial colony of Persian courtier-merchants.
4. K.F.R. circa late 1740s.
5. Om Prakash, 2002, '*Trade and Politics in Eighteenth Century India*' in Alavi 2002: 143. Also mentioned in *Seir Mutaqherin* and by Karim, Abdul, 1964, *Dacca The Mughal Capital*, Dacca, Asiatic Society of Pakistan: 23–24.
6. Om Prakash, 2002.
7. *Seir Mutaqherin* V.1: 422–23.
8. Karim, A. 1964: 23.
9. Islam Khan was chastised of ruling through his own favourites and ignoring Mughal officials dispatched from Delhi. See *Baharistan-I-Ghaybi*: 'The great imperial officers sent a memorial to the Emperor submitting as follows: Up to this time every victory achieved by the Mughals has been attributed by Islam Khan to his own people. He has not yet given up the practice of sending the imperial officers in the company of his own men . . . Shaykh Kamal, an officer of Islam Khan, made peace with the Raja (of Kachar) to suit his own purpose and left the expedition where it was. If this work is entrusted to us, then, with the favour of the fortune of the Emperor, we shall conquer the territory of Kachar . . .' (V. 1: 220–21). Again, when Islam Khan was recalled by the Emperor and Shajaat Khan appointed as subahdar in his place Islam Khan countermanded this order and sent Shajaat Khan off to Orissa instead (*Baharistan-I-Ghaybi*, V.1: 211) .
10. Mir Junlas independence from Delhi is will documented. Bernier, a contemporary traveller, attests to it also.
11. For more on this see Serajuddin, A.M., 1971, *The Revenue Administration of the East India Company in Chittagong 1761–1785*, Chittagong, University Press: 18, 161.
12. Karim, Abdul, 1964: 87.
13. Ibid.: 87–88. See D.F.R. G15 for 1747.

CHAPTER 19: TRADE IN THE 'FAR EAST' – JUGDIA AND LAKHIPUR

1. *Baharistan-I-Ghaybi*, Vol. 2.
2. Karim, Khondkar Mahbubul, 1974, *The Provinces of Bihar and Bengal under Shahjahan*, Dacca, The Asiatic Society of Bangladesh: 116.

3. Abdul Karim's comprehensive *Dacca The Mughal Capital* (Dacca, Asiatic Society of Pakistan, 1964) makes no mention of the place although Abul Fadl mentions Jugdia in the *A'in*.
4. Tarafdar 1965: 57.
5. *Memoire des Etablissements Francais en Asie et Principalement Ceux du Bengale*, par le Capitaine Darrac chef de la loge de Dacca, 1822, C2 115, A.N., Paris. Henceforth C2 115.
6. Ibid., D.F.R., I.O.L.R., London, now at British Library.
7. *Memoire sur le Commerce de l'Inde: Precis de Celui qui faisait l'Ancienne Compagnie des Indes et Celle Etabli en 1785* (written April 7, 1814), Affaires Etrangeres (AE) BIII, 459, A.N.S.O.M., Oudinot, Paris (henceforth AE BIII 459), says: 'L'Europe renoncerait plus facilement aux autres branches du commerce de Bengale qu'a celui de Jougdia, ce commerce roulant presqu'entierement sur des merchandises de la premiere necessite, au lieu que dans toutes les autres parties de Bengale, les objets de luxe en font la base'.
8. Serajuddin 1971: 9.
9. Hossain, Hameeda, 1988, *The Company Weavers of Bengal: The East India Company and the Organization of Textile Production in Bengal 1750–1813*, Delhi, OUP.
10. See Deloche (ed.) (1984), *Les Aventures de Jean Baptiste Chevalier dans l'Inde Orientale 1752–1765,* Paris, Publications EFEO.
11. Martineau, Alfred, 1927, *Dupleix et l'Inde Francaise 1749–1754*, Paris, Societe d'Editions Geographiques, Maritimes et Coloniales: 449–51.
12. In Deloche, Jean, (ed.), 1990, *Statistiques de Chandernagor* (1832, 1827, 1838) by Joseph Cordier and Achille Bedier, Pondicherry, Institut Francais: 20.
13. Hunter, W.W., 1876, *A Statistical Account Of Bengal*, Vol. VI. *Chittagong Hill Tracts-Chittagong, Noakhali, Tipperah, Hill Tipperah*, London, Trubner: 247.
14. See below.
15. Sinha, N.K., 1965 V.1: 6–7.
16. AE BIII 459, A.N.S.O.M., Oudinot, Paris.
17. C2 115 op. cit.
18. Deloche (1990): X., 16–17.
19. See Bedier's note on Jugdia in Deloche (1990) cited later.
20. HMS 804, Fort William dated October 23, 1752 p. 8, I.O.L.R., London and the FEIC letters.
21. *Correspondance du Conseil de Chandernagor avec Divers, 1747–1757*, Societe Historique de Pondicherry, 1 Rue Romain Rolland, Pondicherry. Accession No. F110/AC 164/F156. Letter no.7, Duval de Leyrit in Council at Chandernagore to Albert at Jugdia, April 16, 1751. There letters may be found in Mukherjee, Rila, 1990–1991.
22. Letter No. 7 of M. Duval de Leyrit in Council at Chandernagore to M. Albert at Jugdia, 1751, April 16. See also Mukherjee, Rila, 1990–1991.
23. Sinha, N.K., 1965 V.1: 6–7.
24. Letter 23 of Duval de Leyrit at Chandernagore to Nicholas at Jugdia, 1753, June 20.
25. K.F.R. Vol. G 23/12 Consultation of February 1, 1753, I.O.L.R., London.
26. Ibid.: Consultations of February 1 and June 28, 1753, I.O.L.R., London.

27. February 16, 1753, Duval de Leyrit at Chandernagore to Nicholas at Jugdia.
28. K.F.R. G/23/12 Consultation of February 5, 1754, I.O.L.R., London.
29. Letter no. 23, June 20, 1753, Duval de Leyrit at Chandernagore to Nicholas at Jugdia.
30. K.F.R. G23/12 Consultation of July 18, 1755, I.O.L.R., London
31. Ibid.: August 11, 1755.
32. AE BIII 459.
33. Karim, Abdul, 1964: 87.
34. Based on AE BII 459, Karim, Abdul, 1964: 87–88. See also D.F.R. G15 for 1747, I.O.L.R., London, HMS 456, the Dacca Series by John Taylor 1800–1801: 103–5, I.O.L.R., London. From Tables 21 and 22.
35. HMS 456, the Dacca Series by John Taylor 1800–1801: 103–5, I.O.L.R., London.
36. See Table 11.
37. AE BIII 459.
38. C2 115.
39. Ibid.
40. Cordier in 1823 in Deloche (1990): 16.
41. Hossain, Hameeda, 1988, *The Company Weavers of Bengal: The East India Company and the Organization of Textile Production in Bengal 1750–1813*, Delhi, OUP: 184.
42. C2 115.
43. Toussaint, Auguste, 1974, *L'Ocean Indien au XVIIIe siecle*, Paris, Flammarion.
44. Gokhale, B.G., 1979, *Surat in the Seventeenth Century*, Bombay, Popular Prakashan: 99–101. An EEIC letter from Manila dated December 1, 1644 mentioned that the Chinese sold black baftas to the Cambodians at a huge profit: 100–1.
45. Ibid.: 101.
46. Gordon, Stewart, 1994, '*Burhanpur: Entrepot and Hinterland 1650–1750*' in *Marathas, Marauders and State Formation in Eighteenth Century India*, Delhi, OUP: 163–81. See p.166. White calicoes from Burhanpur were sent to Persia, Turkey, Arabia, Muscovy, Poland and Cairo in the seventeenth century according to Tavernier.
47. Deloche (1990): 154. 'There being no agent at Jugdia since 1817 we can only report what we have been able to reconstruct from the Chandernagore archives. Since the Jugdia factory was swept under the sea M.Chevalier obtained, in 1767, a parwana from the nawab for acquiring land to establish a factory on it. The English having forced the Nawab to retract this parwana, it was only at the time of repossession, in 1785, that M. Joseph Dayot was sent to Jugdia to acquire a new territory. He bought Chandella. The contract of this sale was regularised in 1790, by M. Gilliot, the chief of the Jugdia factory, who obtained an original patta in the name of the King of France. This contract is under the control of Chandernagore'—my translation.
48. See the following chapter.
49. Hossain, 1988: 77.
50. Calculated from ibid.: 100
51. Calculated from ibid.: 98.
52. Ibid: 101.
53. Serajuddin, 1971: 48.

54. Feldbaek, Ole, 1969, *India Trade Under the Danish Flag*, Copenhagen. This fits in with our assertion that the EEIC would let no other European power, except under English aegis, flourish in this region.

CHAPTER 20: THE MARKET AT JUGDIA – TEXTILES, MERCHANTS AND COMPANIES

1. Hamilton, Alexander, 1727, *A New Account of the East Indies 1688–1723*, 2 vols., Edinburgh.
2. Tieffanthaler in Bernouilli, *L'Inde*, refers to these as cotton piece goods costing five to thirty francs a piece.
3. Hunter, 1876, Vol. VI: 288.
4. Although also provincial capitals and port towns, these were originally market towns.
5. Little, J.H., *House of Jagat Seth* op. cit.
6. HMS 804, Fort William dated October 23, 1752 p. 8, I.O.L.R., London and the FEIC letters.
7. See Tables 22 and 24.
8. *Correspondance du Conseil de Chandernagor avec Divers, 1747–1757*, Societe Historique de Pondicherry, 1 Rue Romain Rolland, Pondicherry. Accession No. F110/AC 164/F156. Letter no. 7, Duval de Leyrit in Council at Chandernagore to Albert at Jugdia, April 16, 1751. See Mukherjee, Rila, 1990–91.
9. The FEIC regarded this as an advantage: '. . . l'avantage de ce comptoir est qu'on n'y fait aucune avance aux tisserands, des toiles sont portees aux marches et on les achete comptant', AE BIII 459.
10. HMS 804, Fort William, October 23, 1752: 8. I.O.L.R., London.
11. Hedges, William, *Diary of, During His Agency in Bengal 1681–1687*, R. Barlow and H.Yule (eds). 2 vols. London, Hakluyt Society, M D CCC LXXX. V.I: 152.
12. HMS 456, Dacca Series: 37, I.O.L.R., London.
13. Duval de Leyrit at Chandernagore to Albert at Jugdia, January 13, February 27 and May 5, 1751. See Mukherjee, Rila, 1990–91, op.cit.
14. Ibid. May 5, 1751.
15. Om Prakash, 2002, *Trade and Politics in Eighteenth Century Bengal'* in Alavi, 2002: 136–164: 143.
16. '*Trade and Politics in Eighteenth Century Bengal'* in Alavi 2002: 143. Also mentioned in *Seir Mutaqherin* and by Karim, Abdul, 1964, in *Dacca The Mughal Capital*,Dacca, Asiatic Society of Pakistan: 23–24.
17. *Seir Mutaqherin* V. 1: 422–23.
18. Om Prakash, 2002.
19. HMS 804, Fort William October 23, 1752: 8, I.O.L.R., London, and FEIC letters.
20. C2 115.
21. HMS 804, Fort William dated October 23, 1752: 8, I.O.L.R., London.
22. K.F.R. G23/12, Consultation of February 1, 1753, I.O.L.R., London.
23. Ditto June 28, 1753.
24. Ditto February 5, 1754.
25. Ditto July 18, 1755.
26. Ditto August 11, 1755.
27. Deloche (1990): 16.

CHAPTER 21: THE MID CENTURY TEXTILE CRISIS AT JUGDIA

1. AE B III 459.
2. Letter No. 3 of November 17, 1750; Letter 9 of July 26, 1751.
3. Mukherjee 1990–1991.
4. toiles a quatre file.
5. Letters 10, 13, 14.
6. Cordier in Deloche (1990): 16.
7. Entry No. 3063 of May 27, 1767 22 MIOM/45 at C.A.O.M., Aix.
8. Entry No. 2472, 22MI41, ibid.
9. Entry No. 3152 of June 19, 1767, 22 MIOM 46; entry no. 3154 of July 1, 1768, 22 MIOM 46; entry no. 3155 of September 21, 1768 22 MIOM 46; entry no. 3156 of October 10, 1768, 22 MIOM 46 at C.A.O.M., Aix.
10. Entry No. 3153 June 15, 1768, 22 MIOM 46, ibid.
11. Entry No. 3157 of October 20, 1768, 22 MIOM 46, ibid.
12. Entry No. 2479 of January 26, 1769. 22 MI 41, ibid.
13. Entry No. 3158 of November 10, 1768, 22 MIOM 46, entry no. 3159 of November 26, 1768, 22 MIOM 46, ibid.
14. Entry No. 3160 of December 1, 1768, for Maghs around Chattagram 22 MIOM 46; Entry no. 3161 of September 14, 1768 (69?) for Magh raids 22 MIOM 46; Entry No. 3162 July of 31, 1770 for rising expenses 22 MIOM 46; Entry No. 3163 of August 31, 1770 for expenses 22 MIOM 46; Entry No. 3164 of September 30, 1770 for expenses at Jugdia 22 MIOM 46; Entry No. 3165 of June 10, 1771 for sums due to dalals 22 MIOM 46. All at C.A.O.M., Aix.
15. Entry No. 3077 of May 28, 1774, 22 MIOM/45, C.A.O.M., Aix.
16. Entry No. 3089 of October 28, 1785, 22 MIOM 46.
17. Entry No. 3098 of July 8, 1786, 22 MIOM 46.
18. Entry No. 3101 of August 14, 1786, 22 MIOM 46.
19. Entry No. 3166 of December 1, 1786 22 MIOM 46; entry no. 3167 of December 23, 1786 22 MIOM 46.
20. Entry No. 3168 of July 1, 1787, 22 MIOM 46.
21. Entry No. 3169 of October 9, 1788 22 MIOM 46; 3120 of April 4, 1789 22 MIOM 46; 3121 of April 4, 1789 22 MIOM 46; 3170 of October 15, 1789; 3171 of June 27, 1789; 3172 of July 23, 1789; 3173 of October 8, 1789; 3174 of October 11, 1789; 3175 of October 28, 1789; 3176 of November 1789; 3177 of November 25, 1789; 3178 of March 26, 1790, all of 22 MIOM 46, C.A.O.M., Aix.
22. Cordier (1823) in Deloche (1990): 18.
23. Bedier (1838) in Ibid.: 154.
24. Hunter, 1876, V.VI: 288.

CHAPTER 22: THE END OF THE ECONOMIC WORLD OF THE MUGHAL

1. Datta, K.K. 1963: 56–7. See also pp. 158–9.
2. In 1743, 1745, 1746 were years of repeated failure in the *gara* contracts. See also Datta, K.K.1963: 158–9.

3. Entries 2939 of December 23, 1744 and 2941 of February 27, 1745, 22 MIOM/45, C.A.O.M., Aix.
4. Entry No. 2953 bis of January 3, 1746, 22MIOM/45, C.A.O.M., Aix.
5. Entry No. 3003 of December 28, 1746, ibid.
6. Accounts of Salimullah, Karam Ali and Wafa in Datta K.K. 1963: 107–8. See pp. 104–13.
7. Datta, K.K. 1963: 159–60.
8. In Om Prakash 1985, 1988: 25.
9. Datta, K.K. 1963: 116.
10. Ibid.: 162.
11. Khan, Abdul, Majed, 1969, *The Transition in Bengal 1756–1775: A Study of Saiyid Muhammad Reza Khan*, Cambridge University Press: 171.
12. Ibid: 172.
13. Ibid: 173.
14. Entry No. 3057 of January 10, 1766, 22MIOM/45, C.A.O.M., Aix.
15. Entry No. 3072 November 17, 1768, 22 MIOM/45 ibid. 'A Parwana from Murshidabad ordered the Nawab of Dhaka to find out if we had received arms and ammunitions in large quantities. The Nawab sent many of his agents to inspect our factory. Dangereux wanted to oppose such a dishonourable action. . . . (my translation).
16. Entry No. 3008 of May 27, 1767 22 MIOM/45, ibid.
17. Entry No. 2478 of January 15, 1769, 22MI4, ibid.
18. Entry No. 3009 of February 13, 1768, 22 MIOM/45, Lacheney at Kasimbazar to Chandernagore.
19. Entry No. 2479 of January 26, 1769, 22MI4, ibid.
20. Entry No. 2481 of January 31, 1769, 22MI41, ibid.
21. Entry No. 2572, 22MI41.
22. HMS 176 (5), Letter of Directors to Governor and Council, Fort William, September 10, 1783.
23. HMS 176 (7) Fort William to Court of Directors, April 4, 1783.
24. HMS 173 (12) 259–73.

CHAPTER 23: CONCLUSION

1. See Mukherjee, Prabhati, 2002, *Beyond the Four Varnas: The Untouchables in India*, second ed. IIAS, Shimla for more on this.
2. This has been discussed in *Strange Riches: Bengal in the Mercantile Map of South Asia* (Cambridge/Foundation Books forthcoming).
3. See the account given in Wilson, C.R. *The Early Annals of the English in Bengal*-Surman's Diary, Calcutta, Asiatic Society, 1911, reprints 1963, 1976 2 vols. V.1: 76 for the Surman Embassy.
4. Mukherjee, Rila, 1994.
5. K.F.R., G/23 Series, Consultations, November 19 1755.
6. Mukherjee, Rila, 1990-91.
7. Entry No. 3057 of January 10 1766, 22MIOM/45, C.A.O.M., Aix.

8. Entry 3008 bis, 22MIOM/45, C.A.O.M., Aix.
9. Entry No. 2479 of January 26 1769, 22MI41, ibid.
10. Entry No. 2481 of January 31 1769, 22MI41, ibid.
11. Ibid. April 6 1758.
12. Ibid. May 9 1758.
13. K.F.R. March 12 and April 26 1758.
14. Sinha, N.K., 1965; See Mukherjee, Ramkrishna, 1957, *The Rise and Fall of the English East India Company: A Sociological Appraisal,* 2nd edition, Verlag der Wissenschaft, Berlin. See also Mukherjee, Rila, 1994.
15. See *Strange Riches.*
16. Rennell James, 1780, 1781, *A Bengal Atlas Containing Maps of the Theatre of War and Commerce on that Side of Hindoostan* London.
17. Serajuddin, A.M., 1971.
18. Entry No. 3157 of October 20 1768, 22 MIOM 46, ibid.
19. Bedier (1838) in Deloche ed. 1990: 154.
20. Entry No. 3169 of October 9 1788 22 MIOM 46; No. 3120 of April 4 1789 22 MIOM 46; No. 3121 of April 4 1789 22 MIOM 46; No. 3170 of October 15 1789; No. 3171 of June 27 1789; No. 3172 of July 23 1789; No. 3173 of October 8 1789; No. 3174 of October 11 1789; No. 3175 of October 28 1789; No. 3176 of November 1789; No. 3177 of November 25 1789; No. 3178 of March 26 1790, all of 22 MIOM 46, C.A.O.M., Aix.
21. Entries 3013 of April 16 , 3014 of April 18, 3015 of April 20 1768, 22MIOM/45,C.A.O.M., Aix.
22. Entries 3025 and 3027, 22MIOM/45, ibid.
23. Entry No. 2479 of January 26 1769, 22MI41, ibid.
24. Entry No. 2481 of January 31 1769, 22MI41, ibid.
25. Entry No. 2513, 22MI41, ibid.
26. Entry No. 2572, 22MI41.
27. See Deloche ed. 1984, *Les Aventures de Jean Baptiste Chevalier dans l'Inde Orientale 1752-65*, Paris Publications EFEO.
28. Martineau, Alfred, 1927, *Dupleix et l'Inde Francaise 1749-1754*, Paris, Societe d'Editions Geographiques, Maritimes et Coloniales: 449-51.
29. Deloche, Jean, ed. 1984: 98–101.
30. Deloche Jean ed. 1990: 22, 241.
31. In Bernouilli, V.II.
32. Rinckenbach, Alexis, 1999, 'The French Military Engineers and Geographers in India (1750-1778)' in Mathew K.S. and Stephen S. Jeyaseela eds. *Indo-French Relations,* New Delhi Pragati Publications: 129.
33. In Deloche, Jean, ed. 1990: 20.
34. Entry 3058 of January 11 1766, 22MIOM/45, C.A.O.M., Aix.
35. Entry 3057 of January 10 1766, 22MIOM/45, C.A.O.M., Aix.
36. Entry No. 2479 of January 26 1769, 22MI41, ibid.
37. Entry 2447, 22 MI41, C.A.O.M., Aix. We have no further information on these Frenchmen.
38. PROCES VERBAUX, 22MIOM/22, C.A.O.M, Aix.

39. Toussaint, Auguste, 1974, *L'Ocean Indien au XVIIIe Siecle*, Paris, Flammarion: 170. 'The eastern side of the Bay of Bengal, stretching from Chittagong to the Malay coast, produces nothing that is commercially comparable to the production of the Coromandel or of Bengal. It offers no item of interest-either as colonial produce or as items of 'noble' commerce.' (My translation).
40. Dasgupta, Ashin,1993, *Europeans in India Before the Empire*, Professor A.C.Banerjee Memorial Lecture, 1992, Calcutta, a Department of History Jadavpur University publication.
41. Marshall P.J. *Britain and the World in the Eighteenth Century*: 1 Reshaping the Empire, Presidential Address, *Transactions of the Royal Historical Society*, read November 1997 published in 1999.

Bibliography

I. ARCHIVAL SOURCES

London

Bengal Public Consultations, RI, V.44.
Dacca Factory Records G 15 series.
Fort William Correspondence.
HMS 456, the Dacca Series by John Taylor 1800–01: 103–105, I.O.L.R., London.
HMS 804, from Fort William Correspondence, containing BPC February 25 1747/48 to December 9 1761, I.O.L.R., (now British Library) London. Henceforth HMS 804.
Kasimbazar Factory Records G23 series.

Paris

C2 Indes Orientales Series, A.N., Paris.
Bernier's letter in C2 62 Indes Orientales *Correspendance Generale* 1666–1676 A.N.Paris, now at C.A.O.M., Aix en Provence..
C2 56 *Indes Orientales: Commerce 1686–1788* at above including *Memoire Generale du Commerce que la Cie. des Indes peut faire dans ses etablissements en Inde tant pour l'Europe que les autres parties de l'Inde* by Jacques Vincens, A.N. Colonies C2 197 ff. 1.18/C2 56 ff.22–44 at Aix.
C2 64.
C2 115, Darrac Capitaine de la Loge de Dacca, *Histoire des Etablissemens Francais en Asie et principalement Ceux du Bengale 1537–1822,* A.N., Paris, now C.A.O.M, Aix.
Affaires Etrangeres (AE) BIII 459, of Archives Nationales, Section Outre Mer of Rue Oudinot Paris, now at Centre des Archives Outre Mer, Aix en Provence. *Memoire sur le Commerce de l'Inde: Precis de Celui qui faisait l'Ancienne Compagnie des Indes et Celle Etabli en 1785* (written April 7 1814).

Aix en Provence

Entries of FEIC, including Proces Verbaux, at Chandernagore for the eighteenth century: 22MI/41, 22MI/45, 22MIOM/22, 22MIOM/46, 22MI/60.

Pondicherry

Correspondance du Conseil de Chandernagor avec Divers, 1747-1757, Societe Historique de Pondichery, 1 Rue Romain Rolland, Pondicherry. Accession No. F110/ AC 164/F156.

II. PRIMARY SOURCES: PRINTED

II. 1. Travel Accounts

II.1.1. European

Barbosa Duarte, *The Book of Duarte Barbosa,* Tr. M.L. Dames, London, Hakluyt Society, 1921.

Bernier, Francois, *Travels in the Mogul Empire,* 1656–1668, revised Vincent A. Smith, Reprint, Delhi, Munshiram Manoharlal, 1992.

Bernouilli, 1788, *L'Inde: Description Hisrorique et Geographique de l'Inde qui presente en trios volumes et enrichis de 64 cartes,* 3 vols. Berlin. Contains accounts of Tieffanthaler, Rennell, Father Georgi and Anquetil-Duperron among others. I La Geographie de l"Indoustan par le Pere Joseph Tieffanthaler, II Des Recherches Historiques et Chronologiques sur l'Inde et la description du Cours du Gange et du Gagra avec une tres grande carte par M. Anquetil Duperron, III. La carte Generale de l'Inde, Celle du Cours du Brahmapoutre, et de la navigation interieure du Bengale, avec des Memoires Relatifs a ces cartes, par M. Jacques Rennell.

Bouchon, Genevieve and Thomaz, Luis Filipe, 1998, *Voyage dans les Deltas du Gange et l'Irraouaddy,* 1521, Fondation Calouste Gulbenkian, Paris.

Bowrey, Thomas, *A Geographical account of the Countries Around the Bay of Bengal 1669–1679,* R.C. Temple (ed.), Cambridge, Hakluyt Society, M D CCCCV.

Cesare Frederici's *Travels* in Purchas, Samuel, *His Pilgrimages,* Glasgow, 1905.

Challes, Robert, *Journal d'un Voyage Fait aux Indes Orientales,* 2 vols. Mercure de France, MCMLXXXIII.

Chevalier, J-B, Deloche, Jean (ed.), 1984, *Les Aventures de Jean Baptiste Chevalier dans l'Inde Orientale 1752–1765,* Paris, Publications EFEO.

De Gennes de la Chancelliere, in Subramanian, L. (ed.), 1999, *The French East India Company and the Trade of the Indian Ocean: A Collection of Essays by Indrani Ray,* Centre for Studies in Social Science, Calcutta and Munshiram Manoharlal, New Delhi. Chapter 7 *Journey to Cassimbazar and Murshidabad: Observations of a French Visitor to Bengal in 1743.*

Federbe, Louis Laurent de, Comte de Modave, *Le Voyage en Inde de . . . etc. 1773–1776. Nouveaux Memoires sur l'Etat actuel du Bengale et de l"indoustan* (Tr. and ed.) Jean Deloche, 1971, Paris, Ecole Francaise d'Extreme Orient.

Fitch, Ralph, *Narrative of Ralph Fitch 1583–91* in William Foster (ed.), *Early Travels in India 1583–1619,* London, 1921, Reprint, New Delhi, 1968.

Hamilton, Alexander, 1727, *A New Account of the East Indies 1688–1723*, 2 vols., Edinburgh.

Luillier, *Voyage du Sieur Luillier aux Grandes Indes avec une Instruction Pour le Commerce des Indes Orientales*, Paris, Claude Cellier, MC CC V.

Luillier, *Voyage du Sieur Luillier aux Indes Orientales Avec une instruction pour le commerce des Indes Orientales*, 1705, Paris, Claude Cellier,

Luillier, *Voyages du Sieur Luillier dans des Grandes Indes Orientales*, 1726, Rotterdam.

Manrique *The Travels of Fray Sebastian Manrique 1629–1643*, Luard, C.E. (Tr). 2 vols. London, Hakluyt Society 1926–27.

Marshall John, Shafaat Ahmad, (ed). 1927, *John Marshall in India, Notes and Observations in Bengal 1668–1672*, London, Oxford University Press.

Peter Laval, or Pietro della Valle, *The Voyage of Peter Laval to the East Indies, the Maldives, the Moluccas and Brasil 1601–1611*, Tr. A. Gray, London, Hakluyt Society. 2 vols.

Tavernier, Jean Baptiste, *Travels in India* (Tr). Ball and Crooke, 1925, 2 vols., Oxford, University Press, 2nd edition.

Tavernier, Jean-Baptiste, (Intr). Yerasimos, S., 1981, *Les Six Voyages en Turquie et en Perse*, 3 vols., Paris, Maspero.

Terry, Edward, *Voyage to East India*, London, T. Wilkes, MDCC LXXVIII.

Tome Pires, *The Suma Oriental of Tome Pires: An Account of the East from the Red Sea to Japan, Written in India and Malacca in 1512–1515*, (ed. and tr.) E.A. Cortesao, 1944, London, Hakluyt Society. 2 vols. Reprinted Wiesbaden 1967.

Varthema, Ludovico, *The Itinerary of*. . . Tr. R.C. Temple, London, Hakluyt Society, 1928.

Varthema, Ludovico, *The Travels of Ludovico di Varthema in Egypt, Syria, Arabia Deserta and Arabia Felix, in Persia, India and Ethiopia AD 1503–1508*. (Tr). J.W. John, (ed.), G.P. Badger, London, Hakluyt Society, M D CCC XIII.

II.1.2. Non European

Ibn Batuta, *Voyages*, 3 vols., (Tr). Defremery, E.C., Sanguinetty, B.R., 1982, Paris, Maspero.

Ma Huan, Mills, J.V.G. Tr. and Ed, 1970, *The Overall Survey of the Ocean's Shores* (An Account of Ma Huan's voyage to Bengal), London, Hakluyt Society.

II.2. Contemporary Reports, Documents, Histories-Asian and European

Abdul Hamid Lahori's *Padshah Nama* in Elliot and Dowson's *History of India as Told by Its Own Historians*, V.7, Allahabad, Kitab Mahal. Reprint 1969; Abdul Hamid Lahori, *Padshah Nama* in Elliot and Dowson, *History of India as Told By its Own Historians*, V.7, L.P.P. Reprint, 1990, Delhi.

Ain-i-Akbari. Abul Fazl, Jarrett, H.S. (Tr). *The Ain-I-Akbari By Abul Fazl Allami*, Jadunath Sarkar annotated 2nd edition, Oriental Books Reprint, New Delhi, 1978.

Anisuzzaman, M. (ed.), 1981, *Factory Correspondence and Other Bengali Documents*, London, I.O.L.R. Publications.

Baharistan-I-Ghaybi by Mirza Nathan. 2 Vols. Tr. M.I. Borah, Government of Assam Publication, Guwahati 1936.

Deloche, Jean, (ed). 1990, *Statistiques de Chandernagor* (1832, 1827, 1838) by Joseph Cordier and Achille Bedier, Pondicherry, Institut Francais.

Fathiya-I-Ibriya (or Tarikh-I-Mulki-Asham) of (Ibn Muhammad Wali), Known popularly as Shihabuddin Talish. Tr. By Blochmann, Journal of the Asiatic Society of Bengal, 1872.

Ghulam Hussein Salim, *Riyas-us-Salatin,* Tr. Maulavi Abdus, 1902, Calcutta, Asiatic Society.

Hamilton, Walter 1828, *East India Gazeteer*, 2 vols., London.

Hedges, William, *Diary of, During His Agency in Bengal 1681–87*, R. Barlow and H. Yule (eds.), 2 vols. London, Hakluyt Society, M D CCC LXXX.

Hunter, W.W., 1876, *A Statistical Account Of Bengal*, Vol. VI. *Chittagong Hill Tracts-Chittagong, Noakhali, Tipperah, Hill Tipperah*, London, Trubner.

Master, Streynsham, R.C. Temple (ed.), 1911, *The Diaries of Streynsham Master 1675–1680 And Other Contemporary Papers Relating Thereto*, London, John Murray, Indian Records Series, 2 Vols.

Seid Gholam Hossein Khan, *Seir Mutaqherin or View of Modern Times*, (Tr). Nota Manus, Calcutta, T.D. Chatterjee, 4 vols.

Taylor, J., 1851, *A Descriptive and Historical Account of the Cotton Manufactures of Dacca*, London.

Taylor, James, 1840, *A Sketch of the Topography and Statistics of Dacca,* Calcutta.

The Imperial Gazeteer, 1908, vol. XI.

III. SECONDARY LITERATURE: BOOKS AND ARTICLES

Alam, Muzaffar, 2002, 'Aspects of Agrarian Uprisings in North India in the early Early Eighteenth Century' reprinted in Alavi, Seema, 2002, *The Eighteenth Century in India,* New Delhi, OUP: 84–112.

Alam, M. and Subrahmanyam, S. (eds)., 1998, *The Mughal State 1526–1750,* New Delhi, OUP.

Alavi, Seema, 2002, *The Eighteenth Century in India,* New Delhi, OUP.

Ali, Muhammad Mohar, 1985, *History of the Muslims of Bengal*, 2 vols., Riyadh, Imam Muhammad Ibn Sa'ud Islamic University.

Arasaratnam S., 1987, 'India and the Indian Ocean in the Seventeenth Century' in A. Das Gupta and M.N. Pearson (eds.), *India and the Indian Ocean 1500–1800*, Calcutta, OUP.

Arasaratnam S., 1986, *Merchants, Companies and Commerce on the Coromandel Coast 1650–1740*, Delhi, OUP.

Bagchi, P.C., 1951, *India and China: A Thousand Years of Cultural Relations*, New York, Philosophical Library and Bombay, British India Press.

Bagchi, P.C., 1945, 'Political Relations Between Bengal and China in the Pathan Period', *Visva Bharati Annals*, V. 1, Cheena Bhavan.

Barnett, Richard (ed.), 2002, *Rethinking Early Modern India*, New Delhi, Manohar.

Chaudhuri, K.N., *1978, The Trading World of Asia and the English East India Company 1660–1760,* Cambridge.

Chaudhuri, Sushil, 2002, 'Was There a Crisis in Mid-Eighteenth Century Bengal?' in Barnett, R. (ed.), 2002, *Rethinking Early Modern India*, New Delhi, Manohar.

Chaudhuri, Sushil and Morineau, Michel (eds.), 1999, *Merchants, Companies and Trade: Europe and Asia in the Early Modern Era,* Cambridge.

Chaudhuri Sushil,1995, *From Prosperity to Decline, Bengal in the Eighteenth Century*, New Delhi, Manohar.

Chaudhuri, Sushil, 1986–87, 'European Companies and Pre Modern South Asian Commercial Systems', *The Calcutta Historical Journal*, XI, 1–2: 95–108.

Chaudhuri, Sushil, 1975, *Trade and Commercial Organisation in Bengal, 1650–1720.* Calcutta: Firma KLM.

Chaudhuri, Sushil, 1971, 'Bengal Merchants and Commercial Organisation in the Second Half of the Seventeenth Century', *Bengal Past and Present*, XC, July-Dec: 36–51.

Cipolla, Carlo M., 1976, *Before the Industrial Revolution: European Society and Economy 1000–1700*, London, Methuen.

Coedes, George, 1964, *Les Etats Hindouises d'Indochine et d'Indonesie*, Paris, Boccard.

Das Gupta, A. and M.N. Pearson (eds.) 1987, *India and the Indian Ocean 1500–1800*, Calcutta, OUP.

Das Gupta Arun, 1987, 'The Maritime Trade of Indonesia 1500–1800' in A. Das Gupta and M.N.Pearson eds. *India and the Indian Ocean 1500–1800*, Calcutta, OUP.

Dasgupta, Ashin,1993, *Europeans in India Before the Empire*, Professor A.C. Banerjee Memorial Lecture, 1992, Calcutta, a Department of History Jadavpur University publication.

Das Gupta, Ashin 1987, 'India and the Indian Ocean in the Eighteenth Century' in A. Das Gupta and M.N. Pearson (eds.), *India and the Indian Ocean 1500–1800*, Calcutta, OUP.

Das Gupta, Ashin, 1987, 'Introduction II: The Story' in A. Das Gupta and M.N. Pearson (eds.), *India and the Indian Ocean 1500–1800*, Calcutta, OUP: 25–45.

Das Gupta, Ashin, 1987, 'Upakuler Bharatvarsha' in A. Ray, S. Nurul Hasan, G. Bhadra and A. Das Gupta (eds.), *Madhyajuger Bharat*, Calcutta, OUP. (In Bengali)

Das Gupta, Ashin, 1979, *Indian Merchants and The Decline of Surat, 1700–1750*, Wiesbaden, Steiner Verlag.

Das Gupta, Ashin, 1970, 'Trade and Politics in Eighteenth Century India' from Richards, D.S. (ed.), *Islam and the Trade of Asia*, Philadelphia reprinted in Alam, M. and Subrahmanyam, S. (eds.), 1998, *The Mughal State 1526–1750*, New Delhi, OUP: 370–97.

Das Gupta, Ashin, 1967, *Malabar in Asian Trade*, Cambridge, CUP.

Datta, K.K., 1963, *Alivardi and His Times*, Calcutta, The World Press Private Limited.

Dermigny, Louis, 1964, *La Chine et l'Occident: Le Commerce a Canton au XVIIIeme siecle, 1719–1833*, 3 vols., Paris, S.E.V.P.E.N

Deyell, John, 1983, 'The China Connection: Problems of Silver Supply in Medieval Bengal' in J.F. Richards (ed.), *Precious Metals in the Later Medieval and Early Modern Worlds*, Durham, Carolina Academic Press: 207–227. Reprinted in Subrahmanyam Sanjay (ed.), 1994, *Money and the Market in India 1100–1700*, Delhi, OUP: 112–136.

Eaton, Richard, 1993, *The Rise of Islam and the Bengal Frontier 1204–1760*, California, Berkeley and Los Angeles.

Evers, Hans Dieter, 1987, 'Trade and State Formation: Siam in the Early Bangkok Period', *MAS*, XII, 4: 751–971.

Frank, A.G., 1998, *ReOrient: Global Economy in the Asian Age*, University of Califiornia Press and Sage/Vistaar.

Feldbaek, Ole, 1969, *India Trade Under the Danish Flag*, Copenhagen.

Gaborieau, Marc (ed.), 1986, *Islam et Societe en Asie du Sud*, Paris, *Purusartha*, Vol. 9.

Gill, Sandrine, 1999, 'Mahasthangarh: A Riverine port in Ancient Bengal', in Himanshu Prabha Ray (ed.), *Archaeology of Seafaring: The Indian Ocean in the Ancient Period*, New Delhi, Pragati Publications.

Gokhale, B.G., 1979, *Surat in the Seventeenth Century*, Bombay, Popular Prakashan.

Gordon, Stewart, 1994, 'Burhanpur: Entrepot and Hinterland 1650–1750' in Gordon, Stewart, 1994, *Marathas, Marauders and State Formation in Eighteenth Century India*, Delhi, OUP: 163–181.

Habib, I. 1982, 'Non Agricultural Production and Urban Economy' in *The Cambridge Economic History of India*, V.I (eds.), Tapan Raychaudhuri and Irfan Habib, CUP/Orient Longman, 1982.

Hossain, Hameeda, 1988, *The Company Weavers of Bengal: The East India Company and the Organization of Textile Production in Bengal 1750–1813*, Delhi, OUP.

Hutton, J.H., 1961, *Caste in India: Its Nature, Function and Origins*, London, OUP. Third Edition.

Karim, Abdul, 1964, *Dacca The Mughal Capital*, Dacca, Asiatic Society of Pakistan.

Karim, Khondkar Mahbubul, 1974, *The Provinces of Bihar and Bengal under Shahjahan*, Dacca, The Asiatic Society of Bangladesh.

Khan, Abdul Majed, 1969, *The Transition in Bengal 1756–1775: A Study of Saiyid Muhammad Reza Khan,* Cambridge University Press.

Little, J.H., 1920–21, *The House of Jagat Seth, BPP, 20*: 111–200 (1920) and *21*: 1–119 (1921). Later as a publication of the Asiatic Society, Calcutta.

Lombard, Denys, 1990, *Le Carrefour Javanais: Essai d'histoire Globale,* 3 vols. Paris, Editions E.H.E.S.S.

Lombard, Denys, 1990, *Le Carrefour Javanais: Essai d'histoire Globale,* V.III, *L'Heritage des Royaumes Concentriques,* Paris, Editions E.H.E.S.S.

Lombard, Maurice, 1971, *l'Islam dans sa Premiere Grandeur, VIIIe-XIe siecle,* Paris, Flammarion. In English as *The Golden Age Of Islam,* (Tr). J. Spencer, Amsterdam, 1975.

Majumdar, R.C. (ed.), 1943, *The History of Bengal.* V.1 *Hindu Period,* Dacca, The University of Dacca.

Marshall P.J. 1999, '*Britain and the World in the Eighteenth Century*: 1 Reshaping the Empire', Presidential Address, *Transactions of the Royal Historical Society,* read November 1997 published in 1999.

Marshall P.J., 1976, *East Indian Fortunes: The British in Bengal in the Eighteenth Century,* Oxford, Oxford Press.

Martineau, Alfred, 1927, *Dupleix et l'Inde Francaise 1749–1754,* Paris, Societe d'Editions Geographiques, Maritimes et Coloniales.

Matthew, K.S. and Stephen S. Jeyaseela (eds.), 1999, *Indo-French Relations,* New Delhi, Pragati Publications.

Mohsin, K.M, 1973, *A Bengal District in Transition: Murshidabad, 1765–1793,* Dacca, Asiatic Society of Bangladesh.

Moreland, W.H., 1920, 1962, *India at the Death of Akbar,* Delhi Reprint.

Morrison, Barrie M.,1970, *Political Centers and Cultural Regions in Early Bengal,* The Association for Asian Studies, University of Arizona Press.

Mukherjee, Prabhati, 2002, *Beyond the Four Varnas: The Untouchables in India,* 2nd edn. IIAS, Shimla

Mukherjee, Ramkrishna, 1957, *The Rise and Fall of the English East India Company: A Sociological Appraisal,* second edition, Verlag der Wissenschaft, Berlin.

Mukherjee, Rila, *Strange Riches: Bengal in the Mercantile Map of South Asia* (forthcoming 2006 from Cambridge/Foundation).

Mukherjee, Rila, 2004, 'A Rice Culture of Divine Right in a Celestially Ordered Zone: A Case Study of South Asian and South East Ideologies and Hegemonies from c. 2000 BC to c. 1800 AD with Specific Reference to Bengal', *Campus Social,* Lisbon. Editor Teotonio de Sousa.

Mukherjee, Rila, 1994, 'The Story of Kasimbazar: Silk Merchants and Commerce in Eighteenth Century India', *Review,* XVII, 4, Fall: 499–554.

Mukherjee, Rila, 1990–91, 'The French East India Company's Trade in East Bengal from 1750–1753: A Look at the Chandernagor-Jugdia Letters' *The Indian Historical Review,* 17, nos. 1–2.

Nandy, S.C., 1981, '*Palasi Juger Aage Maphasvaler Bangali Resham Byabshahi*', *Aitihasik*, Jan-March: 72–103. (In Bengali)

Nandy, Somendra Chandra. 1978, *Life and Times of Canto Baboo: The Banyan of Warren Hastings*, 2 vols., Bombay, Allied Publishers.

Om Prakash, 2002, 'Trade and Politics in Eighteenth century Bengal' in Alavi, Seema (ed.), 2002, *The Eighteenth Century in India*, New Delhi, OUP: 136–164.

Om Prakash and Lombard, Denys (eds.), 1999, *Commerce and Culture in The Bay of Bengal 1500–1800*, Delhi, ICHR/ Manohar.

Om Prakash, 1998, 'European Corporate Enterprises and the Politics of Trade in India, 1600–1800' in Alam, M. and Subrahmanyam, S. (eds.), 1998, *The Mughal State 1526–1750*, New Delhi, OUP.

Om Prakash, 1988. *The Dutch East India Company and the Economy of Bengal 1630–1720*, Delhi, OUP. Originally 1985.

Om Prakash, 1984 (ed.), *The Dutch Factories in India 1617–1623*, New Delhi, Munshiram Manoharlal.

Paul, Pramode Lal, 1939, *The Early History of Bengal*, Calcutta, Indian Research Institute.

Pearson, M.N., 2003, Unpublished keynote address to the conference *'Seascapes, Littoral Cultures and Trans-oceanic Exchanges,'* sponsored by the American Historical Association, Washington DC, February 12–15, 2003.

Pearson, M.N., 1987, *The Portuguese in India, New Cambridge History of India*, 1.1, Cambridge University Press, Indian edition, Orient Longman.

Ray, Aniruddha, 2004, *The Merchant and the State: The French in India 1666–1739*, New Delhi, Munshiram Manoharlal Publishers Pvt. Ltd.

Ray, Aniruddha, 1997, 'Middle Bengali Literature: A Source for the Study of Bengal in the Age of Akbar' in Habib, Irfan, *Akbar and His India*, New Delhi, OUP.

Ray Aniruddha, Hasan Syed Nurul, Bhadra Gautam and Das Gupta Ashin (eds.), 1987, *Madhyajuger Bharat*, Calcutta, OUP.

Ray Himanshu Prabha (ed.), 1999, *Archaeology of Seafaring: The Indian Ocean in the Ancient Period*, New Delhi, Pragati Publications.

Ray, Indrani, 1999, 'India in Asian Trade in the 1730s: A Discussion by a French Trader' in L. Subramanian (ed.), 1999, *The French East India Company and the Trade of the Indian Ocean: A Collection of Essays by Indrani Ray*. Calcutta, Centre for Studies in Social Sciences and Delhi, Munshiram Manoharlal: 177–202.

Ray, Indrani, 1999, 'Journey to Cassimbazar and Murshidabad: Observations of a French Visitor to Bengal in 1743' in Subramanian, L. (ed.), 1999, *The French East India Company and the Trade of the Indian Ocean: A Collection of Essays by Indrani Ray*. Calcutta, Centre for Studies in Social Sciences and Delhi, Munshiram Manoharlal: 144–176.

Raychaudhuri, Tapan and Habib, Irfan (eds.), 1982, *The Cambridge Economic History of India*, V.1, CUP/Orient Longman.

Raychaudhuri, Tapan, 1982, 'Inland Trade' in *The Cambridge Economic History of India,* V.1 (eds.), Tapan Raychaudhuri and Irfan Habib, CUP/Orient Longman, 1982.

Raychaudhuri, Tapan, 1966, *Bengal under Akbar and Jahangir-A Study in Social History,* Delhi, Munshiram Manoharlal.

Rennell James, 1780, 1781, *A Bengal Atlas Containing Maps of the Theatre of War and Commerce on that Side of Hindoostan* London.

Richards J.F. (ed.), 1983, *Precious Metals in the Later Medieval and Early Modern Worlds,* Durham, Carolina Academic Press.

Rinckenbach, Alexis, 1999, 'The French Military Engineers and Geographers in India (1750-1778)' in Mathew K.S. and Stephen S. Jeyaseela eds. *Indo-French Relations,* New Delhi Pragati Publications.

Risley, H.H., 1891, 1981 Reprint, *The Tribes and Castes of Bengal,* 2 vols. Calcutta, Firma Mukhopadhaya.

Salles, Jean Francois, Boussac, Marie Francoise, Breuil, Jean Yves, 2002, 'Mahasthangarh (Bangladesh) and the Ganges Valley in the Mauryan Period' in Sengupta, Gautam and Panja, Sheena (eds.), *Archaeology of Eastern India: New Perspectives,* Calcutta, Centre for Archaeological Studies and Training, Eastern India.

Sanyal, Hitesranjan, 1981, *Social Mobilty in Bengal,* Calcutta, Papyrus.

Sarkar, Jagadish Narayan, 1987, *Mughal Economy: Organization and Working,* Calcutta, Naya Prakash.

Sastri, Haraprasad, 1980, *Bener Meye, Collected Works,* V.1. Calcutta, West Bengal State Book Board.

Sen, Sudipta, 1998, *Empire of Free Trade, The East India Company and the Making of the Colonial Marketplace,* Philadelphia, University of Pennsylvania Press.

Sengupta, Gautam and Panja, Sheena eds. 2002, *Archaeology of Eastern India: New Perspectives,* Calcutta, Centre for Archaeological Studies and Training, Eastern India.

Serajuddin, A.M., 1971, *The Revenue Administration of the East India Company in Chittagong 1761–1785,* Chittagong, University Press.

Sinha, N.K. 1965. *An Economic History of Bengal, V.1 From Plassey to the Permanent Settlement,* Calcutta, Firma K.L. Mukhopadhyay.

Subramanian, L. (ed.), 1999, *The French East India Company and the Trade of the Indian Ocean: A Collection of Essays by Indrani Ray.* Calcutta, Centre for Studies in Social Sciences and Delhi, Munshiram Manoharlal.

Subrahmanyam, Sanjay, 2005,'Dutch Tribulations in Seventeenth century Mrauk-U' in Subrahmanyam, Sanjay, 2005, *Explorations in Connected History; From The Tagus to The Ganges,* New Delhi, OUP.

Subrahmanyam Sanjay ed. 1994, *Money and the Market in India 1100–1700,* Delhi, OUP.

Subrahmanyam, Sanjay, 1993, *The Portuguese Empire in Asia 1500–1700: A Political and Economic History,* New York, Longman.

Subrahmanyam, Sanjay, 1992, '*Iranians Abroad: Intra-Asian Elite Migration and Early Modern State Formation*' in *The Journal of Asian Studies*, 51, 2, May: 340–63.

Subrahmanyam, Sanjay, 1990, *Improvising Empire: Portuguese Trade and Settlement in the Bay of Bengal 1500–1700,* New Delhi, OUP.

Tarafdar, M.R., 1986, 'The Bengali Muslims in the Pre Colonial Period: Problems of Conversion, Class Formation and Cultural Evolution', 92–110, in Marc Gaborieau (ed.), *Islam et Societe en Asie du Sud*, Paris, *Purusartha*, Vol. 9.

Tarafdar, M.R. 1965, *Husain Shahi Bengal 1494–1538 AD: A Socio-Political Study*, Dacca.

Thapar, Romila, 1975, *Time as a Metaphor for History*, Calcutta, K.P. Bagchi.

Toussaint, Auguste, 1974, *L'Ocean Indien au XVIIIe siecle*, Paris, Flammarion.

Varadarajan, Lotika, 2006, *Indo-Portuguese Encounters: Journeys in Science, Technology and Culture*, Lisbon and New Delhi, Aryan Publishers. 2 vols.

Wilson, C.R., 1911 (1963, 1967), *The Early Annals of the English in Bengal.* Surman's Diary, Calcutta, Asiatic Society, 2 vols.

Winius, George, 1983, '*The "Shadow Empire" of Goa in the Bay of Bengal*', *Itinerario*, v.vii (2): 83–101.

Xinru Liu, 1996, *Silk and Religion: An exploration of the Material Life and the Thought of People*, OUP.

Index